Remembering
RICHIE

Richie Benaud
& Friends

HODDER

First published in Great Britain in 2015 by Hodder & Stoughton
An Hachette UK company

First published in paperback in 2016

1

A CIP catalogue record for this title is available from the British Library

Paperback ISBN: 978 1 473 62744 4
Ebook ISBN: 978 1 473 62741 3

Typeset in Garamond by Hewer Text UK Ltd, Edinburgh

Printed and bound by Clays Ltd, St Ives plc

Hodder & Stoughton policy is to use papers that are natural, renewable
and recyclable products and made from wood grown in sustainable
forests. The logging and manufacturing processes are expected to conform
to the environmental regulations of the country of origin.

Hodder & Stoughton Ltd
Carmelite House
50 Victoria Embankment
London EC4Y 0DZ

www.hodder.co.uk

Contents

Introduction ix
Foreword by Sir Michael Parkinson xi

I THE PLAYER

1 For the Record
Not merely the voice of cricket by Scyld Berry 3
Wisden Cricketer of the Year 1962 – R. Benaud 6
Wisden Cricketer of the Year 1962 – A. K. Davidson 10

2 A Boyhood Love of Cricket
Life was all about playing sport 14
Better than heaven 18

3 Learning the Ropes
Up a level, but can I handle it? 23
A hole in the head 31
Three greats 36

4 In England for the First Time
Jeezzz, Harv, it's not even level!: Australia in England 1953 46
Lessons from a master 56

5 Turning Points
Confounding the critics: Australia in England 1956 60
Cutting down: Australia in India 1956–57 66
Ivan James: Australia in New Zealand 1956–57 68
The Claw: Australia in South Africa 1957–58 71

6 **Captain of Australia**

The return of the urn: England in Australia 1958–59   74

Learning about life and diplomacy: Australia in
    Pakistan and India 1959–60   89

The Tied Test: West Indies in Australia 1960–61   103

Stumped in the pavilion!   107

A mentor and a friend by Tony Cozier   110

Indulging a hunch: Australia in England 1961   112

7 **Legspin**

Words of advice   117

Shane Warne   121

Dear Richie by Shane Warne   128

Richie Benaud – career playing statistics
    by Benedict Bermange   129

II   THE OBSERVER

8 **Journalism**

A foot in the door   143

Police rounds   146

Shaping a new career   148

Scoop!   155

Mentor, inspiration and friend by Justin Langer   158

9 **Broadcasting**

Training at the BBC, 1956   159

Tales from the commentary box   161

It's been absolutely marvellous: England v Australia
    at The Oval, 2005   177

Richie pitches it just right by Ian Wooldridge   178

10 **World Series Cricket**

The origins of WSC   181

A proposition from Kerry Packer   189

11 **The Spirit of the Game**

Fifty-two years with Benords by Ian Chappell   195
Sledging   198
Walking, or not walking   203
The Spirit of Cricket in Australia   208
No place for violence   211
Having a look for myself   212

12 **Limited-Overs Cricket**

The long and the short of it   216
Four games to remember   218
The future of the one-day game   223

13 **Technology**

DRS and neutral umpires   226

14 **Board Games**

The Barnes business   231
The boots business   235

15 **My Greatest XI**

Being a selector   239

III   THE MAN

16 **Away From Cricket**

Tales of the turf   267
My best friend in life by Jack Bannister   271

17 **Family**

The Benauds and the Savilles: pioneers   273
Reasons to celebrate   282
A splendid piece of advice   283
A sad farewell   284
Another sad farewell   286

IV TRIBUTES

Richie Benaud, cricket's philosopher king by Gideon Haigh   291
A fond farewell to the quiet voice of an English summer
  by Mike Atherton   296
Richie Benaud by David Frith   300
A true one-off by Jonathan Agnew   304
Australia's master commentator by Mike Selvey   306
My friend the colossus by Henry Blofeld   308
What an innings by David Gower   311
A true leader by Geoffrey Boycott   313
Listening to Richie was like having your neck gently
  massaged by Angus Fraser   316
A cry for our lost youth by Oliver Holt   318

Acknowledgements   321
Index   323

Introduction

Hodder & Stoughton have been publishing Richie Benaud's books for over fifty-five years. Throughout that period, needless to say, he has been one of the most respected and successful authors on our list.

When Richie so sadly passed away in April 2015, the British and Australian branches of the company decided we should publish a new book as a tribute to the great man. Daphne and the Benaud family gave us all the encouragement we needed to do so.

Richie wrote with great admiration of a book on the early history of cricket by John Ford. It was called, *Cricket: A Social History*. And I asked John and Tim Waller, another member of my team, to help me select some of the finest writing from Richie's books for inclusion in *Remembering Richie*.

His sad passing prompted a host of tributes – by fellow players and cricket writers – and we have also included a number of these. They rightfully salute his major achievements and reveal the affection and respect in which he was held.

Anyone reading his words will become aware of Richie's abiding passion for Test match cricket and the finest traditions of the game. They will see too that he understood more than most that cricket has evolved – and must continue to evolve – along with the changes in society. The game would die if it were ever to stand still.

In a more egalitarian and affluent society, professional remuneration for cricketers had to increase accordingly. In a society with a multiplication of leisure alternatives, one-day cricket and day-night cricket have saved Test cricket from financial collapse. Shocking as his revolution seemed to many at the time, Kerry Packer's innovations (with some guidance from Richie) can now be seen to have secured the financial future of cricket, ensuring the survival of the game at the highest level.

At the same time, Richie appreciated that the challenges which have faced the modern game are often nothing new. Take, for instance, sponsorship, gambling, corruption, the questioning of umpires and selectorial decisions, administrative failures and sledging (by whatever name it was known). All have occurred before in cricket's long evolution and, like new challenges, they must be confronted and resolved on today's terms. Richie understood and wrote about this, just as clearly as he understood how and why the techniques of batting, bowling and fielding have always evolved in response to new challenges.

All this informed his captaincy, his writing and his commentating and made him probably the most balanced and the wisest guide to the modern game. There can be few individuals in the long history of the game who have been so influential and so universally admired by their contemporaries.

He will long be remembered by all who love the game of cricket.

Roddy Bloomfield
Editor, Hodder & Stoughton

Foreword

by Sir Michael Parkinson

Cricket is about moments.

As a young man the best ball I ever saw was bowled by Richie Benaud at Old Trafford, England v Australia 1961. Australia in danger of losing the Test. Ted Dexter, imperious, aristocratic, flaying the Aussie attack. Benaud went round the wicket bowling into a rough patch and did for Dexter with a topspinner. England 150–2 needing 106 to win. To the wicket Peter May, who had already declared himself England's best batsman with a marvellous 95 in his first innings. The second ball he received from Benaud was the perfect delivery. Of enticing length, it drew May forward, drifted late, pitched outside the line of leg stump and then broke back to bowl him.

From that moment on I was in awe of Benaud. There was May, my favourite batsman, a player of classic technique and impeccable breeding, being made a monkey by the upstart Aussie. It was the best ball I had ever seen until years later at the same ground I saw Warne bowl Gatting with what became known as the Ball of the Century.

I didn't meet Richie until a few years after that when we sat together at Old Trafford – again – for a Yorkshire v Lancashire game. We were in the press box, both reporters for our employers in Grub Street. A young Boycott was batting. I played club cricket with Geoff and I asked Richie how he rated my mate. What he told me appeared in my report, whereupon my editor received a complaint from Mr Benaud along the lines that he was a journalist and no longer captain of Australia and therefore did not take kindly to being quoted by some stranger in a press box. I didn't quite understand what the fuss was about but I apologised and put my indiscretion down to hero worship.

From that point on, while never losing my admiration of Richie, I kept my distance until inevitably and thankfully we became friends. When I went to Oz in the late 1970s to work on the Antipodean version of the talk show, I played golf at the Australian Golf Club in Sydney where Richie was a member. He kindly proposed me as a member and partnered me in my playing-in round, which turned out to be a club competition.

I was a handy sixteen handicap at the time and I think Richie was a tough twelve or so. Anyway, I had a day when, for the first twelve holes, I could do no wrong. Richie, similarly, was playing well and as we approached the thirteenth he said to me: 'Nothing flash from now on. Be sensible and we'll win.' The thirteenth at the Australian is a par four requiring an accurate drive and then a mid-iron second into a well-bunkered green with a treacherous slope. I was on in two with a shot, six feet above the pin facing a quick downhill putt. By now fantasy had taken over and I had become Jack Nicklaus, my golfing hero. Richie said: 'Mike, be careful with the putt. It's downhill and very quick.'

'Got it, Richie,' I said.

Richie continued advising caution. 'I mean it's *very* quick,' he said.

'Richie,' I said, 'it's all under control.'

I putted past the hole and into a bunker. It took me two shots to get out and a potential birdie three became a triple bogey seven. As I walked off, my partner and Captain Supreme was close behind. I could feel him smouldering. I said: 'I know what you are thinking.' He said: 'You could not possibly know what I'm thinking.' So I said: 'How come?' and he said: 'Because you are still here.'

He was an exceptional man. A great and bold captain, a fine

allrounder and a perceptive commentator on the game. Also, along with Kerry Packer, he masterminded the modern cricket merry-go-round.

The essential paradox of Richie Benaud was that for all he lived his life under public scrutiny and was employed for most of that time to volunteer opinion and comment, he didn't give much away. He was a stranger to hysteria, disdainful of hyperbole. He used words like a miser. 'Marvellous,' he would comment, but not elaborate too much on why he thought so. When he bowled Peter May that day at Old Trafford, what I said to myself was 'Marvellous.' Enough said. The art of commentary is sometimes to let what happened speak for itself.

All his other gifts apart, Richie Benaud was the best in the business at doing just that. From his place in the pantheon, reading this book of praise and fanfare for his great gifts, as well as a selection of his finest writing, I think Richie Benaud would allow himself to be gently chuffed – but quietly so.

I
THE PLAYER

‘Flair was his thing. He was a Brylcreem boy. He had the open-neck shirt. He would have been a sensation today.’

Bill Lawry

1

For the Record

Benaud the commentator seldom referred to his on-field experiences and accomplishments – a shrewd expedient which had the effect of making him seem almost ageless – and was amused when young admirers inquired innocently whether he had been a player. In fact, Richie Benaud would rank among Test cricket's elite legspinners and captains had he never uttered or written a word about the game.

Gideon Haigh, *The Australian*

Not merely the voice of cricket
Scyld Berry, *Daily Telegraph*, 2015

As long as cricket is played, Richie Benaud will be ranked as one of its finest captains and one of its finest television commentators. In both careers he was not simply quietly observant, informed and shrewd, but the quintessence of these qualities.

It was asking a lot of the first cricketer who scored 2,000 Test runs and took 200 Test wickets, in addition to his captaincy of Australia, to go on – after his retirement – to an equally successful career. Yet Benaud did so, and not only in his native country, where he became the voice of Channel Nine, but in England too, where he anchored the cricket coverage on the BBC and Channel 4, and even Channel Five, for half a century.

His two great feats of captaincy came in successive Ashes series against England. The first was in 1958–59, when England suffered their most unexpected reverse against Australia before Alastair Cook's tour. Indeed the two stunning defeats had much in common

– except that Benaud acted not only as the captain, like Michael Clarke, but as the coach, like Darren Lehmann, and the leading wicket-taker, like Mitchell Johnson.

But if a single passage of play created Benaud's reputation as a captain, it came on the last day of the Old Trafford Test of 1961. With a touch of wizardry he arrested England's advance to what had seemed an inevitable victory in the match and series, and turned it into the most traumatic loss in their annals.

Benaud's determination to beat England when captain can only have been increased by his early experiences in Ashes series. As a 22-year-old all-rounder for New South Wales he was selected to tour England in 1953; and while his leg-breaks troubled county batsmen, and the Australian fielding was vastly superior to that of their English counterparts, he aggregated no more than 15 runs and two wickets in his three Tests.

In the last game of this tour, however, at the Scarborough Festival, he played an exceptional innings of 135, his only first-class hundred of the tour. Len Hutton, England's captain, was playing in the game – and the opposing captain. When England toured Australia in 1954–55, and Benaud came out to bat, Hutton tried an early form of sledging: 'Here comes the festival cricketer,' he said – not a term of approbation in Yorkshire, or Australia.

Benaud's Ashes experiences were little happier in 1956, when Australia were caught on damp pitches by the offspinner Jim Laker. But when England returned to Australia in 1958–59, Benaud was having lunch with his friend and much senior team-mate Neil Harvey when the news arrived that Benaud had been appointed Australia's captain. They resolved to work together to beat the Poms, who had won the three previous Ashes series.

As a first move Benaud introduced the custom of a team dinner on the eve of every Test. He also had the great advantage of inheriting Alan Davidson as his left-arm swing bowler – and a more dubious left-arm pace bowler in Ian Meckiff, who was banned for throwing after four Tests, but not before he had done damage.

While England's batting disintegrated, Benaud stood quietly at gully, giving the impression of seeing all and hearing all, before clapping his hands and making a move that – often enough – proved effective if not inspired.

Benaud reversed England's sequence of success and won the 1958–59 series 4–0. England's opening batsmen were troubled by left-arm pace; their wicketkeeper and pivot, Godfrey Evans, lost form with the bat and was dropped; England's offspinner, Laker, was vastly less effective than in England; and some of their fast bowlers were living on reputation, past their peak. It was the exact blueprint which Cook's team was forced to follow in 2013–14.

Benaud's major initiatives on his 1961 tour of England were to play attacking cricket in the county games – building on the renaissance which Frank Worrell's West Indians had started in Australia in 1960–61 after a dour decade of Test cricket – and to court the media as never before. Benaud had been working for the Sydney *Sun* himself, and realised its influence. He went out of his way to help not only the Australian but English journalists, by answering questions after close of play or sending his players along to functions. Thus he might have softened the blow which struck in the Fourth Test at Old Trafford.

The series stood at 1–1, after Australia had won the Second Test at Lord's – under Harvey. Benaud's right shoulder had been troubling him all tour, and he had been bowling mostly medium-pace in the county games. England, on his return, won the Third Test at Headingley, and seemed to be winning the Fourth as they raced to 150 for one wicket, powered by Ted Dexter at his most thrilling, in pursuit of a target of 256.

As the last throw of his dice, Benaud tried bowling round the wicket into the footmarks created by Fred Trueman in his follow-through. He dismissed Dexter. England froze. Their captain Peter May was bowled behind his legs, trying a sweep without protecting his stumps with his pads. Brian Close tried what might be now called a slog-sweep and was caught at square-leg. England collapsed in panic to 201; Benaud, from nowhere, had conjured six wickets for 70.

He was not only selected as one of *Wisden*'s Five Cricketers of the Year; he also wrote the profile of another one, his teammate Davidson, another first.

Wisden Cricketer of the Year
1962 – R. Benaud
Harry Gee, *Wisden Cricketers' Almanack*, 1962

If one player, more than any other, has deserved well of cricket for lifting the game out of the doldrums, that man is RICHARD BENAUD. Captain of Australia in four successive and triumphant series to the end of 1961, he has demonstrated to enthusiasts all over the world that the intention to make cricket, particularly Test cricket, attractive and absorbing is every bit as important as skilled technique in batting, bowling and fielding. He has succeeded in his aim to re-create interest in cricket because he loves playing it.

That was, of course, why Benaud junior – to distinguish him from his cricketer father, Louis Richard Benaud – took up the sport which brought him fame as a crusading captain and high commendation as a spin bowler, batsman and close fielder. No wonder that Richie – born Richard – at Penrith, thirty-odd miles from Sydney, on October 6, 1930, showed a fondness for cricket at an early age. He had his father, a first-grade player for twenty years with the unique feat to his credit of twenty wickets in a match, as instructor and mentor. Benaud senior, a third-generation Australian of Huguenot extraction, and a schoolteacher, bowled leg-breaks during a long career for the Cumberland club and so it was natural that he imparted the art of delivering them with the appropriate variations the googly and topspinner to his son.

A small bat and tennis ball, then a bigger bat and hard ball, were the implements used by the eager boy in his formative years as a cricketer under his father's expert eye. When the Benaud family, after living for a while in Jugiong, moved to Sydney, Richie went to Parramatta High School and here he had his first experience of captaincy. At sixteen, he followed in his father's footsteps by playing for Cumberland's first-grade team and, eventually, captained them. The New South Wales State selectors, ever on the look-out for rising talent, first picked him when eighteen as a batsman and this was still his primary role when promotion to international status came his way at the age of twenty-one in the Fifth Test match against West Indies at Sydney in January 1952.

Thus far, his ambition had been realised, but he had no means of knowing that almost ten years later, against the same country, he would lead Australia in the first Test match tie in history. Meantime, Richie Benaud came to England in 1953 and 1956 and he also earned representative honours against South Africa, India and Pakistan. His gradually mounting bowling skill was evident on his first two English trips, but he is remembered chiefly during those ventures for the dashing 97 he hit off the England attack in the Second Test at Lord's in 1956.

The 1957–58 tour to South Africa at length established him as an allrounder of top class, for he took 106 wickets, which surpassed the previous record of 104 by S. F. Barnes, and scored 817 runs, including four centuries, two of them in Test matches. Ian Craig led Australia in this series, but the following year slow recovery from illness precluded his choice for the captaincy against England when they toured 'Down Under'. So Benaud, somewhat to his surprise, but very keen to put his many theories into practice, was appointed to the task of recovering the Ashes which England had held since Hutton wrested them from Hassett in 1953.

Benaud duly completed his mission and fully justified the selectors' faith in him despite fears that the burden of captaincy might affect his form. His fine bowling, which yielded him 31 wickets for 18.83 runs apiece, proved a major factor in Australia's triumph of winning four Tests and drawing the other. Shrewd and inspiring captaincy transformed an ordinary side into an invincible combination bent on revenge – and gaining it.

Eight Test appearances in India and Pakistan a year later and five more during the memorable visit of West Indies to Australia in 1960–61 – all as captain – brought Benaud's total of caps to fifty. In India and Pakistan he excelled by taking 47 wickets (average 20.19) in the Tests and in the ensuing exciting rubber against Worrell's West Indies team he was second in the wicket-taking list, with 23 to the evergreen Davidson's 33.

Having with Worrell flung down the gauntlet to those who considered Test matches could only be grim affairs, Benaud consolidated his position as a cavalier captain when he visited England for the third time as a player last summer and helped his men to retain the Ashes. His inspirational value was graphically demonstrated by the fact that although he missed nearly one-third of the matches – including the Second Test – through shoulder trouble and was handicapped in some others, the Australians won the series 2–1 and maintained an unbeaten record outside the Tests.

When Benaud arrived in England with his team he pledged them to play attractive cricket – winning or losing. He also promised more overs to the hour as an antidote to defensively minded batsmen or bowlers. He promised quicker field-changing and fewer time-wasting tactical conferences during play. He and his men did their best to carry out this positive policy, and their faster scoring alone proved a telling reason for the success of the tour. When unable to lead his term, Benaud planned strategy with Neil Harvey, his able and wise vice-captain.

Pain, for which he had injections, did not deaden Benaud's intense desire to conquer on an English visit. That his playing share was limited to 32 innings for 627 runs and 61 wickets for 23.54 apiece spoke eloquently of his influence and worth in other directions. Nevertheless, his contribution of six wickets for 70 in the second innings of the Fourth Test at Manchester when the issue of the match and series lay in the balance, was a traditional captain's effort

made at a crucial time. He explained the achievements of his side by
declaring that they had risen to the occasion, but, modestly, sought
no credit for his part in them.

It was a great pity that, because of his shoulder injury, Benaud
could not give his admirers last summer other than rare glimpses of
his best form, but he had already done enough to make sure of a
high place in cricket history. He came with the reputation of being
one of the finest close-fielders in the world – either at gully or in a
silly position – and appreciative of the hazards thus entailed he
would never ask a man to take up a dangerous post he would not
himself occupy. As a forcing batsman, Benaud, tall and lithe, has
always been worth watching. His drives, powerfully hit and
beautifully followed through, are strokes of especial joy to those
whose day is made if they see a ball sent hurtling over the sightscreen.
At Scarborough in 1953 Benaud hit eleven sixes and nine fours
while making 135.

Still it is as a bowler that Benaud, in recent years, has touched the
heights. An advocate of practice and yet more practice, the erstwhile
youngster from the backwoods has long had a bulging quiver of
arrows for attack. The leg-break, the googly and the topspinner have
been used most often, and lately Benaud has added the 'flipper' to
his armoury. This is a ball, spun out of the finger-tips, which flashes
across from off to leg – in effect an offspinning topspinner. For his
discovery of this unusual and effective delivery, Benaud thanks Bruce
Dooland, who perfected it while assisting Nottinghamshire after
making his name in Australian cricket.

The urge to trick the batsman has developed in Benaud the ability
to evolve many more ways of getting a man out than his four basic
deliveries. Changes of pace and flight, with the ball released from
different heights, angles and lengths, have combined to make Benaud
a perplexing rival for the best of batsmen. He really likes bowling as
it affords him more chance than batting to keep in the thick of a

fight he relishes. A fighter, indeed, he has been all through his cricket career, which nearly came to a tragic end almost before it had begun when, as a youngster playing for New South Wales Second XI, he suffered a fractured skull in failing to connect with a hook stroke. Fortunately, he recovered to bring pleasure to cricket followers all over the world and to attain a place among the great players, a distinction earned by his taking of 219 wickets and scoring 1,744 runs in fifty-four Test matches to the end of 1961. Only three other Australians – M. A. Noble, Keith Miller and Ray Lindwall – have scored 1,500 runs and taken 100 wickets in Tests, and Lindwall alone (228) has captured more wickets for Australia.

By profession, Benaud, who is married and has two sons, is a newspaper reporter on the Sydney *Sun*. He writes as well as he plays and his self-written book *Way of Cricket* will act as a spur to aspiring young players to tread the road which leads to Test fame.—H. G.

Wisden Cricketer of the Year 1962 – A. K. Davidson

Richie Benaud, *Wisden Cricketers' Almanack*, 1962

When a cricketer can make fifty runs in a Test match he immediately becomes a valuable commodity to his side. When he has the ability to add to that five wickets and a brace of catches he is beyond price to his associates and skipper. Such a cricketer is ALAN KEITH DAVIDSON, born on June 14, 1929, of cricket loving parents at Lisarow on the Central North Coast of New South Wales, and latterly one of the great allrounders in the history of the game.

Davidson is a dynamic cricketer! A superb left-hander with both bat and ball. Many of his exploits are legendary among his fellow modern-day players. New Zealand tourists tell of the match at

Wairarapa where he took all ten wickets for 29 and then made a brilliant 160 not out to complete the day. The following game he relaxed by merely throwing out a scuttling batsman from the boundary with one stump at which to aim.

'Davo' played most of his early cricket in the Gosford district of New South Wales. There he was part of what was almost a family team with Davidsons and Cliftons putting a well-nigh unbeatable side into the field. A completely natural cricketer, he soon became a star player at Gosford High School and represented Northern High Schools for three successive years, vying with his present Test captain, Richie Benaud, who played for City High Schools. In those far-off days fast bowling was far from his mind. He was one of the unorthodox Fleetwood-Smith variety that seem to appear regularly in Australia. Not until the year after leaving school did he turn to fast-medium bowling, and with such success that he was selected the following season, 1949–50, for the State side.

With the Australian team in South Africa there were many opportunities for young players; the more so with a second eleven to be selected later in the year for a tour of New Zealand. Davidson grasped every one of them. He had a good match for NSW Colts against Queensland Colts and then bowled a future Test opener, George Thoms, first ball when he appeared against the Victorian Second Eleven. A week later, with his second ball in first-class cricket, he trapped the South Australian opener, Bob McLean, lbw, and, with consistent batting and bowling allied at times to almost unbelievable fielding, forced his way later in the season into the earlier-mentioned side for New Zealand. Four years later, he stepped on to the Trent Bridge ground at Nottingham to play for Australia in his first official Test match.

This, then, is the brief chronological account of a gifted cricketer, but who could care for statistics where there is concerned a player of the calibre of Davidson? Teammates and spectators prefer to recall some of his paralysing bursts with the new ball for Australia and the sight of his batting in full cry, preferably to some slow bowler. 'When you see that big right foot coming down the wicket, brother, you duck,' is an accurate and revealing recommendation given by an Australian bowler one day when asked how he felt about the carving just administered by the burly New South Welshman.

Like ten other Australians, one of his greatest moments in Test cricket was when he bowled Brian Statham to win the Ashes at Manchester in that fantastic Test of 1961. And rightly so, for without Davidson's magnificent 77 that day, Australians may well have been drinking their champagne from paper cups a couple of hours before the scheduled finishing time. That day the 'big right foot' was well in evidence. Placed close to the line of the ball and with bat swinging majestically alongside it, he belted David Allen out of the attack – and Allen had just placed Mackay, Benaud and Grout in the pavilion for a paltry number of runs. One of the sixes which assisted a twenty-run over flashed above cover's head; the next crashed against the brickwork alongside the railway line.

Every bit of six feet and fourteen stone went into those shots in the same way it has gone into all that Davidson has done over the years for Australia. Over one thousand runs, 162 wickets and nearly fifty close-to-the-wicket catches in Test matches give some idea why Australian players are prepared to argue about some of the 'old-time greats' as compared with this player. The beauty of an almost perfect fast-medium action with a disconcerting late swing has caused untold worry to opening batsmen the world over.

Peter Richardson, Watson and Graveney will long recall the day he took three wickets for one run in a sensational over in the Second Test at Melbourne in 1958–59 – just as vividly others will remember a burst with the second new ball at Pietermaritzburg in 1957–58 when he whipped three Natal batsmen back to the pavilion in one over for no runs, among them Test player Roy McLean.

Thirty-nine Test matches for his country have brought the left-hander to the top of the cricketing tree, though for many of those he was playing in the shadow of the great Australian pair, Miller and Lindwall. It was not until these players were out of the side that Davidson came into his own.

In South Africa in 1957–58 he left batsmen floundering and critics advising as he savoured the delights of the new ball for the first time as an Australian bowler. England, in 1958–59; India and Pakistan, in 1960; and the West Indies, 1960–61, all felt the lash of his talents. Indeed, one of his greatest performances was to take 33 wickets against the Caribbean visitors at a cost of 18 runs apiece when the next best average was 33 per wicket and five of the West Indians scored over 350 in the Test matches.

Davidson has announced that he will not tour again with an Australian side, but with his fitness restored and some sterling performances against his name in the 1961–62 Sheffield Shield season, Australians are looking to him for a great season against England later this year and justifiably so; for he has never let them down yet.—R. B.

2
A Boyhood Love of Cricket

‘It's a good lesson for everyone: that a youngster who throws a tennis ball up against a wall in a country town can still go on to captain his country at cricket, watch more than 500 Test matches, see cricket played in daylight and, as well, at night. It's been a fortunate life and one which has been very much enjoyed.’

Richie Benaud, *My Spin on Cricket*

Life was all about playing sport
Richie Benaud, *Over But Not Out*, 2010

Those first two summers gave my father a good grounding in Sydney club cricket, and the following summer, in 1939–40, he did very well, falling only four wickets short of the first-grade club record of 56 wickets established in 1913–14 by Rupert Coogan. In the *Cumberland Annual Report* it was mentioned of Lou that 'he achieved a marvellous feat to obtain 52 wickets, and although one of the club's most successful bowlers, he is also one of the most unfortunate as numerous catches were dropped off him.'

I was only nine at the time, but was already playing backyard cricket and back verandah Test matches at Sutherland Road, using the 1938 *NSW Cricket Association Yearbook* for my teams. That yearbook contained all the scoreboards from the 1936–37 Test series in Australia. I had an *Unrivalled Pocket Cricket Scoring Book* and used to take it to the matches with my father and, in the same way as you see some of the youngsters doing on television these days, I would score throughout the match.

Nine-year-olds had a good time in those days, not understanding what people were talking about when they mentioned a World War was about to start. Life was all about playing sport: non-stop cricket in the summer, and football in the winter in the paddocks across the way from Sutherland Road. Cricket was always a real challenge. Sometimes we would play on the pitch we had manufactured in the paddock, using a shovel as a leveller, and occasionally we were allowed to borrow a tennis court roller to flatten down a few of the humps. We also played down at Belmore Park, a few hundred yards away from my parents' home, where now there is the sign 'Belmore Park and Richie Benaud Oval'.

For children like me, everything was geared to sport, to listening to the radio, mystery stories on the airwaves, comedies like *Yes What?* where the pupils were allowed to be cheeky to the teachers, but then invariably were caned for being so. It was the radio, in those days called the wireless, which kept us all in touch with the world. There was a lot of sport on the radio throughout the week, and in the winter Andy Flanagan gave a wonderful rendition of the game of rugby league he had watched that day, referees' whistles and all. The cinema was popular in Parramatta. There were three of them, the Roxy, which was the high-class one, the Astra and the Civic. I secretly wanted to go to the Civic because it might be showing something like *Dracula's Sister Meets Frankenstein's Brother*, but my parents only allowed me to go to the Roxy, or sometimes the Astra, where, as though by magic, the electric organ and organist would appear from the area below the stage, and play tunes.

It was during the 1939–40 season that I saw my first Sheffield Shield match. It was between New South Wales and South Australia and it was played at the Sydney Cricket Ground, a place up to that moment

I had never seen. The game had a profound effect on me. It was played early in January 1940 and the participation of Bradman and other stars like McCabe and O'Reilly produced the second 75,000 match crowd that summer for a Shield game. That was the day when I first felt the urge to bowl leg-breaks, after watching Clarrie Grimmett bowl out NSW, taking 6–118 from 22 overs. The NSW spinners, O'Reilly and Pepper, took ten and six wickets respectively in the match and NSW won by 237 runs, after Grimmett had bowled them out in their first innings for 270.

The NSW victory gave them the Sheffield Shield, though that didn't mean a great deal to me then; nor did I know that the NSW opening batsman, Mort Cohen, who was making his debut and joined a select group of cricketers by making the two highest individual scores in the match, was later to be my accountant and a very good friend. I didn't see much of Bradman on the first day because NSW won the toss and batted, although he did come in late in the day and was 24 not out at the close of play. Bill O'Reilly took his ten wickets in wonderful attacking style, but it was Grimmett who caught my imagination because I actually watched him do it in the first innings, bowling from the Sheridan End, where we were seated on the stairway of the stand of the same name. It was a delightful day, very much a wide-eyed nine-year-old's day, and when we arrived back at Sutherland Road I had wondrous stories to tell my mother. I can still remember the names of the players in that match and the twelfth men; for many years they held pride of place in my little scorebook.

In those days there were no club games for Cumberland when there were top-line Sheffield Shield matches, so we were able to go to the SCG again when Victoria were the visitors a fortnight later. I watched Doug Ring take four wickets, without dreaming for a moment that I would tour England with him and Lindsay Hassett thirteen years later. This was the match where Hassett made 122 in each innings. Because of the war, this was the last such competition until 1946–47. In retrospect, one of the interesting things about the match was that Keith Miller didn't bowl at all. In fact, he didn't bowl in any first-class match up to the war. It was with the Services team in the UK in 1945 that he first began bowling and *Wisden* said of him, 'As an opening bowler he was the liveliest seen in England during the summer.' The Almanack added, with an eye to the future, 'He is destined to become one of the great men of Australian cricket.'

During my penultimate year at Burnside School, where my father was still teaching, we won our own little competition. I was hoping to do well enough scholastically at Burnside the following year to be able to gain a place at Parramatta High School, which my father had attended. The Burnside team had some great games at different grounds and against different schools. Generally the outfields were of paspalum, sometimes mown, sometimes not, and the pitches were always concrete, which was an interesting exercise because there was a great deal of bounce from the surface. The match was usually played with a ball made of cork and some rubber. I was bowling offspin and slow medium pace at this stage – my father wouldn't allow me to bowl leg-breaks because of the damage I might do to my muscles, ligaments and tendons at such a young age. That was some of the best parental control I ever had, although, like all youngsters, I occasionally sneaked a leg-break in the garden cricket at Sutherland Road.

Two of the players in the Burnside team were brothers, Harold and Laurence Barnes, both good cricketers. In 1997–98, when ACT made their debut in the Mercantile Mutual Cup in Australia, the match was played at the beautiful Manuka Oval in Canberra. Before the match started, a chap came to the commentary box and said, 'You won't remember me. My brother and I played with you at Burnside.'

'Then you must be a Barnes,' I said. 'But which one?'

'Harold,' was the answer, and he lived at Eugowra, eighty-five miles north of Jugiong. It was fifty-six years since I had seen him.

Better than heaven
Richie Benaud, *Over But Not Out*, 2010

In the 1942–43 season, which spanned my first year at high school and the start of the second, I scored for Cumberland second-grade team, a jump up from the *Unrivalled Pocket Cricket Scoring Book* to the *Unrivalled Scoring Book, Full Size*. I had a wonderful season, because in addition to the scoring I was allowed to field if any of the players either turned up late or hadn't been able to get leave from the Services; once I was able to field throughout the match, which meant someone else scoring, but it was heaven.

Sometimes I went to the matches with Jack O'Donoghue, the second-grade captain. I always dressed carefully in white shirt, light fawn or white shorts, white socks and sandshoes so that I could have some fielding practice with the team before the start, and if it happened someone had been unable to turn up on time, I was dressed properly to go on the field.

Better than heaven was when the team was one short and, aged twelve, I was allowed to bat for Cumberland against Petersham in 1942, at Petersham Oval. I took quite a good catch off my father's bowling when they batted and then, with nine wickets down, I went out to bat. We needed four runs and I had one ball to play in the over. Everyone was crouched around, I played forward and dropped the ball at my feet. Milton Jarrett, the big hitter and medium-pace bowler, took strike at the other end, smashed the first ball for six and the game was over. It was like playing in a Test match, or so it seemed at the time. When I walked off the field Milton Jarrett looked ten feet tall. I felt the same, and there was no happier twelve-year-old in Sydney.

The season commencing October 1943 was a great one for me. I was in second year at Parramatta High School, had just turned thirteen years of age, was captain of the fourth-grade cricket team at school, played again for a schools' representative team and was told by my parents I was about to have a brother or sister. This was excellent news, even though, if the former, it would be a few years before we were able to play cricket with one another, but it all sounded good. Certainly it did nothing but good for my fitness because apart from playing cricket in the daylight, there were long walks to be undertaken every evening as part of my mother's fitness regime.

My mother and father were approaching forty at this time, and John's birth in May of 1944 was great for both of them. We didn't know it at the time, but JB was to go to Parramatta High School eleven years later, play cricket for NSW and Australia and become one of the most respected journalists and editors in NSW newspapers.

The schools' representative match was played at Chatswood Oval between a Combined High Schools' team and the premiers, North Sydney Boys' High, managed by Arthur Henry, a prominent rugby and cricket figure. I returned home only half happy, having made a few runs but having 40 smashed off 10 overs. At the other end, Phil Tresidder, later to become a close friend of Daphne's and mine, took 8–32 from 15 overs of excellent pace bowling.

I scored again for Cumberland seconds that summer, and Doug Milner and I had a wonderful day at North Sydney Oval No. 2 when the side was two men short and we had to go in to bat at a crucial time, with wicketkeeper Joe Anderson the last of the recognised batsmen at the crease. Doug made ten and I made five, more off the edge than the centre of the bat, but it didn't matter at all to us, nor to the skipper Phil Bowmer, who had a 'well done' and a pat on the back for us.

For Doug and me it was a marvellous afternoon. At the end of the summer it was very sad to realise there would be no more cricket for several months, though there was always football, and Doug and I went off to play for our respective clubs, and against one another when that local derby came along.

The first two years at high school had been wonderful: I thoroughly enjoyed the schoolwork, and every other available moment was taken up either playing and practising cricket, or, in the football season, having long practice sessions with a very good friend, Lloyd Blain. Lloyd played for St Andrew's at right-half, and we would ride our bikes a few miles down into Parramatta Park, where the soccer goalposts had been set up by the Parramatta Council, and practise taking penalties and dribbling the ball.

The summer of 1944–45 was a little different. It was decided I would play cricket at school as usual, and rather than score at weekends for Cumberland seconds, I would play in the local junior competition on the matting pitches, where instead of bowling spin, I would bowl with the new ball, something I thoroughly enjoyed. I also liked batting on coir matting, the aim of this being to improve my back-foot play, because the ball lifted relatively sharply off the mat. As the usual flat and grassless turf pitches meant front-foot play was the norm, particularly early in the summer, this matting cricket was to provide a different type of challenge.

It was a successful summer, and, aged fourteen, I played Green Shield (Under-16) matches as well, making 177 runs at 25 and taking 20 wickets at 17 apiece from 57 overs, but with most of our team only fourteen years old, we weren't a real contest for the other clubs.

In the holidays we went to the SCG to watch matches between Combined teams and a Services side, and two of our Cumberland players, Bert Alderson and Brian Bowman, were chosen to play. It was a slightly sobering experience watching from the Sheridan Stand as I suddenly realised there were some really fast bowlers in the world. One bowler named Ray Lindwall took the new ball against Bert and gave him a torrid time. Lindwall took four wickets and could have had more and they said he was likely to go on to greater things in cricket.

During these summers I went with my father to the weekly practices at the Cumberland Oval in Parramatta; I was allowed to field all afternoon, which was a real treat. Doug Kennedy, a Cumberland first-grader and great friend of our family, would keep a running total of the runs I had saved, and this stiff examination at practice every Thursday afternoon was, more than anything else, the reason I fielded so well when I moved into the higher level of cricket.

The following summer, 1945–46, I went to Cumberland's preliminary practices at Lidcombe Oval, this time as someone trying out for selection, and I made it into third grade. It was a good place to start and my father stressed that at fifteen years of age and in the fourth year at high school it was time to find out a few things about my cricket. It was excellent experience; we played on some *very* bad pitches when we were away from Parramatta and Lidcombe Ovals. *The Cumberland Annual Report* of the pitch for the final match, at St Paul's University, described it as 'a natural grass pitch, innocent of any treatment from the roller', but it gave me the chance to be competitive against higher-class players.

I was promoted to second grade for the last match of the summer against Gordon, and before I left for the game my father gave me a piece of good advice. 'Jack Prowse,' he said, 'is a very good bowler and I've played against him for many years. He is a legspinner, but hardly turns the ball at all, it's his topspinner you must watch, it hurries off the pitch like lightning. You must play forward at him even if the ball is short.'

When I went out to bat at number seven, Jack was bowling. The first ball *was* short, I played forward and it hit my bat as I was still bringing it forward. He stood there mid-pitch, hands on hips, and said, 'Your father's been telling you about me.'

My father had again topped the club's first-grade bowling, most wickets, best average and best strike-rate, where he was averaging a wicket every twenty-five balls – not bad for someone who turned forty-two years of age just before the end of the summer!

3
Learning the Ropes

❝After attending Parramatta High School, Richie made his New South Wales debut on the final day of 1948. Three years later, against the West Indies at Sydney, he first played for Australia. His selection was frequently questioned in those early years, when much other flowering talent was evident in domestic cricket. In 1952–53 Benaud played against South Africa, recording a duck and having his front teeth smashed while fielding at gully in the Sydney Test, which coincided with his honeymoon. It was not the first time he had been hospitalised by a blow to the head. Four years previously he had been hit in the face while batting for New South Wales 2nd XI in Melbourne.❞

David Frith, *Guardian*

Up a level, but can I handle it?
Richie Benaud, *Anything But . . . an Autobiography*, 1998

Nineteen forty-six to forty-seven was the season when everything seemed to be happening as far as I was concerned. I was in my last year at high school and studying for my Leaving Certificate, as it was called in those days, and I was selected for first grade with Cumberland, playing in the same team as my father. In addition, I was the captain of the Green Shield team and captained the Combined Sydney Green Shield team against Newcastle, as I had done the previous summer. When a New South Wales 2nd XI team visited Newcastle in the Christmas vacation, I was named twelfth man when the team was announced. Soon afterwards came the news that I had passed the Leaving Certificate. Not by much, mind you – it was known as the sportsman's pass, with four Bs. Even so, it was a relief to have made it, a feeling reciprocated in heartfelt fashion by my parents, who had agonised through every moment of the last few weeks of cramming.

Although the ultimate personal ambition of every cricketer is to play for his country, Australian cricketers share an ambition only a little short of this, in that they are desperate to play for their state and to win the Sheffield Shield. When I first played Sheffield Shield there were five teams in the competition; Western Australia and Tasmania were admitted in 1947 and 1977. Gaining a place in a team was a cut-throat business, and holding your place in the side was dependent on a combination of skill, potential, some law changes, and on whether or not there was a youth policy in the state in which you lived. As it happened, I was extremely fortunate that all four things applied after I left Parramatta High School, and the NSW selectors were constantly on the lookout for young players.

In 1946, the year I left school, aged sixteen, the NSW selectors named me in a strong team of youngsters to tour Forbes, Dubbo and Wellington, three country towns in NSW, to see how the players shaped up in a team environment. Although I didn't realise it then, the state selectors were way ahead of their time in their policy decisions. The MCC team were about to arrive in Australia for the first Ashes battle after the war, and while NSW and the other states had plenty of experienced cricketers, the youngsters were very much an unknown quantity. The selectors decided to find out about them.

It was a wonderful experience for a sixteen-year-old, the cricket was very good and very competitive, and the selectors saw enough of the youngsters in the team to get a good idea of which players might be put into a 'possible' category for the State Colts' XI Interstate matches when they resumed.

I started the 1946–47 cricket season in third grade and had two very good matches, one second-grade game against Western Suburbs, and then was rapidly promoted to the firsts. We were well beaten by Glebe in my debut match, but the second game provided some happier moments. Cumberland had lost 4–34 when I walked out to bat to join allrounder Gordon Clark. We added 111, and by the time I was close to the nineties my father was in with me batting number nine. I missed the century by two runs, being stumped off NSW Sheffield Shield offspin bowler Vince Collins. My father was disappointed, as I was, but he took 4–22 the next Saturday, bowling out Marrickville to give us the victory in what was a good family effort.

At Parramatta Oval that summer I shared in one of my most enjoyable partnerships. I was in with Arthur Clues, and it was his final innings before boarding the ship for England, where he was going to play rugby league for Leeds. Arthur was one of the greatest rugby league footballers produced by Australia and I had watched him as a youngster. When I started going to the Cumberland practices in 1939, Arthur was always in the practising group.

Arthur looked a good cricketer and he also had a flow of language that brought either envy or the raised eyebrow, whichever way you looked at it, or listened to it. It was fascinating to a youngster to hear Arthur's penetrating voice ringing out across the Oval with one of his milder entreaties: ' "Bowie", you stupid bastard, catch the bloody thing . . .' 'Bowie' was Brian Bowman, a mate of Arthur's. Jack Jeffery, our family doctor and Central Cumberland offspinner, had a slightly disapproving look, and my father would cast one eye at Arthur and keep the other on me, trying to judge whether or not I was within hearing distance. I promise you, the stationmaster at Parramatta railway station was in fact within hearing distance, but each time I caught my father's eye I kept a perfectly straight face. No chance of me providing a reason not to be at the practice.

This day at Parramatta Oval, Cumberland had to follow on against a strong Manly bowling attack, and Arthur and I shared a century partnership. Arthur made 115 not out in 89 minutes, and I watched, slightly bemused and in admiration at the other end, and made 40 not out. It was one of the best exhibitions of strokeplay I had seen, and that after he had also top-scored in the first innings. It was some farewell to Cumberland.

The Cumberland Club and its practices, and the manner in which it embraced the players, was an example to all. I'm sure there were other clubs in the Sydney metropolitan area which were also good, although even fifty-eight years later, it is quite impossible to conceive that anything could have been better. There had been three Test players at the stage, of whom W. P. (Bill) Howell was most famous. He was born at Penrith, NSW, in 1869, and was an apiarist, and played eighteen times for Australia. In his first match in England, against Surrey at The Oval in 1899, he took all ten Surrey first-innings wickets for 28. The other Test players were Gerry Hazlitt, who toured England in 1912 after playing against them in Australia in 1911–12, and Frank Iredale, who played in 1894–95 in Australia and then in 1896 in England.

Cumberland had been one of the founder members of the district cricket competition in Sydney, beginning in 1893 with seven other teams. As far back as 1840, the year Captain Jean Benaud arrived in Australia from France on the *Ville de Bordeaux*, cricket was played and the event recorded at Parramatta; it was a match 'for 25 pounds and a supper at mine hosts of the Royal Exchange'. Five years later teams were complaining the opposition used unfair tactics, including having recourse to their own umpires. There is a delightful account of a match between the Currency Club and the Parramatta Club in

1845 where the Currency team won by 112 runs, but were upbraided for the fact that the ball they used had been deliberately soaked in linseed oil for a long time so that it was *completely non-elastic*. Tough times.

At the beginning of December 1887 Mr Vernon's touring England team played against Eighteen of Parramatta at the Parramatta ground, and in 1891–92 W. G. Grace captained Lord Sheffield's team to Australia. Their fourth match was against Twenty of Cumberland at Parramatta. It got away to a bad start when the local captain, Kirby, and 'WG' went out to toss. Kirby called and Grace picked up the coin, pocketed it and told Kirby Cumberland were to bat on a wet pitch. Kirby protested that he had called correctly, but Grace said, according to the *Parramatta Argus* report of 12 December 1891, 'That sort of thing won't suit me, I won't stand it from anyone!' When Grace was bowled for a duck by the Parramatta man 'Joe' Wilson, the England captain was cheered off the ground in lively fashion by more than 1,000 spectators.

My father told me a lot about the rich tradition of the club and talked about those three Test players and the others who had played in some representative cricket. When MCC beat NSW by four wickets during the Bodyline tour, Cumberland player Ray Rowe, making his debut, had double-figure scores, 70 and 11, in the two low-scoring innings. There were only four other double-figure efforts, from Bill Brown, Don Bradman and Jack Fingleton, all Test batsmen then or later.

Ray Rowe was my first captain when I made it into Cumberland's first-grade side in 1946. He was also captain seven years earlier in a match which will always stick in my mind as a spectator, Cumberland v Northern District at Waitara Oval.

A Sheffield Shield match between NSW and South Australia was played in blistering heat that same weekend at the SCG, and it was the game when Don Bradman, playing for SA, equalled C. B. Fry's feat of making six successive centuries in first-class matches. This Cumberland match was on 14 January 1939, the time of appalling bushfires in Sydney, which destroyed homes all around the metropolitan area and turned the tinder-dry bushland to ash. My father said he had never played cricket on a hotter day. Cumberland's bowlers were thrashed for 420–5 at Waitara in front of seventeen spectators.

Seven thousand turned up to see Bradman fourteen miles down the road, but with Charlie Walker nursing a broken finger, Bradman kept wicket and then was twenty-two not out at stumps. He eventually made his century to equal Fry's record, but not until the fourth day of the match because the second and third were washed out with wonderful, delightful, glorious and so badly needed rain, which thankfully put out every one of the awful bushfires.

Nineteen forty-seven to forty-eight was a very heavy season and a most successful one for the Benaud family. I finished second in the club batting averages and aggregate, but again my problem was with my bowling. I had a strike-rate of a wicket every 72 balls, which was poor, and took only nine wickets in the season.

I was in my second year of employment at the time, in Alan Savage's chartered accountant's office in Pitt Street, Sydney, having started there under the watchful care of John Maloney and Mr Savage. I was never sure I was cut out for accountancy, but at Parramatta High School, in keeping with all other secondary schools, they provided tests for pupils to see for what they would be best suited. I loved English but the testers said I was outstanding at mental arithmetic, so accountancy it was.

My father and I started cricket practice in July 1948 out at Bert Alderson's home at Northmead and by the time the official practices began at Lidcombe Oval on the first Saturday in September, we were all in reasonable form, though mine was more in the batting department than bowling. I was hitting the ball very well, but my legspinners weren't coming out right at that stage, in retrospect possibly because I was trying to bowl several different types of ball each over.

I made 20 against Gordon in the first match of the summer which Cumberland won, then 86 against St George, 57 against Manly and 69 against Western Suburbs and was chosen for the NSW Colts team for the match to be played against Queensland. This was a wonderful adventure. I had just turned eighteen, had been out of Sydney only when on holidays and visiting relatives in the country, or with NSWCA teams on their country visits when staying in an hotel was an adventure in itself.

After I had arranged leave from Mr Savage's accountancy firm, the team assembled at Central railway station and we travelled by train to Queensland. That NSW v Queensland game was a triumph for Alan Walker, the fast left-arm bowler who later was to play Sheffield Shield cricket and tour South Africa with the Australian team in 1949–50, and also for Ron Briggs and Jim Burke, who made centuries, both later played Sheffield Shield and 'Burkie' played for Australia.

I batted and bowled well enough to be satisfied with the week. NSW won the match with ease, and for many of the young players it was the start of careers at a level above grade or club cricket in Sydney. It was exciting and I wanted to continue to be part of it.

Don Bradman's all-conquering team had returned to Australia, and at the conclusion of the season Bradman played his last match for South Australia in a game which was designated as a testimonial for former Test player Arthur Richardson. Bradman fell and twisted his ankle on the second day of the match and took no further part in the game.

I once said to Keith Miller how disappointed I was to have made my debut in the same year as Bradman finished. How wonderful it would have been to have watched him play at the SCG in 1940 and then been able to bowl at him on the same ground. Nugget looked at me and remarked drily that everyone has one lucky break in a lifetime and that may well have been mine!

> ⁶A bleeding ring finger at the end of every training session was not only normal but essential for my development as a wrist spinner.⁹
>
> *RB on what it takes*

Bradman had announced he intended to retire from the game which he had graced for such a long period and a testimonial match was arranged for 3–7 December at the Melbourne Cricket Ground. It drew 94,000 spectators and it was a batsman's match, with 1,672 runs coming in the four days' play and the game itself finishing in a tie.

Television wasn't to hit Australia for another eight years, so I listened to the match on the radio, although my main interest was in the Sheffield Shield; NSW were playing Queensland on the same ground where I had recently played in the Colts match. Their performances in that Colts game had earned Alan Walker a place in the Shield team and Jim Burke the position of twelfth man. It was significant that the Colts match was being seen as a genuine path to first-class cricket in NSW. While the NSW–Queensland Shield game was being played in Brisbane, I made a good 69 in a grade match against Western Suburbs at Parramatta in front of state selector, Selby Burt.

The traditional New Year fixture at the SCG in those days was always NSW v Queensland. I was walking back to the office after my lunch break when I saw in the Sydney *Sun* the story of my selection for the NSW Sheffield Shield team. It wasn't your normal run-of-the-mill match either because the ground was hit by a cloudburst the night before the scheduled start and then more heavy rain in the early morning meant the abandonment of the opening day. The curator started work at 4 a.m. on the second day and had the very grassy surface rolled hard enough by the start of play, but Arthur Morris had no hesitation in putting Queensland in when he won the toss and I was happy not to be in the centre, batting. It was really difficult and Ray Lindwall and Alan Walker were very fast and dangerous. I failed with the bat in the first innings but I wasn't required to bat again, nor was any batsman in the NSW side other than Morris and Burke, and I never looked like being called to the bowling crease.

Arthur later said, 'Sorry about that, son, but I didn't think the pitch would suit you all that much.' Even at that young age, and keen as I was to bowl for t he first time in a Sheffield Shield game, I realised the batsmen's eyes would have lit up had they seen a debutant legspinner coming on to bowl instead of Lindwall, Walker or Miller. I was happy enough for the reprieve.

A hole in the head

Richie Benaud, *Anything But . . . an Autobiography*, 1998

If luck had played a part in my selection for the state team, it then immediately turned the other way because I had at the same time been chosen in the NSW 2nd XI team to play Victoria in Melbourne. This was slightly unusual, but because I was only eighteen at the time, and a rather immature eighteen at that, the selectors had decided I needed as much experience as possible. I suppose you could say I was one of the NSW 2nd XI's more experienced players, having played one Sheffield Shield match, albeit without having had the slightest success. I was soon to realise cricket was a much more punishing and painful game than it might have appeared in the backyard at Parramatta or when playing for Central Cumberland.

In the *Sydney Morning Herald* and the Sydney *Sun* over the previous ten days there were minor reports and abbreviated scores of matches between Victoria and Tasmania. The name Jack Daniel cropped up twice, once when he took 6–37 to rout the Tasmanians for 132 on Christmas Day and then, six days later, when he took 6–20 and bowled them out for 65. Born in Yorkshire and brought to Australia as a youngster, he was classed as 'fast bowler J. Daniel'. The Victorian wicketkeeper was I. H. McDonald. I had no cause at that stage to know about either of them, but I was to know them much better within a few days!

We arrived in Melbourne by train on the morning of 10 November 1949, a team full of hope for victory and future selection after what our dreams told us might be a series of splendid performances over the three days of the big game. These were two strong teams, with future Test players in Colin McDonald and Jack Hill in the Victorian side, plus nine other Sheffield Shield players of the future. NSW had Graeme Hole, Jim de Courcy and me as future Test players, though we weren't to know this at the time, and there were five others who would play Sheffield Shield. It was always likely to be a tough contest and, even in those days, a Victoria–NSW game stirred the players' blood, whether it was at Sheffield Shield level or just below that exalted position.

NSW bowled Victoria out for 276 and again I didn't reach the bowling crease. Ron Briggs and Graeme Hole opened the innings with less than an hour to play and Brian Dwyer asked me to pad up as nightwatchman. I was very happy to do it, otherwise I might have been down at six or even seven. When the first wicket fell at 35 that evening, I went out through the gate to an atmosphere I had never before encountered on a cricket field. It was sheer aggro which, some time later, was transformed to friendliness when we were back in the dressing-room and the day's play was over. It was the first really good lesson which showed me that on the field the game should be fair but very hard, and off the field it should provide the chance to meet people and to sit down and chat over a drink.

The following morning, Jack Daniel bowled a bouncer before I had added to my overnight score and I was carried off the field on a stretcher. Ian McDonald, who had been behind the stumps at the time, had seen exactly what had happened and described it to me some years later. The ball was thumped in short and I went for the hook shot, but didn't move far enough inside the line. My memory of it was that I was trying to pull the ball, which I thought would arrive at about chest height, but that it lifted more than I expected and left me stranded. I saw a blur of ball, and then there was a very nasty thud against my forehead, just above the right eye. In that, I was lucky: two inches lower and I might well have lost an eye, or worse. McDonald later said he had never heard a worse sound on the cricket field than that ball hitting and splintering bone.

As might be imagined, everything was a bit hazy after that, although I can clearly recall two things to this day. The first was the sight of Jimmy de Courcy, the next man in for NSW, standing impassively at the gate as I was carried past him. He gave me a slight nod and then I was on my way into the dressing-room. The other was that once I had been put on the massage table, what I wanted most in life was to take my boots and socks off as I had pins and needles in my feet. What my team-mates thought about all this scarcely bears imagining. This was the guy who, a few minutes earlier, had walked out of the dressing-room full of confidence, hoping to make a packet of runs and a name for himself, and now here he was, stretched out with his legs kicking, asking people to take off his boots and socks. In addition, he had a hole in his forehead exactly the size of half a cricket ball.

They took me off to hospital, where doctors and nurses gave the impression that in a matter of minutes they would have X-rays which would show the extent of the damage, although it was nothing like as simple as that.

There is a true story of a cricketer hit by a ball who went to the hospital for X-rays and the media bulletin handed out in the press box a couple of hours later said the X-rays of his head showed absolutely nothing! That brought a deal of hilarity at the time, and the first part was repeated this day in Melbourne. The X-rays showed nothing. Twenty-eight X-rays and there was still nothing on film, although the doctors, who by now were a little perplexed, did say there had to be something there, you couldn't have a hole that deep in a forehead without something being fractured.

Ian McDonald was very concerned and Brian Dwyer made me promise to go to my own GP, Jack Jeffery, the Cumberland cricketer, and to make sure more X-rays were taken. Like all young people I took note of the advice, though not straight away and not until I had been home to see Mum and Dad, or rather Mum first, as she was the one who opened the door to me. I can't recall exactly what she said, but she told me later she needed all her pioneering instincts to keep a level tone in her voice. I'm not surprised. In the space of a couple of days the injury had bled internally, and my face was a mixture of black and yellow, and the colours had run down into the neck area. It wasn't a pretty sight Late in the afternoon I went down to Parramatta town to see Jack Jeffery, who took one look and phoned the hospital, then took me there himself for further X-rays.

The next day Cumberland's first-grade team were playing at Lidcombe Oval, so, as I couldn't play, I did the next best thing and cadged a lift down to see the match. While I was there Jack Jeffery arrived at my parents' home in Sutherland Road with the new X-rays and the information that I had a very badly shattered frontal bone in my forehead. When told where I was, he organised a very quick phone call to officials at Lidcombe Oval to tell me not to do anything to jar my head and under no circumstances to get anywhere near a cricket ball.

I had been only moderately worried up to that moment; at my stage of life youthful optimism told me it was little more than a medical quirk that I had a hole in my forehead, but no fracture had shown. Now it was very different and the urgency in the various voices sent a little tremor up my spine, because of the implication that another blow in the same spot could be fatal. When I got home to Sutherland Road I went into my room and had a look in the mirror. What previously had been merely multi-coloured, now had about it a menacing and ugly touch, and although it was only fear of the unknown, the mirror showed that fear.

Jack Jeffery lined up the best man in Sydney, surgeon George Halliday, to perform the necessary operation, and without going into too many gory details, it all worked, even down to what the surgeon told me about scarring. He said, 'After we've opened you up from outside your left eye across to outside your right eye and sorted out the bits of bone, within a couple of years the operation scar will be nothing more than a thin line across your nose. People will assume it is a mark left by your spectacles. Just say, "Yes, of course!"'

After a two-week stint at the Royal Prince Alfred Hospital in Sydney, I discovered very quickly I was allergic to penicillin. Two weeks of penicillin shots in the backside whilst in hospital hadn't been a problem, but no one had completely prepared me for arriving back at Sutherland Road and waking up the following morning, having not had a shot for the first time in fourteen days, and being unable to open my eyes properly. There was a very good reason for this. When I took a glance in the bathroom mirror I looked like a Michelin tyre advertisement with great folds of swelling. The only difference was, unlike the ad, I wasn't smiling. That lasted just a week, but it was enough to have me carry a note from then on and an instruction on a medallion that says 'NO Penicillin'.

Musing about these medical matters later, it did cross my mind to ask the doctors what might happen, when I started playing cricket again, if I collected on the same spot another blow from a cricket ball. I decided it might be better not to know.

Three greats
Richie Benaud, *My Spin on Cricket*, 2005

Arthur Morris, Keith Miller and Ray Lindwall were everything any young cricketer could want as mentors, at a time when there was intense competition for places in an extraordinarily strong New South Wales team in the late 1940s. That strength continued through the 1950s and early 1960s, with the Sheffield Shield being won twelve times in fourteen years. Those three brilliant and experienced cricketers always had time for the younger players and they knew precisely what would be of assistance to them in improving their all-round games. All-round doesn't just mean batting, bowling and fielding, but thinking came into it as well. Sitting in the dressing-room after the day's play was always a great experience. It was a case of listening more than talking, though there were always questions to be asked and answers to be remembered. All this was priceless for any youngster lucky enough to be in the NSW team at that time.

When I was chosen in the NSW team to go to Queensland for the traditional opener of the season in 1951, Ray was the opening bowler. The pitch at the 'Gabba was always magnificent for batting, but we contained Queensland to 316, with Ken Archer making a magnificent 106. Lindwall's bowling figures were 26.1–7–45–7 and it was one of the greatest exhibitions of pace bowling I had ever seen to that time. He bowled fast, had perfect control of swing and movement off the seam and his changes of pace constantly had the batsmen in trouble. In the second innings his figures were 13–5–23–2 and again he bowled magnificently. Facilities at the 'Gabba in those days were rather ordinary and the two teams had their dressing-rooms side by side. The flooring was of weather-beaten timber, scarred over the years by the long spikes of the players as they walked around and did their loosening-up exercises. Don Bradman's spikes had left their mark on the floor when he had made his Test debut twenty-three years earlier.

Ray was a splendid footballer as well as a great cricketer and he was always super-fit, always looked after himself. Before bending and stretching became fashionable in the modern game 'Lindy' was doing it, but without the aerobics! He always finished up with running on the spot, something that was almost unnoticed in other dressing-rooms around the world, but not at the 'Gabba, where the timber floor allowed the noise to bounce across and off the walls and then up to the corrugated iron roof, where it doubled in sound in our room and trebled in the Queenslanders' room. He only ran on the spot for one minute but it must have seemed more like an hour to the two batsmen next door padded up and ready to open the innings.

Ken Archer was a fine cricketer, one of the more brilliant fieldsmen ever to play for Australia and a very good opening batsman. More credit to him this day then for having held out against Lindwall, caned the other bowlers, including me, and made his century. When NSW batted, Arthur Morris, the skipper of the side, made 253 out of the 400 innings total, an innings to be matched with anything I had seen in Sheffield Shield cricket. The third member of the group, Keith Miller, missed out with both bat and ball in the game, which was eventually drawn, but he had other great all-round performances in the past and there were certainly more to come at the 'Gabba in the future.

Lindwall had made his debut in first-class cricket against Queensland at the 'Gabba in November 1941 and I watched him bowl in a match at the SCG that year which was shortly before Japan entered the Second World War, and then I watched him play in some Services' matches when he came back to Sydney from the jungles of New Guinea. He bowled against one of my Central Cumberland team-mates, Bert Alderson, who was an opening batsman and had been chosen to play for NSW in one of those games. Bert, who had been a champion schoolboy cricketer, was also a very heavy scorer in club cricket and for many years was at the top of the first-grade batting figures at our club. It was quite an experience for him batting against Lindwall because he had a slightly unusual grip of the bat, with the index finger of his left hand resting on the back of the bat, down the spring. Ray, bowling at blistering pace, yorked him but not before he had severely jarred that index finger through the ball thumping into the blade.

Test cricket resumed in Australia in the 1946–47 season and, although Ray was a certainty for the opening Test against England at the 'Gabba in 1946, he contracted chicken-pox and had to miss the Second Test in Sydney, which was the first Test match I ever watched and in which Don Bradman and Sid Barnes each made 234. Ray's absence from this Sydney match was a great disappointment to me but he was back in the next Test in Melbourne, taking three wickets and making a century. Although Ray was always listed as a fast bowler in any tour guides, he was in fact a fine allrounder, one of the best ever produced by Australia. He is one of only four Australian players to take 200 wickets and score 1,000 runs in Tests*. He went on in that first series after the war to take six wickets in the Fourth Test in Adelaide and nine in the final game in Sydney.

* As of June 2015, seven Australian players have achieved this: Shane Warne, Brett Lee, Mitchell Johnson, Jason Gillespie, Merv Hughes, Ray Lindwall and RB.

At the same time Miller was hitting a half-century and a century and Morris hit three successive Test centuries at the top of the order, so the heart of a sixteen-year-old was able to beat a little faster. Ray and Keith had developed into a feared pace bowling combination, Ray already being spoken of as the finest fast bowler since Jack Gregory and Ted McDonald in their prime. I played under Lindwall's captaincy in 1956 in Bombay, as it was then called, in the series we played on the way back from England, and then he played under my captaincy on the first-ever official tour of India and Pakistan in 1959–60, as well as in the series against England in 1958–59 when he went past Clarrie Grimmett's Australian Test wicket-taking record of 216.

Ray always produced plenty of apprehension among opening batsmen and some of his greatest tussles were with Len Hutton, the great England opener. I can still remember the stunned silence with which the Yorkshire crowds twice accepted their hero being bowled by Lindwall for a duck. His bowling arm was slightly lower than normal but this gave him the opportunity to bowl a very dangerous outswinger, even if it did restrict the inswinger which he eventually developed when playing in the Lancashire League, where he found the snicks were not easy for the fieldsmen to hold.

Lindwall was a model for all young cricketers, fast but very rarely furious, and a role model for the acceptance of umpires' decisions and attitude. That attitude was do your best on the field but, whether you've made a duck or a hundred, make sure you are still in the dressing-room of the opposition team at the close of play saying 'well played' or 'thanks for the game'.

I first met Arthur Morris at the back of the old Members' Stand at the Sydney Cricket Ground when I went with my father to see a match before the Sheffield Shield restarted after the war. I had read a great deal about this left-hander, described as one of the best and most elegant players Australia had produced, and had also been following his name after his record-breaking debut in first-class cricket in 1941. The last of the Sheffield Shield games had been played in the 1939–40 season and the games between then and the resumption had been mainly between NSW teams and Services' sides.

My father knew him because of having bowled to him when playing for Central Cumberland against St George, which was the very strong team captained by Bill O'Reilly in the Sydney grade competition. I had been mentioned a few times in the newspapers as a promising Parramatta High School cricketer who had played in schoolboy representative games in Sydney and Newcastle. When introduced I said very politely, 'Hello, Mr Morris', as one did in those days, and, after chatting for a minute or so, he said he hoped my cricket continued to go well and he went up to the dressing-room to get ready for the day. It would be a better story if I had vowed that I would one day play in the same team as him but, although that actually happened a few years later, I was more interested at that moment in going to watch the players practise in the nets which used to exist on the old SCG No 2, just twenty yards away.

The next summer, 1949–50, had the Australian Test side in South Africa, but a glaring omission was the dropping of Keith Miller, which meant he would be captaining NSW in the Sheffield Shield. No one seemed able to fathom the fact that he had been dropped and it later transpired all three selectors, in private conversations, indicated they had voted for him, not against him. A slightly bizarre sequence of events. At any rate, it meant that two of my cricketers, Morris and Lindwall, were in South Africa, the other, Miller, was in Australia, though that was soon to be changed because Bill Johnston was injured in a road accident in South Africa and Miller was flown over as the replacement player.

He had captained NSW to a stirring 15-run victory over Queensland at the 'Gabba in the opening match of the summer, making 80 and taking six wickets, and, in grade cricket with Cumberland, I had made a good start to the season which included 160 against Gordon at Lidcombe Oval. I had been retained in the NSW practice squad and after making those runs I was included in the twelve for the game at the SCG against Western Australia, carrying the drinks successfully and very happy to be back again. When Miller left for South Africa, the selectors made Ron James captain of the state team for the southern tour, which meant I was about to play my second game of first-class cricket, something of a relief after the predictions that I might not play again.

The selectors also included Alan Davidson, the former left-arm over-the-wrist spinner from Gosford High School who was now playing with Northern District in the Sydney club competition and had changed himself into a left-arm pace bowler, genuinely quick and with wonderful control of swing. It was an inspired selection. 'Davo' took the wicket of Bob McLean with his first ball in first-class cricket and had such a good summer with the ball that the Australian selectors named him in the Australian team to make a short tour of New Zealand under Bill Brown's captaincy. The team was to be named at the conclusion of the NSW–South Australia match at the SCG and Alan and I both had reasonably good matches. He took six wickets and I made 93 but I'd found wickets hard to come by. I was a chance for selection in the line-up for New Zealand but, when I looked at the final touring party nominated, I could see clearly I had yet another level to climb. I might have been promising, and certainly I had made something of a comeback after serious injury, but it was a case of translating promise into something more concrete when the Sheffield Shield was at full strength, with all the Test players available.

Nineteen forty-nine to fifty then was a summer of considerable learning, but it was also a summer without Miller, Morris and

Lindwall, all of whom had a successful tour of South Africa, even though Lindwall was dropped for the final Test there, despite having had match performances of 5–32, 3–47 and 4–89. Morris hit two centuries and Miller, although not making a century, turned in excellent all-round performances. Not least of the mysteries was that the man for whom he was sent as a replacement player, Bill Johnston, was far and away Australia's best bowler, with 23 wickets in the series, having made a very quick recovery once Lindsay Hassett and his tour selection committee had ensured Miller would be on the next aeroplane! One of the more devious and clever Hassett and Morris moves to circumvent an originally poor selection.

It was great to go to the NSW Sheffield Shield squad practices the following summer starting in October 1950, and meet up with the six players who had returned from South Africa. Alan Walker, Jack Moroney and Ron Saggers were back in the team, as well as Morris, Miller and Lindwall. The one thing patently obvious to all the players from the previous Australian summer was that it was going to be very difficult to catch the selectors' eyes and, having done that, performances would need to be at a peak to remain in the side. I scrambled in as twelfth man for the first two games against Queensland at the 'Gabba and then the SCG. In the game at the 'Gabba, 'Davo', who beat me for a place in the final eleven, excelled with 7–49 from 20 overs in the Queensland first innings. The second match produced the extraordinary Melbourne Cup broadcast declaration. NSW went on to win that game after Don Tallon declared the Queensland innings so that all players could listen to the Cup and Morris and Miller then opened the innings and hit an astonishing 225 off 29 overs to win the match. Each of them had already made a century and a half-century in the game in Queensland and Lindwall took wickets in both matches. I might not have made it into the final eleven, but it was just as fascinating in 1950 to hear the three of them discussing tactics and advising the young players in the dressing-room or at the dinner table, moving salt and pepper shakers around to illustrate the advice and make a point.

I was an avid listener and I was also doing well enough in the grade cricket matches to retain my place in the twelve for the southern tour, with the first match to be played at the MCG. Selection was so tough that Alan Davidson was made twelfth man for that game, and the subsequent one in South Australia, though he returned to the side when the First Test was being played in Brisbane and the top players were out. It was a tough summer. In the Melbourne game I made 55 and took 3–46, the latter including Lindsay Hassett lbw. I'd like to be able to say I dismissed the Australian captain and great player of over-the-wrist spin with a beautiful delivery, dipping and spinning, but, in fact, it was a topspinner which landed on one of the famous cracks in the Melbourne pitch and ran along the ground, hitting Lindsay on the foot.

I had caught the eye of the selectors to the extent that I had been named in the Australian XI team to play England at the SCG, so too Jim Burke, who made a century and then gained a place in the Test side. I couldn't play because I had broken a bone in my right thumb fielding the last ball of the day in a club match the Saturday prior to the Australian XI fixture.

The summer of 1951–52 was no easier as regards selection. The West Indies were touring after their triumphant series in England, where they beat England for the first time. When NSW played West Indies at the SCG immediately after the First Test in Brisbane, I put on 100 in an hour with Ray Flockton. West Indies had put NSW in to bat and, when I walked out, the green pitch and some spirited West Indian pace bowling had us 96–7. Flockton was an outstanding schoolboy cricketer and, when given the chance, did very well in the state team. In one later season, 1961–62, he played in the first two matches and then was twelfth man in all the others; such was the strength of NSW that year that only twelve players were used in the summer where the Sheffield Shield was again won.

In that West Indian year Sid Barnes, who captained the team when Miller and Morris were on Test duty, gave me two great opportunities with my batting. He batted me at number six in the game against South Australia in Adelaide and I made 117, and then he put me up to three in the return game against them at the SCG and I made 93. I was lucky to have the chance. In the first of those matches the century gave me an inside berth to the Test team if the selectors were intending to make any changes for youth. It didn't appear likely.

> ‘1952–53, Sydney. My first wicket was Alf Valentine . . . I don't think he ever got over it.’
>
> *RB on his modest bowling return in his first Test: the wicket of West Indian No 11 A. L. Valentine*

The Test rubber was still alive when West Indies seemed certain of winning in Melbourne, having set Australia an interesting challenge. With Valentine, Ramadhin and Worrell taking nine wickets, it looked highly unlikely that the Australians last-wicket pair, Doug Ring and Bill Johnston, could make the 38 needed for victory. They did it with a mixture of swashbuckling batting and adventuresome running between the wickets which completely demoralised John Goddard and his team. It was at this moment, with the series won, the selectors decided to experiment and they brought in Colin McDonald, George Thoms and me, leaving out Arthur Morris, Jack Moroney and Ian Johnson, none of whom deserved to be omitted but it was something the selectors were looking at for the future.

It was George Thoms's only Test. He decided to stay in the medical profession, which was a full-time job, and he became one of

Australia's leading gynaecologists. It was a safety decision to retire from cricket. Surgeons cannot afford to take risks with injuries to do with the hands. Colin McDonald became one of Australia's finest opening batsmen and a great thinker on the game, and I moved along in the all-round sphere for another twelve years.

4

In England for
the First Time

The 1952–53 Tests [v South Africa in Australia] had been an interesting if sometimes disappointing series for me, but at the end of it I gained a place in the team for the England tour, which turned out to be an education in every sense of the word.

Richie Benaud, *Way of Cricket*

Jeezzz, Harv, it's not even level!
Australia in England 1953
Richie Benaud, *Over But Not Out*, 2010

We had a day in Perth after the game against Western Australia for some last-minute shopping and then it was down to Fremantle to join the ship as the last passengers for what was going to be a fast and, in the end, record-breaking trip by sea to Tilbury.

My room-mate for the tour was Graeme Hole. 'Olley' was a fine cricketer, at the time playing with South Australia but originally from NSW, and a good chap, generous and quiet and very keen indeed on his cricket. We didn't know it at the time, you never do when faced with having a room-mate for months on end, but we were to become good friends in a short space of time, a friendship that would remain for many years until his untimely death, aged fifty-nine, in 1990.

Shipboard life might not suit a lot of people, I suppose, but after a hectic summer I very much appreciated the drop in tension, and the chance to have myself really fit for the start of the tour.

There are a lot of things you can't do on a ship because of the rolling motion; even with good stabilisers on board you must be careful you don't suffer an injury. Neil Harvey, with his experience of the 1948 tour, was the one who was able to explain to us what we might be able to do, and he and I developed a very good fitness regime on that tour and later in 1956 and 1961. The days might sound boring to some, but for a cricket team they worked out very well. Some of the players wanted nothing more than complete relaxation, and I could understand that, particularly the pace bowlers like Miller and Lindwall who had gone through a gruelling summer. Others like Neil and I wanted relaxation plus some specific exercise during the twenty-one days on board, and that in itself needed careful planning. We also had 15,000 autograph sheets to sign, all of which had to be accounted for to George Davies, the manager of the team.

George's sense of humour had already appealed to us on our way from Essendon airport to the Windsor Hotel in Melbourne. Suddenly the bus stopped, not long after we had left the airport, and George got out.

'Where are you going, George?' we enquired.

'Well, home of course,' was the reply. 'I live in the next street. No point in going to stay with you jokers. You know the Windsor Hotel, it's in Spring Street.' Not what you would call Plan A in the managerial stakes, and George's sense of humour was looked on with a slightly wary eye for some time.

The relaxation and exercise programme I worked out with Neil Harvey involved taking second-sitting breakfast before moving to the private lounge where the whole team assembled to sign the autographs, something like 750 a day. Then we went up on deck for a relaxing hour before a game of over-the-net deck tennis with the circular quoits. This game resembled a combination of squash, tennis and badminton with its constant but careful turning and twisting, bending and jumping. We would enjoy a quiet hour on deck after lunch, then another two hours of deck tennis, again to our own rules, where we caught everything and used it as a fitness tool. A hot shower or a sea bath was followed by dinner, more relaxing on deck and bed. This meant plenty of relaxation but also three hours of solid fitness training every day. When we arrived at Tilbury on 13 April I had never been fitter, even though it was not in keeping with my previous personal strictures about training for cricket almost exclusively with cricket exercises.

I couldn't sleep the last night out of port and I was up early looking at the land as it appeared through fog and filmy mist. I was a long way from Parramatta, and a long way too from Jugiong and the little store room, a considerable distance for a Parramatta boy who had played in the paddock across the road, had hit a ball through Mrs Vidler's window and had scored for Cumberland seconds during the war years, hoping all the while there might be a chance of fielding for ten minutes if one of the soldiers or airmen didn't turn up. A lot of people might think of it as a dream come true, but it was more than that. It was almost beyond belief that in two days' time I would be walking into Lord's, referred to in all those wonderful books I had read as 'The Home of Cricket'.

'Jeezzz, Harv, it's not even level, *it slopes*!' It wasn't something that would have bothered Thomas Lord had he heard me say it, because the man who had created the ground would have been well aware of this. Neil and I, with Alan Davidson and Ron Archer, had stepped out of our car at the Grace gates at Lord's and walked inside. Neil told us to turn slightly right so we were looking at the ground from the area of the Old Tavern. Neil had been there in 1948 and he stood back as we, the newcomers, saw it for the first time.

'Not level, eh,' he said. 'And it slopes. So would you if you were 139 years old!' The slope in fact is eight feet, left to right if you are looking from the Members' Pavilion, a fall of 1 in 56. It works out at something like a two-inch slope in one pitch, and generally it means that pace bowlers at the Pavilion End would be wise to have, as their line, six inches outside off stump, rather than directly at it. That morning and the following two weeks confirmed for me it was a delightful old place.

After one indoor practice session at the Television Centre at Alexandra Palace, an arrangement with BBC Television which was excellent publicity for the team, we had a fortnight of practices at Lord's, as well as lunches, dinners and receptions. The evening functions were mostly black tie and some of the speeches were magnificent. Sir Norman Birkett, who later became Lord Birkett, first Baron Birkett of Ulverstone, was said to have one of the world's greatest legal minds. I can't vouch for that, but he was the best after-dinner speaker I ever heard. He spoke at Skinners' Hall at the Cricket Writers' dinner.

The Cricket Writers' Club was the brainchild of E. W. Swanton, who came up with the idea when he was covering the MCC tour of Australia in 1946–47. Wally Hammond was captain of that team, and it was a brave move by MCC to undertake the tour so soon after the end of the war. Jim Swanton was a fine writer. Concentrating more on cricket than anything else, he worked first for the London *Evening Standard* from 1927 to 1938 and then painted word pictures of cricket for more than fifty years in the *Daily Telegraph*. He was with BBC Radio from 1934 onwards and with BBC Television from 1946 through to the 1980s, and also on *Test Match Special*. The Cricket Writers' Club began as a loosely woven group of cricket writers, most of them skilful as wordsmiths and in their command of the English language, and they wrote for conservative broadsheets or for English newspapers of massive circulation.

Sir Alan Herbert, MP and *Punch* columnist, was in fine form at the British Sportsman's Club lunch at the Savoy, and I heard him speak on later tours as well. He was able to remind Lindwall and Miller, 'When you rub the ball on your groin or belly . . . remember how it looks on telly!'

The opening of the Lord's Imperial Cricket Memorial Gallery was an exciting event, and in those days there was nothing anachronistic about the Royal Empire Society giving a cocktail party for the team. None of the cocktail party circuit worried me: as a responsible twenty-two-year-old playing for his country, I wouldn't dream of allowing alcohol to pass my lips, because in a couple of weeks I had a cricket match or two to play and I didn't want to do anything that might in any way have an effect on my performance. Rather prissy!

The practices went well and the practice pitches were excellent, though not covered, which was a good idea because in those days match pitches in England weren't covered. We needed all the practice we could manage on what was, for most of us, a new type of surface. I still think it is a great pity that there is total covering of pitches now in England, and I believe the reliance on covering has affected some areas of English batting skills. Harvey told me I would find it quite an experience playing against top-line bowlers on slightly grassy pitches and then finding rain had completely changed the character of those surfaces. Hassett spent a lot of time with the younger players making certain we knew what we should be doing and how we should be practising, even if we couldn't always manage it as he suggested.

The younger players tended to stick together in this early part of the tour. If we were teetotallers we weren't to be found in the bar having a beer, although this was no different from the Sheffield Shield matches in Australia, where after the game Jimmy Burke and Ian Craig and I might go to the cinema and afterwards have a glass of orange juice. In London we stayed at the Park Lane Hotel in

Piccadilly, and the first night we were there Neil Harvey said he knew of a little sandwich bar at Piccadilly Circus where five years earlier he had found outstanding sandwiches made to order. We walked up past Eros and a few yards into Shaftesbury Avenue, and he was right. Iced coffee and a roast beef and English mustard or chutney sandwich, or any other variety, turned out to be a delightful and inexpensive meal, the latter of some importance as money was scarce for me in England and for my wife in Australia for the eight months I was away from home. One thing we never lost sight of, though, was the fact that in some areas in England at that time, rationing and coupons still applied, better than in 1948 Neil said, but still something to be borne in mind.

It was at the Park Lane during our first week that Lindsay, having ordered a double ice-cream for dessert, was unfortunate enough to have the waiter drop it in his lap; they looked at one another and he sensibly declined the waiter's offer to retrieve it with a metal scoop. Instead, he stood up, removed his trousers, handed them to the waiter and asked, poker-faced, to have them cleaned and returned in time for coffee. Oh, and could he please have another double ice-cream? Wouldn't get away with it these days, would he?

Our first match, only a one-day game, was against East Molesey, and Bill Johnston and the team had the most appalling luck when he damaged his right knee so badly he wasn't able to play for a considerable time and even then could only show a glimpse of his former skills.

Our first trip out of London was to Worcester, the ground about which I had heard so much, and where Bradman had made 236, 206, 258 and 107 in his four appearances. There were good cricketers in the opposition and we knew we would need to be in good form. Worcestershire made 333 in icy and wet conditions. I fielded in four sweaters and bowled in two and if I could have fielded in six I would have done so. It was impossible to get warm, and had they been around at the time, I would have worn a couple of T-shirts underneath my cricket shirt. I took 2–66 in 29 overs but found it difficult to grip the ball, let alone spin it. We started in abysmal fashion, losing McDonald, Morris and Hassett for 28 before Miller began to dominate and made 220. I made 44 and thoroughly enjoyed it. Miller was down to talk to me at the end of every over and his main advice was to 'Get forward, son, this is a slow low pitch, get forward.' Ron Archer heeded his advice a little better than I did and he made a dashing 108 including 18 boundaries.

Our match against Yorkshire was played at Bradford where, unbelievably, it was colder than Worcester. Fortunately, in the dressing-room was a wonderful, glorious, log fire. We didn't actually huddle around it, but we sat there in wicker chairs, keeping warm and keeping the blood circulating.

We were away to a reasonable start, and I again shared a partnership with Miller. 'Different pitch, son, you still need to be forward because the ball's moving off the seam but you'll need some back-foot play here as well.' Keith and I put together 152 in two hours. I made the most of Miller's advice and was three short of a century when Norman Yardley came on and had me caught behind by Don Brennan.

We closed at 453–6, and shortly afterwards I saw one of the finest sights of my life and heard one of the strangest sounds. The sight was Len Hutton's stump cartwheeling towards Gil Langley and the sound was silence. I'd never experienced this before: normally a wicket would bring a roar from a crowd, but this one brought a hush, matched only by what happened up the road at Headingley eleven weeks later when Lindwall bowled Hutton with his second ball in the Test match. I followed Lindwall at the Pavilion End at Bradford this day and took 7–46 in the Yorkshire first innings, and up to this time I had every cause to be happy with my form.

At The Oval in the game against Surrey we were all superfluous to the short but exciting battle between Ray Lindwall and Peter May. It was important, Lindsay told us, to dent Peter's confidence after his successes against South Africa and India. Ray was given the job and completed it successfully with one of the greatest overs I have seen. It was a maiden for starters and it consisted of five outswingers which went past the outside edge and one inswinger which came back between bat and pad and missed the off stump by a whisker. Ray had him caught behind for 0 by Don Tallon in his next over. It was wonderful bowling and was the main reason Peter played only two Tests that summer.

I made my first appearance at Lord's against MCC with a big crowd present. It was a wonderful moment to walk on to the ground as a player representing Australia. I top-scored with 35 in a low-scoring game, and then took 1–20.

Our match against Nottinghamshire was reduced to two days due to the Coronation.

We were told that unfortunately there was no chance at such a late stage of being able to see the procession 'live', but then Ronnie Cornwell was able to organise seating for us in a building still to be completed. Ronnie was the father of David who, as John le Carré, was later to become one of the outstanding mystery and spy writers of our time. The elder Cornwell was a business entrepreneur who had thrown a lunch party for us earlier in the tour. He was a businessman in the millionaire class, although when things went wrong he was a little below that, but it was a very interesting day, made more so by our manager George Davies.

At that country-house lunch, George and I decided we needed to go to the loo but there was only one available and, when we arrived, there was a queue around eighty yards long. Eventually, after what seemed hours, George and I arrived at the point where the queue turned at right angles and ten yards further on was the prize. I glanced at George and thought I detected a desperate look in his eyes, perhaps partly brought on by the tight crossing of his legs. Around the corner, with what *definitely* seemed a desperate look in his eyes, came a peer of the realm, hopping. He was a very nice chap and a very important peer, but like George, he was also wearing an intense look, in his bid to arrive at the right place at the right time.

Being very important is only relative at times like that: out snaked George's arm and it landed on the shoulder of the peer and turned him around face to face with our manager. George muttered to him through gritted teeth, 'Down the back of the queue . . .'

From the playing point of view, I was starting to find some difficulty in the non-stop on-field action and travel, although I had said to Lindsay Hassett at the start of the tour that I would be quite happy to play in every game. He had nodded and given a half-smile. He knew better. As a team we were struggling with our batting. Bill Johnston's injury was a real problem and I was in trouble with both batting and bowling.

When we came to the First Test at Trent Bridge it could hardly be said I was in form and full of confidence. The match was a disappointment because of the rain, but from a personal point of view, it was worse. Alec Bedser was too good for most of us except the experienced players, and the remainder of our batting disintegrated. I was caught behind glancing Trevor Bailey in the first innings and then Bedser got me in the second innings with a leg-cutter, which almost did, pitching on leg stump and hitting middle. The match finished in a draw, with rain intervening, and the only worthwhile thing I did was to take two very good catches.

Perhaps that's not quite right about the catches being the only good thing to happen to me that week, because Lindsay Hassett gave me a very good lesson in loosening up – 'taught me a lesson' might be more accurate.

Whilst in Nottingham we went to the home of Bert Edwards of Nottingham Lace. Chatting with Lindsay at the function. I mentioned, 'I couldn't possibly have a drink, thanks, we're on a cricket tour.' Even more prissy than earlier on the tour!

Lindsay nodded sympathetically at the youngster offering him a stricture on how to play cricket, before I compounded things by agreeing to try a sip of his proffered Scotch and venturing the opinion that anyway it was tasteless stuff. His poker-faced answer was to ask the perfectly dressed barman to give Mr Benaud a Scotch his high-class taste buds may be able to savour. I began to like the taste after half a dozen doubles, the disappointment of the batting failures faded and I had six more from my new very best friend, the generous bartender.

It proved to be a painful experience, as the next day I suffered my first ever hangover. I still don't drink Scotch these days, although I am partial to a glass or two of high-quality white Burgundy, Chardonnay or Shiraz, a gin and tonic with ice and lemon, or a beer from a green bottle. And, I think I'm able to say that Hassett's poker-faced lesson made me a little less prissy!

On the Saturday night of the Second Test at Lord's we had an official function with a difference, as Prime Minister Menzies threw a dinner for the team in the River Room at the Savoy. Douglas Jardine was one of the guests and it was a most convivial evening, with splendid speeches from Menzies and Hassett.

The match was the scene of the epic draw when Trevor Bailey and Willie Watson played so well and we couldn't separate them until too late. Watson for Peter May turned out to be an inspired selection. I did little with the bat or the ball and was dropped for the Old Trafford Test, which was marred by rain and in which we reached only 35–8 in our second innings.

I made 52 against Middlesex and was back in the side for the Headingley Test, during which Trevor Bailey distinguished himself again, on this occasion, however, for deliberately wasting as much time as possible and bowling to a packed legside field. Bill Johnston, almost recovered from injury, took 6–63 against Glamorgan after this Test and was selected for the final Test at The Oval ahead of Doug Ring and me.

With the final Test, England regained the Ashes after a break of nineteen years, and, understandably, there was great jubilation around the country. We even had a drink or two ourselves, but it was more in disappointment than anything else after we had congratulated the England players on what was a splendid victory.

Lessons from a master

Richie Benaud, *Anything But . . . an Autobiography*, 1998

We had other games to play to finish the 1953 tour. They went off without incident and with mixed success, until we arrived at Scarborough for the Festival game against T. N. Pearce's XI and I hit 29 in the first innings. It was on the second evening of this match that Bill O'Reilly gave up a convivial night with Hassett to have dinner with me, something organised by Tom Goodman, who was with the *Sydney Morning Herald* as their cricket correspondent. Tom was a real gentleman and a fine cricket writer, constructive and thoughtful. He knew a lot about the game and was able to translate that into print for his readers. He told me Bill O'Reilly

> *Some bowlers and wicketkeepers, and others for that matter, are better at appealing than their mates . . . Bill O'Reilly, they tell me, was terrifying.*
>
> *RB on appealing*

had become increasingly frustrated watching the methods I was using in my bowling, and if it was OK, he would like to have a talk to me. The only problem I had was Bill giving up an evening with

Hassett, but I grabbed the chance of being offered some advice by the greatest bowler the world has seen. We had a meal in the hotel dining-room at Scarborough and then repaired to Bill's room for an after-dinner beer or two and a bowling lesson.

It remains one of the most beneficial events in my cricketing life. We talked, or rather Bill talked and I listened. The upshot was that I needed to take stock of what I was trying to do and how I could relate that to whoever was captaining me and others. Bill was a mate of Hassett's but he made the point, and forcibly too, that Hassett was such a wonderful player of spin bowling that he had no proper respect for it. I went away and summed up the advice and pointers I had heard during the fascinating two hours.

Give the batsmen absolutely nothing!

Develop one ball as your stock ball and perfect it. Spend a year, even two years, doing that and don't be swayed by anyone – friends, captains, selectors, hangers-on, do-gooders, ear-bashers – into doing anything else.

That ball should be your leg-break, and from your point of view it should be both an attacking and defensive weapon; attacking because, if you are pitching it as you want, you will be giving yourself a chance of taking a wicket; defensive because, if a batsman is in full flow, you have the chance of stopping him if you have complete control over your bowling and your own mind.

Don't try to take a wicket every ball.

On the surface that may seem poor advice, but it's not. If you are bowling six different balls an over, as you are at the moment, or eight different balls, as you were in Australia last summer, you will bowl one loose one in the over, and by the time you have bowled a spell of eight overs, you could have none for 32. Yet, at the same

time, you might have bowled forty very good balls. The captain will
take you off.

Never forget, even for one moment, that the batsman is an enemy on
the field. You might have a beer with him at the end of the day, and
that's good. On the field, attack him, but above all, give him nothing, absolutely nothing.

Bear in mind that almost every captain under whom you will play
will be a batsman. Batsmen know a lot about many things, including
batting. With very few exceptions they know nothing whatsoever
about the technique of spin bowling.

They often have a good or very good idea of how to bat against it, but
about the technique, the field-placings needed for particular batsmen and the best methods and the thought processes of a spin
bowler, they know very little.

If you read that at normal speed you are able to finish it in seventy
seconds. That's the way good advice should be – brief and simple –
and that is precisely the way Bill conveyed it to me that evening. It
was to form the basis of my bowling for the next ten years and, allied
to my father's advice, it was one of the reasons why, for a time, I
became Australia's leading wicket-taker in Test cricket and was able
to reach the bowling part of the statistic of being the first Test
cricketer ever to do the double of 2,000 runs and 200 wickets.

Because I believe in apportioning credit where due, I always said
publicly what Bill had done for me. When Bill was asked about it by
journalists, he was inclined to gloss it over with a wave of the hand
and say, 'Anyway, advice isn't worth anything if the person can't use
it properly.'

The final part of that Scarborough match provided me with a
great finish to the tour: I opened the Australian second innings with

Arthur Morris and we put on 163 for the first wicket, I finished with 135 including eleven sixes to equal the then record and we won the match.

When I returned to Australia and told Lou about the chat with his fellow schoolteacher 'Tiger' O'Reilly, he was delighted. 'Greatest bowler of all time and a good bloke,' he said. 'You won't be given any better advice than that.'

Whether or not I would be able to carry it out was another matter, because I did need to turn in better figures. Although the tour had been very much a learning process, I had had a disastrous time in the Tests, and even though I had managed some decent performances in other matches they were spasmodic rather than consistent. I had started out as a promising allrounder and that was where I had finished the tour, though I had tried to learn as much as possible. My spinning fingers were still raw after every day's play.

5
Turning Points

❛His gradually mounting bowling skill was evident on his first two English trips, but he is remembered chiefly during those ventures for the dashing 97 he hit off the England attack in the Second Test at Lord's in 1956. The 1957–58 tour to South Africa at length established him as an allrounder of top class, for he took 106 wickets, which surpassed the previous record of 104 by S. F. Barnes, and scored 817 runs, including four centuries, two of them in Test matches.❜

Harry Gee, *Wisden*

Confounding the critics
Australia in England 1956
Richie Benaud, *Anything But . . . an Autobiography*, 1998

The First Test was something of a fizzer. It was marred by rain, produced fewer than 700 runs and the pitch looked odd, with a real reddish look about it until rain changed its colour. England had played Laker, Lock and Appleyard but, in the end, although the ball turned sharply, the rain and lack of time, plus some excellent batting from Jim Burke and Peter Burge, saw us through.

In that game we had suffered a dreadful double blow as regards injury, with Ray Lindwall straining a muscle early in the first innings and Davidson slipping in a bowler's footmark and chipping his ankle. He was carried off, the ankle was put in plaster and we were in real trouble, with the Second Test at Lord's starting only nine days after the completion of the one at Trent Bridge. Davo couldn't play again until the match against Surrey in August, and then, with a combination of solid batting and left-arm orthodox spin bowling, forced his way into the team for the Fifth Test at The Oval.

The Second Test at Lord's produced a great win for Australia, and although it was everyone's victory, it was really Miller's match. Keith made 28 and 30 at critical times, and took ten wickets in his 70 overs, all in the knowledge that Lindwall, Crawford and Davidson would not be at the other end. England had changed their side for the firm, well-grassed Lord's pitch, bringing in Brian Statham and Johnny Wardle for Bob Appleyard and Tony Lock; Alan Moss was also omitted from the team which had taken the field at Trent Bridge.

We knew this was to be Miller's last tour and that he planned to retire from the game on his return to Australia, where he would continue writing and would be the Channel Nine sports correspondent, with television about to start in Australia. This then was his last major appearance at Lord's, which he had first seen as a competitor when he walked out to play in the Services game in 1945. He was the greatest allrounder I played with or against, bearing in mind Garry Sobers had started his career just two years earlier and I was destined to play only one further Test series against him.

Miller was the best captain I played under, and he was the best captain never to lead Australia. In those days it was of vital importance to the Australian Cricket Board that what they perceived as their own image should be perpetuated, and it was unlikely someone with Miller's personality and extrovert nature, and his popularity with the public, would have been chosen by the Board to captain Australia. The things I saw and learned from Miller may not have been apparent all the time to those watching from the outside. A move in the field might have come with a slight nod, or an even slighter head-shake.

This victory at Lord's was a tremendous confidence boost for the remainder of the Test series, and we reckoned that, given decent pitches, we were in with a big chance of regaining the Ashes. There were many complimentary notes in the media about the part I played in the unfolding events of the five days, including the Colin Cowdrey catch, the innings of 97 and the bowling in both innings despite my fingers being a mess.

So, if Miller was the greatest, what kind of rating do I give Ken 'Slasher' Mackay? Well, a champion is generally regarded as a cut above the rest of the field, so it is a matter of taking care in the world of hyperbole when one talks of a cricketer being a champion. Slasher Mackay in his own way was a champion, though not for the generally accepted reasons. He may have been a better player had I not interfered with his career when I was his captain. I turned him from a high-scoring batsman into an allrounder because it suited me to do so. Only fifteen Australian cricketers in the history of the first-class game have made 10,000 runs and taken 250 wickets in their career, and Slasher is one of them.* When he retired it was with 1,507 Test runs and 50 Test wickets, something that makes good reading, as alongside him in 121 years of Test cricket the only Australians to have achieved that double are Warwick Armstrong, Ray Lindwall, Greg Matthews, Keith Miller, Monty Noble, Bob Simpson, Steve Waugh and Richie Benaud.

Ken Mackay was a number of things to me: he was a good tough cricketer, and in all the years I played and watched the game, he remained one of the finest of men and proudest Australians ever to walk on to a cricket field. He died of a heart attack on the rest day, the Sunday, of the Lord's Test in 1982 when England were playing India, the same ground where, a little more than quarter of a century

---

* This list now extends to seventeen Australian cricketers.

earlier, he had played such a staunch part in 'Miller's match', one of Australia's greatest Test victories.

It was in that Lord's game in 1956 that Slasher and I started our partnership, although at that stage I had no idea I might one day be captaining him. The wicket he took in England's first innings was that of Colin Cowdrey and I was the man who took the catch with England's score at 60. It is the one often shown in later years, depicting the ball in my left hand as I am knocked over with the force of the blow. In fact, I caught it in both hands right in front of my nose and was knocked backwards.

'Slash' seemed to be pleased with the effort, although he never used to say a lot. When he walked up to me and said, 'Caught, "Benords",' it was the equivalent of a politician's speech, and there was even a half smile on his weather-beaten countenance.

On the Monday morning of that match and not out over the weekend, I was caught with many others in an awful jam around Marble Arch on my way to the ground, eventually arriving at Lord's with no time for a spell of batting practice. On the way out to the centre I said to him, 'Slash, if ever I've needed a hundred it's today.'

He looked straight ahead and said, 'Don't let's get run out . . .' Several indifferent strokes later he came up to me and said, 'Benords, you don't have to hit everything out of the ground, let's just take our time . . .'

One thing I did know about Slash was that he would upset the England players with his skill at leaving the ball alone, sometimes when it was only a matter of a couple of inches outside the off stump, but I didn't know until later how much he was upsetting them.

Peter May, without smiling, said very quietly to him at the end of one over during which he had allowed three to pass by an inch, 'You must really enjoy batting, Slasher.'

Slash looked at him and said just as quietly, but with the hint of a smile, 'I enjoy it so much, Peter, I'm going to try to be here all day.' It didn't work out like that but when he was out his innings had taken up four hours and twenty-five minutes and he had outlasted me.

The runs I made that day provided the single most important happening in my Test career to that time, far more so than the century I had made under no cricket pressure at Sabina Park the previous year against the West Indies, or, for that matter, any other innings I had ever played. The game was critically balanced, we were hampered by injuries and desperately needed to make enough second-innings runs so the target was difficult for England. To make 97 at Lord's was good enough, but it was the way I made them which mattered most to me after the most indifferent start imaginable to the innings.

Keith Miller had taken me to John Arlott's home the previous Sunday when our team were playing against Kent at Canterbury and the two of us were being rested. It was a convivial day and Neville Cardus was present. I had met him before, but only briefly, and it was interesting to listen to him, and even more interesting to hear him discussing classical music with Miller. The following Wednesday, the day before the Lord's Test began, Cardus wrote an article in the *Manchester Guardian* concerning some of the Australian players – Harvey, Miller, Archer, Burke and Benaud.

In general terms he said:

A great cricketer, once he has known greatness, if only momentarily, can again be visited by greatness as long as he remains capable of reasonably healthy physical motions and responses. No team can be taken for granted as beaten before the match begins if it contains Harvey, Miller, Archer, Burke and Benaud.

A slight raising of the eyebrow may well be caused by the mention of Benaud's name in this context, for this young cricketer's performances in Test matches against England have not been, in Mr Attlee's terminology, outstanding.

I doubt if any English player would be trusted by our selection committee so far and for so long, with no more practical or visible contribution to the cause than Benaud's. Yet, he is plainly gifted.

When he first came to England in 1953, Benaud in the third match of the tour against Yorkshire at Bradford scored 97 in two hours, then took seven wickets for 46. Now it is not possible for mediocrity ever to rise to the level of this kind of mastery. And what a man has done once he can do again.

I thought I was able to play, but it was certainly true that what I had promised so far had not been translated into deeds.

I had practised hard at the nets at Lord's on the Tuesday and had hit the ball well. Cardus had been there and he finished his preview of the game with the theme that it wouldn't surprise him if I did something quite reasonable: 'I saw him at the nets at Lord's on Tuesday, defending seriously, scrupulously behind the ball; and his strokes, when he liberated them, were clean, true, strong. His reactions were swift and natural. Benaud is twenty-five and looks every inch a cricketer. It will be no matter for wonder if at any moment he confounds those of his critics who have more or less written him off.'

That Cardus article and what I did to live up to it is one of the reasons I have always considered the Lord's match in 1956 a turning point for me. In the following Tests, played on some strange pitches, I didn't bat too badly and I was prepared to try a few things I might not have had the confidence to try without Lord's.

Cutting down
Australia in India 1956–57
Richie Benaud, *Way of Cricket*, 1961

Most youngsters tend to run too far. Especially when at school, they seem to think the longer they run, the faster and more hostile the delivery. Very probably the imagination has been fired by watching the fast bowlers in action at the Sydney Cricket Ground, or wherever their local ground happens to be. To youngsters, it always seems these fast bowlers go right back to the sightscreens for their run-up, and they try to emulate their heroes. I am afraid all this is youthful imagination and a useless expenditure of energy.

Wasted effort largely afflicts the quicker bowlers, but the same set of rules can apply to spinners, as well I know. When in England in 1956, by which time I had been playing in first-class cricket seven or eight years, I bowled off nine or ten paces. I was not feeling satisfied with my bowling results, so when we got to India to play three Tests there on the way home I decided to experiment. In the nets at Madras I tried bowling off five paces. I soon sensed that my balance and rhythm were better, even though at first the new run was strange to me after so many years of bowling with the longer approach.

Anyway, I felt I was getting somewhere and after several hours in the nets decided to try the new method in the morrow's Test. I did, and took seven wickets. Perhaps it was just as well I cut down to conserve energies, for on the eve of the Test at Bombay I developed a fever that was later diagnosed as a form of dengue. I did not know what the trouble was at the time. I thought I had a spot of stomach trouble and chill which was afflicting many of our players trying to adjust themselves to the new conditions. All I knew was that I felt lousy and every night my temperature shot up well above the 100 mark with a consistency I could never hope to match with a bat out in the middle. One night it was 104 degrees but I still had to bowl something like 28 overs the next day. It was just as well I was bowling off five paces for my feet would never have dragged me back the extra four or five steps!

I still find it hard to believe what a transformation came over my bowling through rationing my run-up. But I think the figures speak for themselves. In 24 Tests up to Madras I had taken 50 Test match wickets. If I had not occasionally made runs, I could hardly have kept my place on those results. Then, in the three Tests in India I had 23 wickets followed by 30 in five Tests in South Africa. When Peter May's team came out to Australia the following season, I took 31 wickets in the series. In eight matches in Pakistan and India at the end of the year there were another 47 victims. So, in 21 Tests I increased my 'bag' by 131 wickets.

The new run seemed to open up the whole secret of bowling to me. It not only gave me greater control of the ball, but control of myself. With the revised approach, I decided to walk back to my mark more slowly, rather as did Jim Laker. I noticed in 1956 that even when he was taking all those wickets, Laker never rushed back to his mark. He was the master of the situation and was not going to allow anything – not even the prospect of 10 wickets in an innings – to jostle him out of his groove.

Being 'in the groove' is the key to good bowling. It is as much a thought process as anything else. Some people, however, have said they find my leisurely step irritating, and that I am trying to upset the opposition by wasting time. This is nonsense. Even when I had a long run, I recall an occasion at Adelaide when Jimmy Burke and I bowled 24 eight-ball overs between us in a 40-minute session. Even if I take just as long with my shorter approach, I still reckon I am getting through my overs in a reasonable span of time.

The real reasons for my measured tread are very different. In the first place it is, as I have stressed before, a matter of getting into the groove. To me, this matter of going back to the bowling mark and returning to deliver the ball is as important as intricate steps to a professional dancer, and require just as much care and effort. You may notice I go back and return in exactly the same way for every ball. I turn from the bowling crease, take deliberate steps, turn with left foot alongside bowling mark, take one step forward with the right foot (it used to be the left foot) and break into my run. At the end of a day's bowling, if the grass is at all damp and shows footmarks, my boots will have made just five marks on the turf, in exactly the same spots, with variations, of course, for using the crease. One uses the crease for varying the angle of delivery, sometimes getting near the stumps, other times going wide towards the return crease. But my approach is always the same. I find that with a short run I must not rush matters, as I need a little time to think what I am going to try to do with the next ball, and I also want the fellow bowling at the other end to have the chance to regain his breath. I must emphasise, however, that I take my time only because I use a short run and still get through an over in a couple of minutes. If a bowler needs to go back a long way, however, he should go back quickly. It is important that the game should be kept moving.

Ivan James
Australia in New Zealand 1956–57
Richie Benaud, *Anything But . . . an Autobiography*, 1998

There were two things I wasn't to know about this summer and the following six months, the first of which was that dengue fever is quite a nasty ailment: suddenly I would start sweating and need to find my way to the nearest resting place. Secondly, that same dengue fever and its treatment of those days, with sulphanilamide, was, purely by accident, to be the saving of my spin-bowling career and the end of the McCool pain barrier.*

We flew out to New Zealand two weeks later with Craig as captain and Harvey as vice-captain. The opening match was at Christchurch and I had all my normal cricketing gear plus a stock of the tablets I had been taking from the moment the dengue had been diagnosed back in November [in India with Australia]. In my wallet was a prescription written by Dr Jack Jeffery to purchase the last two batches of sulpha tablets. Our fourth match on the tour was at Timaru against the Combined Minor Associations. It was supposed to be a two-day game but the first day was totally washed out.

That evening, checking through my gear in the bedroom, I decided, for no particular reason, I would take some exercise and wander off to the chemist shop I had seen down the road and have him make up the next lot of sulpha tablets.

I was cranky and frustrated, my fingers had ripped open again a few days earlier bowling in Dunedin, and although I had cleaned them up a little they were painful. They were not necessarily a pretty sight when I handed the prescription over the counter to the chap who recognised me and asked how I was enjoying the tour. His name as it turned out was Ivan James, though at that moment he was to me another man in a white coat, this time dispensing medicines rather than decisions out in the centre of the ground.

'What's the matter with your fingers?' he asked.

'Aw, it's from the way they get ripped about from bowling, it's when the seam of the ball cuts through the skin.'

---

* In 1952, Queensland legspinner Colin McCool had seen the state of RB's spinning fingers and told him if he wasn't prepared to bear the pain, he might as well give up playing – but he should never stop searching for a remedy: 'Son, find some bloody way to fix those or you'll have an extremely short career.'

'What do you use on them?'

'I've tried everything – hardening them, softening, everything – and I've just got to live with it, I'm afraid.'

'I have something that might be a help. I've found it very beneficial for the treatment of leg ulcers for ex-servicemen, particularly if they are suffering the after-effects of being gassed.'

I said to him, 'I think I've tried everything, but I'll try anything new, anything at all. A fellow named Colin McCool once told me never to let a day go past without trying to find a remedy.'

He handed me the sulpha tablets, which I put in my pocket, and then gave me a small wide-mouthed bottle, plus a container with white powder and a piece of paper with his suggested remedy written on it. It said:

OILY CALAMINE LOTION BPC '54
BORACIC ACID POWDER

Rub the lotion into the wound and then dab off the oil which comes to the surface.

Rub in the boracic acid powder so that it forms a waxy filling in the wound.

Keep doing this as much as possible and definitely whenever there is a recurrence of the skin tearing. Make sure you keep the waxy substance filling the hole all the time.

He added that I should carry with me a piece of fine sandpaper so that before using the remedy I could sand off any bits of dead or torn skin.

I looked at this with a very wary eye, but as he had taken the trouble to ask me about my fingers and then make up his remedy and write out the details and instructions, I thanked him courteously, paid the bill and walked out of the shop and back to the hotel. It seemed a long shot and much too simple, but I'd give it a go.

The word genius is much over-used in our society.
Mr Ivan James turned out to be a genius.

It is difficult to convey what a difference it can make to a bowler used to bowling with raw fingers suddenly to be free of that pain and inconvenience. It was like beginning a new bowling career. The treatment instantly worked and the skin was toughened so that even prolonged bowling spells didn't produce cracking, which was easily the worst part of the problems I had been going through. I was always careful to have the containers in my cricket bag wherever I travelled. Meeting Ivan James was a remarkable piece of luck and there has never been one moment of doubt in my mind that walking into that chemist's shop in Timaru saved my bowling career and was one of the key reasons why from that moment I moved into top gear as an important allrounder in Australian cricket.

I don't know enough about medicine to understand why it should have been so successful, only that it was. Others who asked for the remedy were given it with the greatest of pleasure: for some it worked, for others it didn't, although I suspect some were nowhere near as dedicated in its use as I was. My dedication might have seemed a bit boring to others, but never to me. 'Jeez, Benords, you're not using that stuff *again*!'

The Claw
Australia in South Africa 1957–58
Richie Benaud, *Anything But . . . an Autobiography*, 1998

Alan Davidson, known generally as 'Davo', but also, because of his astonishing fielding, as 'the Claw', was a player with whom I almost grew up. We lived fifty miles from one another: he was at Lisarow near Gosford and I was at Parramatta, fifteen miles out of Sydney. He was a left-arm over-the-wrist spinner at Gosford High School, and I was a right-arm over-the-wrist spinner at Parramatta High. Alan and I used to work together in our practice sessions, although, because of the obvious differences in our bowling style, I would get through more physical work than he did. At the SCG we would be concentrating on bowling flat out in our own ways, and on accuracy. Somewhere along the line someone with a gift of foresight had turned Davo into a left-arm pace bowler who had a devastating inswinger and a ball which angled across towards the slip area. We were both hard hitters, 'dashing batsmen' was one term used about us when we were at school, and we both practised our fielding hour after spare hour until we were able to influence the selectors with that aspect of their team nomination.

We played together in the NSW team from 1949 onwards, with enough success to persuade the selectors there was some form of long-term investment to be made, but, as so often happens with this kind of thing, it wasn't until we were thrown in the deep end that we suddenly started to turn potential into reality. By the time that chance came along I had 73 Test wickets and Davidson had 16.

That tour of South Africa in 1957–58 was the turning point*, and although statistics don't always tell the true story, they do in this case. From the moment we started as a double act in South Africa, and then bowled together over the five years to his retirement at the conclusion of the 1962–63 series, between us we took 333 Test wickets. He had a remarkable bowling average over that time; each of those 170 wickets cost him only 19.25 runs. At the other end I was far more liberal and conceded 25 runs per wicket, but the overall

* Australia won the five-Test series 3–0. RB took 30 wickets at 21.93 and scored 329 runs, including two centuries; Alan Davidson took 25 wickets at 17 and scored 127 runs.

picture was one of being slightly on the niggardly side of things as regards offering runs to batsmen and taking wickets as well. Offered a choice, I suspect any legspinner would have felt as I did, and given anything for the opportunity to be at the end opposite to a bowler of Davidson's quality. Certainly, it made an enormous difference as captain to have him in my side.

I don't doubt, bowling my legspin at the other end, I was of some benefit to Davidson. I never had the slightest doubt that his left-arm pace bowling and skill was of immense benefit to me, and it showed over the six years of our combination. Not only was he a wicket-taker, but the pressure he applied with his accuracy allowed me great scope with tactics. Instead of having two spin bowlers on at the same time, I found opposition batsmen were keen to avoid facing Alan.

He will remain in Australia's history as one of the greatest cricketers ever to set foot on a ground for NSW and Australia.

6
Captain of Australia

> ❝Captaincy is 90 per cent luck and 10 per cent skill. But don't try it without that 10 per cent.❞
>
> Richie Benaud on the art of captaincy

The return of the urn
England in Australia 1958–59
Richie Benaud, *Anything But . . . an Autobiography*, 1998

This was to be another chance for us to try to regain the Ashes, having lost them in 1953, which seemed not five years ago, but fifty. England, since the 1956 tour and Jim Laker's triumphs, had gone very well in the Test arena, playing series against South Africa, West Indies and New Zealand, fifteen Tests in all with nine wins, four draws and only two losses, both against South Africa. As we had the three-nil victory in the recent series, our confidence level was lifted by the fact that South Africa, with much the same team, had managed to draw their series against England in 1956–57, the season before we had gone there with Ian Craig as captain.

In the prelude to this 1958–59 season we had plenty of publicity in Australia from cricket writers in England, most of it along the lines of what England would do to Australia and how good the England side actually was. There was one article which even said that a better idea than England playing Australia would be for England to play the World, thus making more of an entrancing spectacle for everyone. The point about that article was that it wasn't written in jest: they really meant it and believed every word of the sentiments noted!

One major thing happened to England's detriment, however. One of their finest cricketers, who I believed could easily be their trump card, had been dropped from the side for disciplinary reasons. Johnny Wardle of Yorkshire had troubles with the county and, having been told he was not to be retained by them for the next season, he criticised his employer's administration in a series of articles in the *Daily Mail*. Yorkshire had already told MCC he would be available to tour Australia, but they then dispensed with his services and, under the system operating in England at the time, he was automatically dropped by MCC from the seventeen invited to participate in the tour – very much master–servant. Jim Laker had been chosen, but withdrew, and later agreed to make the trip. It all sounded a bit of a dog's breakfast, if that isn't too harsh a term for cricket administration. Wardle, in the 1958 season in England, was Yorkshire's leading wicket-taker with 76. He was also the fourth Test cricketer in twelve months whose services were dispensed with by Yorkshire, at a time when they had a new captain, Ronnie Burnet, who was a very good, strong character, a nice guy, no star as a first-class cricketer but almost certainly the no-nonsense type of amateur cricketer Yorkshire needed at a time when dressing-room squabbles were not unknown. Yorkshire only had to wait twelve months to find out what Burnet could do, because he captained them to winning the County Championship the following summer. They beat Sussex in an exciting encounter in their final game of the season by five wickets, after they had been set 215 to make in 105 minutes. Fred Trueman, Ray Illingworth and Doug Padgett were the stars of the season, and so too, definitely, was the captain, whose appointment had triggered the Wardle articles in the *Daily Mail* and his subsequent omission from the tour of Australia.

If those things were having some effect on the futures of various players in England, then there were other happenings, partly out of the public eye, partly in it, which were to have a marked effect on my own cricketing life, though I had absolutely no idea of this at the time.

The first was that in the previous season, 1956–57, Neil Harvey had captained Victoria very well, had topped the national batting averages with 836 runs at 104.50 and had finished second in the aggregates although he had batted only ten times. He was in excellent form, then we all toured South Africa with the seasons coinciding.

Now Harv was back in Australia at the end of the South African tour and, like the rest of us, if not broke, then in an alarmingly impecunious state and faced with the prospect of receiving the grand total of £375 plus £50 expenses from the upcoming Test series against England. On a television show in Melbourne, when asked about his future, he said he was very unsettled as regards employment at that time and it had been necessary to think seriously about leaving Australia because of financial circumstances. There had been a possibility he might go to South Africa, the original home of his then wife, Iris. When the same television programme was shown in Sydney the next week, it underlined for a lot of people the problem facing Australia's cricketers at that time. Here was our best batsman thinking of going overseas because of financial difficulties directly associated with playing the game, despite playing it so well he was an automatic choice in every side since he had starred in Bradman's 1948 team ten years earlier.

If this were in any way embarrassing to the Australian Cricket Board they managed successfully to conceal that state of mind and found no cause why players' remuneration should be increased from £75 a Test with £10 expenses.

It was almost twenty years later that Alan Barnes made his famous statement to say, if Rod Marsh thought remuneration in 1976 was too low, there were 50,000 others around Australia who would play for nothing. That quote was very well publicised. However, the same thing was often said to players in private many years ago, and it was deliberately emphasised as a way of making everyone toe the line.

Twenty years after that, in 1997, they were at it again in a different style but in the most disgraceful manner imaginable, when the Australian Cricket Board published details of players' earnings so as to put preasure on them and influence the manner in which they might then be perceived by the public.

The second thing to affect me was that the Melbourne television programme in 1958 brought a swift reaction from a good businessman, Joe Ryan, who ran John Dynon and Sons, high-class glassware manufacturers in Sydney. He was so upset at what he had seen and heard that he instantly phoned Neil and offered him a job with his firm and trained him to be a sales supervisor. Neil moved to Sydney in August 1958, not long before the arrival of the England team in Perth in early October. I was delighted Neil was to play with NSW, something which was likely to make our grip on the Sheffield Shield even more secure, as indeed it turned out.

The third thing to happen was that Ian Craig was diagnosed as having hepatitis.

The outcome of all this was that Neil Harvey had moved to Sydney, Ian Craig was ill, and the state selectors chose me to lead NSW in our Sheffield Shield match at the 'Gabba.

This was logical enough, although it was arguable that Neil should instantly be made captain of NSW over me, as the current state vice-captain to Craig, but it was all becoming very, very complicated.

As captain I made 29 and took 3–78 in the Queensland first innings, and on the last afternoon we were in with a shout of victory when they suddenly lost 4–18 and Lindwall and Walmsley had to defend desperately. I was able to set attacking fields and I was happy with the way the captaincy challenge had gone. This was only the second time I had captained NSW in a full match.

Ten days later we played Western Australia at the SCG and Ian came back to captain us for that match but made a duck. He didn't look well to me. The game seemed to be out of our reach on the final day when they were batting soundly but then I took 6–5 in 33 balls and we managed to scramble our way to an outright win with an hour to spare. I finished with 7–65 and it was a heartening start to the summer.

Ian was again captain a week later for the game against MCC, and although he was looking a little better it did seem as though he might have been trying to make a comeback too soon. Hepatitis was said in those days to be a very tough illness and very debilitating – it still is. He made another duck, caught at slip by Cowdrey off Tony Lock. Neil made 149 in a wonderful innings and Jim Burke 104.

I set myself to bowl well when we went out on to the field. Tony Lock had turned the ball a little and I reckoned this was a good chance to see if it were possible to gain some kind of an advantage over the batsmen I was likely to meet in the Test. At one stage I bowled five maiden overs and had the wickets of Graveney, Cowdrey and May, finishing with 5–48 from 28.4 overs, a performance which was a real boost in confidence.

There was no such confidence for Ian. He knew from the fact he was very weary during the game that he had tried to come back to big-time cricket too soon, and he notified the selectors that he didn't intend to play again during the season. It was a cruel blow for him. Taking the side to New Zealand and South Africa was one thing, but to captain an Australian team in an Ashes battle is the ultimate and here it was, sheer bad luck, through illness, had deprived him of the chance.

The captaincy position was now that, with Ian out for the season, I was captain of NSW and Neil was vice-captain of the Australian team. Had we been about to leave for an overseas tour, there is not the slightest doubt Neil would have stepped into the position of captain of the touring team. In fact, he was about to lead an Australian XI against MCC at the SCG but it proved to be a disastrous match as a prelude to the First Test. Fred Trueman and a few others sometimes weren't over-caring of where they put their feet, and this time Fred gouged out two holes in the pitch at the Members' End during the Australian XI's first innings, after MCC had made 319.

It had no effect in that innings, but when Tony Lock bowled into the footholes in the second innings, he took 6–29 from sixteen overs. To go with their first innings of 128, the Australian XI were bowled out for 103. It wasn't the same as Laker bowling us out two years earlier in England, but it must have sent a shudder through the Australian selection committee.

The defeat wasn't in any way Neil's fault, but the next day, 26 November 1958, it was announced I had been made captain of the team for the First Test in Brisbane. It wasn't a case of being underwhelmed by the appointment, but there were a few little things that held me back from total celebration. First there was the fact that Harv had been overlooked again; then there was the background of information that gave me the knowledge that my appointment was regarded by some administrators as being forced on them by a series of accidents. From that moment I always looked with a wary eye on any beaming administrator who came up to me and said he knew I was the man for the job.

I was standing by the telex machine in the *Sun* sports department when the announcement came through, and I phoned Neil straight away. We had been good mates for the past five years and had already arranged, whichever way the announcement went, we would lunch together at the Cricketers' Club and chat about what was looming as the most important match we had played together in many years.

We talked very briefly about the fact that if Ian Craig had been fit and well, and had been in any sort of form, then he would have been captain, and that if Harv had stayed in Melbourne, as Victoria's captain and Australia's current vice-captain, equally there was no doubt he would have been captain after Ian pulled out of the season.

It could not have been otherwise and, even though I have been told since by cricket officials and media that I would still have been captain, what they say is untrue, sometimes deliberately so. They are merely saying it in hindsight and there was absolutely no way the selectors would have overlooked Neil had he been captain of Victoria. Why would they? Why choose ahead of the then Australian vice-captain and recently Victorian captain, someone who was only NSW captain because of Craig's illness? It would have lacked common sense and been very much in the too-hard basket. Trust me! That was my view then and I have had no cause, even for a moment, to change it since that time. Also my view is that Harv paid the cruel penalty solely because he was trying to do the right thing by his family and himself as regards some worthwhile form of employment and remuneration.

One really jarring note on being made captain came in some of the congratulations which were directly along the lines of how great it was to have a captain from NSW. I love NSW but that was a very parochial touch!

At the Cricketers' Club bar we had a drink and talked. Harv started it with, 'Mate, I'm with you,' and by recalling sitting on the balcony at Old Trafford in Laker's match, and what a lousy feeling it had been, bowled out by a fine bowler on a bad pitch. We had said then that 1958–59 would be our time.

The lunch wasn't in any sense a planning meeting, but rough ideas were laid down in the knowledge that Alan Davidson and I would be the main bowlers. One of Australia's big plus marks was that Ray Lindwall was in form, but would he make it back into the side? It seemed more likely it would be Davidson and Ian Meckiff to take the new ball, as had been the case in South Africa, and, I was hoping, with Ken Mackay as the third seam bowler. As the selectors had left Ray out of the side for South Africa it seemed unlikely at this stage they would change their line of thinking.

When the team was announced it was Benaud (c), Harvey (v-c), McDonald, Burke, O'Neill, Burge, Mackay, Davidson, Grout, Meckiff, Kline and Simpson, the latter being made twelfth man on the morning of the match.

I had a lot of good friends in the Australian side over the years, all of them different personalities. When I became captain, all of them needed to be treated in a slightly different fashion without moving away from the team concept. I was a team-mate of Colin McDonald's from the time we first toured England in 1953 through to the end of the 1961 tour of England and he was great. He kept us all on our toes, which is always a good thing, and he was one of the most courageous cricketers I saw. Send out McDonald and Jim Burke to open the innings and you knew you had a good pair. When I became captain Neil was my vice-captain and Colin was the third selector. I couldn't have asked for better, nor for more support. There are many good things to remember in a lifetime of cricket; one for which I'm especially grateful is that I was a part of that trio. Once I had seen the team announcement I could make some plans and think about a few ideas concerning the game, and some not necessarily associated with the cricket.

As a side issue, I had heard on the grapevine Peter May had proffered the opinion in the nets that I might not cause much trouble to batsmen who played straight down the line, that I didn't spin the ball a great deal and that I had no worthwhile wrong'un. I was very cranky about this. One remark was said to have been 'he bowled me a Benaud' when a young practice net legspinner wasn't turning the ball. It had the effect of spurring me on to a considerable degree, on the basis that none of the England batsmen had seen me since Laker's series in England. I had changed my run-up, improved my delivery stride, I now had a flipper, I had been working on a wrong'un. I had broken records formerly held by Grimmett, O'Reilly, Wardle and S. F. Barnes, I had a spinning-finger remedy that was brilliant, and our opposition were merely inclined to consider it amusing. I might, to England, be the same old bowler, but to me I was a very different one! That was one of the reasons I was so keen to do well in the state match against MCC, hence the pleasure at taking 5–48 from 28.4 overs.

Whatever minimal pleasure might have been engendered for the Board at the thought of having me as captain would have been very much balanced by their worries. Apart from the reasons they may have believed noteworthy after the 1956 tour of England, there was the real worry that I was a journalist, and a hard-working one at that. Being on the Police Rounds beat with Noel Bailey, and against Bill Jenkings of the *Daily Mirror* and others, had given me a good grasp of how to file stories and what angles to take, and taught me to try hard to be constructive.

The Board had nothing in its fifty-three-year history to this time which indicated in any way they would be looking in kindly, or even constructive, fashion at a captain of Australia who was also a journalist. They didn't look in kindly fashion at journalists anyway, and had a history of ensuring cricketers had no right to make comments to the media. Their brows knitted when anyone like Jack Fingleton tried to combine a career in cricket with one as a writer, which he was when chosen for the 1935–36 tour of South Africa and the 1938 tour to England. In Australia it was worrying to officialdom that a journalist should be permitted to walk over the imaginary white line at the doorway of the Australian dressing-room, and the same went for overseas tours.

I wanted to change that.

The master at work – Richie Benaud commentates for Channel 4 at Old Trafford in 2004.

'It's been absolutely marvellous for 42 years.' Soaking up the atmosphere at The Oval in 2005 – the final Test of his favourite Ashes series, and the last one he covered for British television.

Padding up in 1950, aged 19, at Sydney's Central Cumberland CC, where his father was still playing first-grade cricket well into his forties.

Not long after making his debut for Australia against West Indies in 1952, RB hits out for New South Wales.

A treasured family photograph – skill, determination and natural timing from the Benaud trio. From left to right: Jeffery, Gregory and Richie.

In the nets at the SCG with younger brother John, who also represented both New South Wales and Australia, before becoming a national selector.

Lou Benaud – here at Sutherland Road, where he and Rene lived for over 50 years – was determined that his sons should have the chance of a career in cricket, something that was denied to him.

Proudly standing in the village of his French ancestors. The first Benaud journeyed to Australia on the *Ville de Bordeaux* in 1838.

'Everything any young cricketer could want as mentors.' Opening batsman Arthur Morris, *above left*, in the middle of a match-winning 196 in the 5th Ashes Test in 1948; Ray Lindwall, *above right*, about to unleash his pace at The Oval in 1953; *below*: MCC wicketkeeper Billy Griffith can only watch as flamboyant allrounder Keith Miller hits another six for Australia during his 163 at Lord's in 1948.

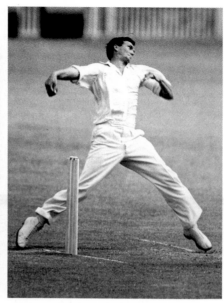

The dedication the young cricketer put into practising and perfecting his bowling technique would later be seen in the meticulous preparation of the journalist and broadcaster.

England captain Peter May congratulates RB after he leads Australia to an unexpected victory in his first Test as captain, in Brisbane in 1958. In 19 Tests he would dismiss May eight times.

RB shares a glass with Frank Worrell in Brisbane before the 1960–61 series. Little was expected of the West Indians, but by the end of the hard-fought tour, their captain had turned them into a close-knit team, hailed as heroes.

At the 'Gabba, on the final day of the 1st Test of the 1960–61 series, when his attack-minded captain told him that he was going for a win, the response of Chairman of Selectors Sir Donald Bradman was 'I'm very pleased to hear it.'

'And then that last unbelievable throw from Solomon, side-on to the stumps, and needing to hit them to save the game for his country.' Test cricket enters a new era of popularity as Ian Meckiff is run out and the 1st Test is tied.

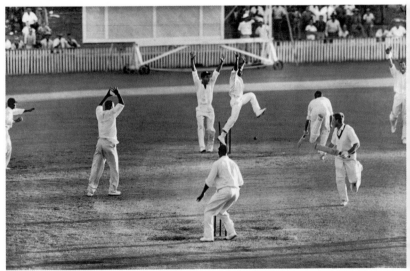

In 1961 with 'The Claw', indispensable bowling partner Alan Davidson. Between 1957–58 and 1962–63 he and RB took 333 Test wickets.

'Good morning, my name's Cowdrey.' The two captains inspect the Edgbaston pitch before the 1st Test in 1961, as RB sets out to defend the Ashes he regained for Australia in 1958–59.

Fred Trueman, 'one of the finest fast bowlers of the post-war period', watches from the safety of the non-striker's end, but he was soon to be one of RB's three victims in the first innings of the Edgbaston Test, which ended in a draw.

After deciding to bowl round the wicket, aiming at Trueman's footmarks, RB takes the crucial wicket of Ted Dexter in the 4th Test at Old Trafford in 1961, initiating an England batting collapse.

RB and his vice-captain, Neil Harvey, are congratulated by team-mates after the captain's six second-innings wickets at Old Trafford bring an unlikely victory and the Ashes are retained.

While we had been in South Africa we had a good rapport with the small Australian press contingent: Keith Butler was the AAP representative, R. S. Whitington was there, and Ray Robinson also. Now I was looking for some constructive team publicity from what was again a small press contingent, although in those days, wherever you went there was always a local press representative, and most newspapers would send their own men on tour inside Australia.

One of the reasons I was thinking of doing something to bring players and press closer together was that it would provide good coverage for the players. A second reason was that the game needed the media. We had gone through some ordinary times in Australian cricket during the 1950s, with the loss of the Ashes in 1953, the dirge-like over-rates of 1954–55, when a big part of England's tactical play revolved around making the batsman wait a long time for every ball, and then the Jim Laker series in 1956. In between times our successful tours of the West Indies and South Africa had been more low key – much better than being beaten, but not the same as being on top of England.

At any rate, for better or worse, I said quietly to the Australian press that they would be welcome to come in for a drink at the end of the first day of the Brisbane Test, and there they were. Soon word spread around that it was possible to have a beer and a chat in the Australian dressing-room at the close of play, bearing in mind it would cease to be an invitation the instant anyone quoted a player, because that was against the Board's rules and against our contracts. What journalists could do, and did, was chat and listen and derive some useful background information for the future. We were happy and so were the journalists, and it did indeed produce beneficial publicity for the team. How it would have gone had we been beaten in every Test is another matter, but the players were mature enough to handle criticism in the media in the same way as they handled praise. Sadly in my view, it's not something which could be done in these modern times.

My second decision was that we would have a team meeting the evening before every Test started, not too protracted, although there was never a curfew while I was captain and every player knew he would be judged on what he did on the field. Anyone whose performance might be affected by what he had done the previous night was simply stupid, and with a tough series in front of us, I was confident everyone would concentrate. No curfew.

My pre-planning included a policy of hemming England in with close-in fieldsmen, making certain they were unable to get at us with the bat. When Peter May and Colin Cowdrey were at the crease, bowlers knew they faced a very tough task. The general feeling I had was that the England batsmen could be contained. Hem them in. We wanted our running between the wickets to be purposeful, even brilliant, I wanted them bustled. What I had seen of England indicated to me they shouldn't be able to match us in the field, not even come within a bull's roar of us in that department. It was my job to put into place the basic planning for the bowlers and the field-placings, and we discussed all these

❝Captaincy is the ability to think ahead of play, not to be left responding to it.❞

RB on captaincy

things at the team meeting. The other thing I wanted was enthusiasm throughout the team, and enjoyment. I reckoned a happy team, and an enthusiastic one which was supportive of good bowling, batting, fielding and brilliant catches, would do well.

I had watched the Australian XI match against MCC at the SCG a couple of weeks earlier, and I was determined, if possible, that no one would run down the line of the stumps, as had happened on the second day of that game, resulting in Tony Lock being close to unplayable in the Australian XI's second innings.

'Burkie and Colin,' I said, 'whichever one of you is at the non-striker's end, I want you to call the umpire's attention to Brian

Statham or Peter Loader, whoever takes the new ball, and ask the umpire to keep them further out off the pitch. I don't give a stuff where their feet were, make the point first ball.'

I'm sure it was mystifying when it happened, because Brian had taken the first over and, as far as we knew, he had never before been spoken to by umpires in that regard. Burkie carried out his orders perfectly though, made a song and dance about it and it was picked up very quickly by the media. And what was more, we kept it going whenever there was the slightest hint of anyone running on the pitch, even to the extent that Jim Laker, when I was batting on the third day at the Vulture Street End, deliberately walked straight up the centre of the pitch. I watched this with pursed lips from the other end and caught his eye as he came nearer. I was opening my mouth to give him a burst when a sixth sense had me look down. He was wearing rubber-soled shoes . . . and a smile, by the time I lifted my eyes to meet his again. We said nothing.

Before a ball was bowled at the 'Gabba, England had a problem when Fred Trueman, their best bowler, had to pull out of the match with a bad bout of lumbago. Fred had also missed the game against Queensland. These days it would be classed as a stress fracture and there would be weeks of treatment, but years ago, if bowlers missed a game, they played the next one otherwise their place might be gone for good.

This opening Test was played on a pitch where you could hardly select the cut portion from the rest of the square. At the same time, because of the heat and the humidity, there was something there for the spinners all the time and spinners in fact took eleven of the wickets to fall.

The match itself was wonderful because we won, boring because it produced some of the slowest and worst cricket imaginable, with Trevor Bailey the star, if that's not a contradiction in terms. Five years earlier Trevor and Willie Watson had combined to frustrate us

at Lord's, and now they frustrated the spectators. The scores were
Australia 186 and 147–2, England 134 and 198. Trevor batted 7
hours and 38 minutes for his 68 and he scored off 40 of the 426 balls
he received. And he ran out Tom Graveney, with assistance from
Neil Harvey who made a brilliant pick-up and throw.

Most of the play was dullsville for the paying spectators, and it
was not at all what we had in mind for what I was hoping would be
some form of cricket renaissance. It was best summed up at one
stage during Trevor's innings by journalist Percy Millard who called
to scorer George Duckworth, 'How long since Bailey has scored,
George?'

'Twenty past two,' was the reply.

Ron Roberts's voice floated over the press box, 'Today or yesterday?'

The Second Test was a victory by eight wickets for Australia after
Alan Davidson took 6–64 in the first innings, including Richardson,
Watson and Graveney in his second over. Peter May made a brilliant
113 after I dropped him off my own bowling at 20. Accounts of the
fielding lapse generally were along sympathetic lines that Benaud
had missed a difficult diving chance. Although the photographs
showed I was crouching in the end, it was only because I had tried
to grab at the ball a second time as it was falling. It was an awful miss
– I tried to take the gentle lob by pulling my elbows in to my waist,
they hit my body and jolted the ball out of my hands. It was the
easiest catch I missed in first-class cricket. I also had a sinking feeling
that I might have cost Australia the match.

By the end of the first day England had only lost four wickets and
had 173 on the board, with May and Cowdrey in charge. We took
wickets with the second new ball and then Neil Harvey and Colin
McDonald saw the team through to the close of play after Jimmy
Burke had been bowled by a beauty from Brian Statham. Brian
bowled well to take 7–57, including me for a duck, Peter Loader

took the other three and then England were bowled out by Ian Meckiff and Alan Davidson in their second innings for only 87 and we made the necessary 39 for the loss of McDonald and Grout.

The Sydney Test finished in a dull draw, with England declaring their second innings closed at 287–7, and we were 54–2 off twenty-five overs when the game finished. Rain marred much of the game. The second day, in front of a crowd of 50,416, couldn't begin until after 4 p.m. and Ian Meckiff was able to bowl only three overs in the second innings because of a bruised heel. For modern-day followers, a summing-up of the statistics of the England second innings, when it is said Australia played defensively, is that Colin Cowdrey's century, to that point, was the slowest in eighty-two years of Ashes battles. In that innings Australia bowled 106 balls an hour and England scored 33 runs per 100 balls.

The Ashes were regained in Adelaide in the Fourth Test where England again were at a disadvantage because of injuries; this time Godfrey Evans broke a finger and Tom Graveney kept wicket for the remainder of the match. The worst thing, however, from Peter May's point of view, was that Jim Laker was unable to play, which left England with Statham, Tyson, Trueman and Bailey as the bowlers, with Lock as the spinner. Laker had bowled more than fifty overs in the Test at the SCG and his finger was in bad shape, the corn cracked and the finger itself arthritic enough for him not to be able to straighten it. He had a net in Adelaide the day before the Test and told Peter May he would be unable to play. That evening we heard the team, with Laker included after May had persuaded him to hold off until the next morning. Supposedly this was a ploy so we Australians would not gain a psychological advantage in knowing England would take the field without him.

Australian journalists told me there was something funny going on, in the sense that Freddie Brown, the manager of the team, was on the surly side of diffident when answering the question, 'Is Jim Laker fit to play?' His reply was, 'He's in the twelve.'

On the first morning Freddie arrived at the press box which, in those days, was below the Australian dressing-room, and announced, 'Laker has come along and said his finger is no good and he can't play.' The general impression given by Freddie was that Jim didn't care. It was poor reward for a man who was one of the greatest bowlers and triers to play for England.

In the Adelaide match I made 46 and took nine wickets, Ray Lindwall made a comeback to the Australian side, and for me, it was a real thrill to captain him. He was a wonderful cricketer who had given me very good advice over the years, and it was a delight to see him take a wicket with his second ball. I made England follow on in this match, despite being met at the top of the stairs by Sir Donald, who pointed out, with a smile, it was the only way we could lose the match. I didn't feel as though we could lose, and on the final and sixth day, they began at 198–5 and we bowled them out for 270 then made the necessary runs with an hour to spare.

The last Test, at Melbourne, was awful for England. Some of the players were involved in a nasty car accident a couple of days prior to the game: Peter Loader had a cut arm, Brian Statham a badly bruised forearm and shoulder and then Willie Watson badly strained a groin muscle the day before the match. Godfrey Evans and Arthur Milton were both still suffering from broken fingers, so it could hardly be said as a team they were in good physical shape. In addition, there had been heavy rain in Melbourne as a lead-up to the game, and when Sir Donald Bradman told me as I was going out to toss that Les Favell would be twelfth man, I decided, on the run so to speak, to put England in to bat if the coin came down the right way.

It was in this match that Lindwall passed Clarrie Grimmett's wicket-taking record for Australia, a reward for the man who was the finest fast bowler I had seen to that time. I ripped a side muscle in the match, trying to swing Jim Laker to leg, but finished with 64 and took five wickets. I was very happy, first of all with the regaining of the Ashes, and also with the fact this was the first time since I had started playing first-class cricket in 1948–49 I had been in an Australian team which had won a series against England. Ten years actually seemed like an eternity. Also, I had been able to debunk the pre-series statements that it was merely a matter of batsmen playing down the line to counteract my bowling.

The not-so-good part was that my batting hadn't been as successful as I had hoped following the tour of South Africa, something I could partly ascribe to the fact that I was now captain and that I had determined to bat Davidson and myself on either side of Ken Mackay when the occasion warranted. I didn't think the captaincy had affected my bowling, but dropping down the batting order did have an effect on my batting.

It was a wonderful summer, and the first thing Neil and I did in the dressing-room at Adelaide, after congratulating the opposition and then our own players, was to sit down and have a cold beer, gently clink glasses and murmur that it was better than Old Trafford 1956.

Learning about life and diplomacy
Australia in Pakistan and India 1959–60
Richie Benaud, *Over But Not Out*, 2010

Captaining the first official team to India and Pakistan was quite an experience, but we managed well and won both series against the odds. We achieved that without the hardly believable number of support staff which are part of every sporting team these days. Ten years after Partition all we had was Sam Loxton, formerly a 1948 Invincibles player and, eleven years later, manager of my team. We had Dr Ian McDonald, an expert in tropical ailments. We had Benaud as captain and we used our brains without bothering with today's compulsory bonding sessions.

One of the problems we faced in 1959 was that although the Pakistan cricket authorities told the Australian Board of Control that the matches would be played on turf, did they mean it? Woven into the equation was whether or not our Board would have the courage to pursue the matter with Pakistan if it suddenly became something in the too-hard basket. There were various answers to that, all of which added up to the fact that I should assume nothing, be careful, and think along the lines that if telex communication broke down or was delayed between the two Boards, then we would be flying blind. I was lucky no Board member had the slightest intention of going anywhere near Pakistan or India.

Most times there is a queue to be manager of a team to various areas; for India and Pakistan there was only the nomination of Sam Loxton. Sam had moderate managerial credentials from the Board's point of view, in that he was perfectly forthright, calling a spade a bloody shovel if he wished. He had never been noted as being a great lover of traditional administration. He could be abrasive at times, particularly if he knew someone was trying to put something over him; he was known as a fine cricketer for the things he had done in Sheffield Shield, where the war zones of Victoria and NSW often met; he had been a member of Bradman's 1948 tour of England; and he was a great mate of Neil Harvey's. He was also a good organiser and he had toured India with that Commonwealth side in 1953–54 when Iverson had eventually gone as a replacement for Ramadhin. He knew the country well, and from the stories he told of that Commonwealth tour, he was aware of the nuances on a continent where various negotiations might be easy or extremely difficult.

I was now in a completely different area, because although I had captained Australia at home against England I had only toured with an Australian team under another captain, vice-captain and third selector, and with absolutely no position of responsibility or influence. This would be very different. It was only three years since we had visited Pakistan and India and played one Test at Dacca and three at Madras, Bombay and Calcutta.

Conditions would not have changed in that time, turf pitches would be roughly the same, although we couldn't be certain of the exact type of surface which would be provided in the various centres. It would be educational and there was a chance it would be a difficult tour, notably with possible medical problems, the types of pitches and any political overtones, about which we might know nothing in advance.

I was keen that we should have some medical assistance on the tour. The Pakistan and Indian doctors, pharmacists and general medical people would be very good and helpful on such a long tour, but my feeling was that we definitely needed a doctor travelling with us so he would be able to liaise with his local counterparts, and, more important, be instantly available at all times of the day or night, if needed. My unofficial recommendation to the Board was that they should find out who was available and see what could be done. They did better than that. They went to Ian McDonald, who was the wicketkeeper for the Victorian 2nd XI when I was hit in Melbourne that day and who had played with distinction for Victoria before retiring to pursue his medical career, and persuaded him to take the job. It was something of a master-stroke, even to the extent that in a crisis we might have an extra player available. My biggest worry was hepatitis, something which these days is still a real problem in many countries; at that time it was the illness I feared might rip through the team. We struggled during the tour but, without McDonald, we wouldn't have made it.

With a turf pitch you are sometimes at the mercy of the groundsman, sometimes of the administrators, as we found out a couple of times during the tour. Matting pitches in Pakistan, though, were an entirely different matter, and on an unofficial basis, I constantly nagged the various Australian Board members I met to persuade them to ensure they had something in writing for me to take with me so that we would be playing on turf in the three matches in Pakistan. The Board insisted they were having trouble with those assurances, although they were continually told the games would not be on matting. That was almost all we could do.

On diplomatic matters I had written to Prime Minister Menzies, asking if the Department of External Affairs could let me have some detail of any known problems we might encounter during the tour, and also anything that was blowing in the wind. The reply allowed me to arrange a meeting with Peter Heydon, who had been Australian High Commissioner to India when we played there in 1956. He was now an Assistant Secretary in the Department of External Affairs, which was the department of Richard Casey, within a few months to become Lord Casey. While I was doing this, Sam Loxton had a stroke of inspiration and arranged for 4,000 cans of Foster's lager to be sent to the Australian High Commissioner of the day, Ray Gullick, who was then based in New Delhi. That sounds a lot of Foster's, but it worked out at two cans a man per day, often at the end of a long slog of six hours in the field. Sam's second most important job was to ensure, before a ball was bowled in any Test match, a bank receipt was placed in his hand signifying the local Cricket Association secretary had banked £6,500 (in Australian currency) and had listed it as a telegraphic transfer to the Australian Cricket Board.

Attached to the team was a media contingent which was minuscule when you compare it with the hustling, bustling press boxes of today. Michael Charlton was the Australian Broadcasting Commission's commentator who would also be doing other non-cricketing jobs during the tour, and Australian Associated Press sent Wally Parr as their man on the spot.

We were looking forward to the tour, although we were not quite certain what it would all entail, because this was the first time the Australian Cricket Board had sent a team on tour to the subcontinent. I reckoned, at that stage, we could have done no more by way of preparation. You hear of people beating their chests and intoning those slightly pretentious words, 'We are ready.' We, in fact, had absolutely no idea if we were ready, but we were available and had been chosen, so it was a case of let's get at it.

There had still been no telex messages concerning the type of pitch on which we would be playing by the time we arrived in Singapore, where we played a couple of one-day matches. We moved on to Dacca, where we were met by the local Pakistan officials and were given a very warm welcome. Fazal Mahmood was there to greet us, looking fit and happy, possibly with good reason, recalling the manner in which he had demolished us on matting three years earlier.

On our way to Pakistan we played a centenary match at the 'Gabba and I took a calculated gamble and every morning had the team practise on matting over closely mown outfield turf. I was particularly interested in the way Slasher Mackay bowled. Conditions weren't exactly the same, but on a pitch with canvas matting over short cut grass which was watered and rolled in the outfield it wasn't far away from what I remembered as the manner in which the surface had played in Karachi three years earlier. It would have been no use at all putting down a mat on an ordinary 'Gabba net pitch, as the under-surface would have been far too hard and the bounce of the ball would have been much higher than in Pakistan.

It's not often you can say in cricket that whatever planning you might have envisaged comes off, even to a certain degree. It did this time. When we left Dacca airport we asked to be taken to see the ground on the way to the hotel, and lo and very much behold, right in the centre of the most beautifully grassed square you have ever seen, was a cream dirt strip just waiting for a mat to be put on it. We were told there had been a problem in growing the grass on this particular section, there had been a problem with the water, there had been a problem with the roller, there had been a problem with the telex machine in sending a message to the Australian Board of Control to say the match would be on matting, problems abounded that day in Dacca. However, the fact that this came as no surprise to us was a plus-mark because we knew we had done all we could in Brisbane on matting with a soft surface underneath, and we were the only ones who knew this. Those who had decided the game was to be on matting might have believed we would be coming in cold, as had been the case in Karachi in 1956.

And I had Slasher. In Brisbane on the matting surface he was bowling the leg-cutter in a way which looked like a faster version of a leg-break but with his own method, which was merely by holding the seam upright and using his index and second fingers for the cutting action. He was cutting the ball more than I was spinning it. In the match itself in Dacca we did win the toss and we did put Pakistan in to bat, and we did bowl them out for 200, which wasn't a bad score. I finished with eight wickets for the match but the champion bowler was Mackay with match figures of 64–39–58–7. We bowled together most of the time in the match – I had 77–36–111–8 – but it was the pressure and accuracy of Mackay which undid them.

So, too, did Slasher's mate, Lindsay Kline, who was down at the ground every morning superintending the tightening of the matting. He was sent off in a taxi, or a second team bus, an hour before the rest of the team and his twelfth-man duties involved nothing to do with water, food, boot spikes or anything else like that. He was the tightener, the 'enforcer' of the mat, only that. Both lengthways and widthways, that mat was to be tight as a drum when we arrived at the ground, and so it was. Whether the hot sun then tightened it more I have no idea, but it was a perfectly fair surface and those of us on the tour will never forget stepping off the bus and hearing the ringing cries of 'Pull, you bastards, pull,' floating across the ground. Not politically correct, but effective!

We won in Dacca because of a number of things. Most important, Neil Harvey played one of the greatest innings of all time, making 96. He was several times physically ill on the ground, and was suffering from a bout of flash dysentery and half a dozen times had to leave the field, make some necessary adjustments and then go back out on slightly rubbery legs. No one had broken Ian McDonald's eating and drinking restrictions, but there were still problems and Harvey seemed to have most of them this day. It was a wonderful innings, a great win and a tough match.

So was the one in Lahore when Kline, back in his playing rather than rug-pulling role, bowled beautifully to take 7–75, Norm O'Neill hit a splendid century and we made it with a few minutes to spare after a one-a-minute run chase over the last two hours. Some blatant time-wasting didn't help, with Nasim-ul-Ghani and Haseeb Ahsan crossing from cover on one side of the ground to cover on the other, at walking pace, each time a single was made. Harvey, having played that innings in the First Test, now stepped away and deliberately allowed himself to be bowled so we could have two right-handers batting.

I played my part by going out to join Norm O'Neill and, on the way to the crease, diverting far enough to chat with Imtiaz Ahmed, the skipper, and set out for him, in very gentle but also descriptive fashion, what I thought about the tactics, which I said I knew were not being planned by him but were coming from the pavilion. He was the one instructed to fire the bullets.

These days, the diversion and the one-way conversation through a stump camera microphone would have brought a red card, a fine of the total match fee and a possible suspension for a month. Instead, things came back to a normal state and overs were bowled at a proper rate, though no faster than would usually have been the case.

In Karachi we played a draw, again on the matting, and this time in front of President Eisenhower, who was on a state visit to Pakistan. Sam and I took the opportunity to press with Pakistan President, Ayub Khan, the matter that no Test should again be played on matting. It was duly decreed after Sam had a final gentle go at him, working on the basis that continuing to play Tests on matting would hold Pakistan up to ridicule in the cricket world. Sam was brilliant and that was the last time a Test was played on the mat.

Between the Second and Third Tests three desperadoes or heroes, as you will, made the trip from Rawalpindi to Gilgit in Kashmir. Colin McDonald, Richie Benaud and, memory suggests, Ian McDonald, were picked up at the hotel and driven in an air force jeep to the airport. You need to realise Col was going through his slightly left-wing kick at the time, and part of this involved going to see what was happening in Gilgit, to see if there was an easy solution we could offer to the Kashmir problem between India and Pakistan; also to check how the people coped as regards accommodation, food, water and general living conditions, and if we three could do anything to improve it.

We also went back in time as regards transport. When we were at the airport, and were looking at the aeroplane scheduled to take us to the frontier, I said to the captain of the craft that the make of the plane reminded me of one in which I had travelled many years ago in Australia, ten years to be exact. He replied, 'Yes, how very observant, Mr Benaud, it is an Australian plane, a DC3, and we are indebted to you and your government for letting us have it. It had been used so much in Australia it was time to pension it off, your government passed it on to us, and here we are.'

We certainly were, and I was trying to catch Colin's eye, but he was studiously avoiding me. We walked over to the aircraft steps, climbed up them, and I knew instantly why he hadn't looked at me. It was because he had been told by the pilot there were no seats in the Australian 1950/Pakistan 1959 DC3 and he thought I might kill him – no seats, but thin rope nets to which we should cling en route.

Something worried me about the flight and I didn't properly work it out until we were about to board for the return trip. In Gilgit we had an interesting look around and a delightful potato and vegetable curry with rice for lunch.

'CC' was delighted. 'I knew you'd love it,' he said enthusiastically.

I said, 'Col, I've asked the pilot what the ceiling of a DC3 is and it's 20,000 feet. When I asked him about the radar on the plane on the way up he said there wasn't any. I've now asked him about the weather and he tells me thick fog is forecast. And we both know the peaks of all the mountains on the way up were 20,000 feet. How will the pilot be able to see the mountain peaks in the fog?'

'Don't worry about it,' Col said. 'The main thing is that we're doing the right thing and showing how much we appreciate what they've done for us.'

'I'll tell you something else,' I murmured grimly. 'I didn't pay much attention when he told me earlier because it was a perfectly clear sky and a beautiful day, but the pilot did say the weather forecast was so bad for later in the day they would never have taken off in normal circumstances. It was only because they knew how much we wanted to see Gilgit!'

On the way back the fog swirled around the windows, when, that is, the mountain peaks weren't appearing alongside them. CC, on landing safely, told me I should feel happy as I had gone through a character-building experience which would serve me well later in life.

To win that series in Pakistan was a triumph, though it may not seem so these days. It wasn't the fault of the Pakistan people that it was tough for a touring party because it was only ten years or so after Partition and independence, with its good moments and some horrifying undertones. The fact that there was a tour at all said plenty for the diplomatic endeavours of those in Canberra, and we had kept to our side of the bargain to date, with our own form of diplomacy, and Australia's High Commissioner in Pakistan, Sir Roden Cutler, had been magnificent with his assistance and advice.

The team had performed brilliantly, Neil Harvey had played one of the best innings seen at Test level, Slasher Mackay had done what I wanted in the two Tests on the mat and we had used him only as a batsman on turf in Lahore. We had managed any problems with enough laughs at one another to keep us going, and our management team of Sam Loxton and Dr Ian McDonald had been resourceful, thoughtful and very, very efficient.

My fingers had stood up wonderfully well on this tour to the rigours of having the seam rip across them in delivering the ball, thanks to Ivan James's finger remedy. However, I did have a shoulder problem which may possibly have been the start of similar troubles which were to bring to an end my career at Test level. On the first day in Karachi, I had slipped when throwing in from the boundary and damaged something in my right shoulder. It was the first such problem I had experienced and I needed injections before I was able to bowl on the second day. It wasn't a good omen.

The team had been very popular in Pakistan. A big crowd saw us off at the airport and when we arrived in New Delhi well over 10,000 people were there to welcome us, an extraordinary and heart-warming sight.

Our first Test against India was at Delhi and we won by an innings and 127, with Harvey making a brilliant 114. I picked up eight wickets for the match, Lindsay Kline four and Alan Davidson three, and the local players not only took plenty of stick from their supporters, but three of their bowlers were dropped for the Second Test.

At Kanpur they had a turf pitch on the ground for the first time, and India turned the First Test result around and thrashed us by 119 runs, a bowler new to us and picked out of the blue, Jasu Patel, taking 14 wickets in the match. He played in other matches in the series but then never again played for India after that summer.

It was the first time Australia had been beaten in a Test in India. When we had lost on the last afternoon in Kanpur, I walked out on to the field and shook hands with Gulabrai Ramchand, their skipper, and all my players stood at the entrance to the playing field and clapped the Indian team into the dressing-room. The whole of our team went to their dressing-room and congratulated them. Then we watched as they were garlanded and fêted around the ground, cheered by thousands and hit by a few unripe guavas hurled or shanghaied by some of the happy students. There was not the slightest doubt within our team that we had been beaten by a better side and it was a matter now of organising ourselves for the next game.

We were helped in this by the article written and published in Kanpur by the Maharaj Kumar of Vizianagram, who had captained India in England in 1936, extolling the virtues of the Australians and saying what good sportsmen we were. He said as well, though perhaps a touch flamboyantly, that India's victory was 'in keeping with other great events of 1959: man's first rocket to the moon, Khrushchev's visit to the United States and President Eisenhower's visit to India.' He added that the win was 'as incredible as the cow jumping over the moon. It was one of the most exhilarating moments in Indian history, parallel to the scene when, in 1947, India gained independence. The Australians,' he said, 'had been dragged from the ethereal heights of invincibility to the dust and din of defeat.' Never had he seen a team lose with better grace and spirit than the Australians.

As it turned out, however, in another article for the *Northern Indian Patrika*, a border newspaper, he had slated me and the Australian team for being the worst sportsmen imaginable. I would never have seen the article had not a good friend of mine, an Indian journalist, handed it to me. It takes a lot to have me in explosive mood but this was one of the days.

On the first day of the Test match in Bombay we had two little incidents, the first when Sam Loxton, our manager, came to me and said, 'Don't rush out for the toss. I haven't seen the receipt for the lodgement of the guarantee money yet. We might have a small problem.'

As Sam sat down alongside me, in bounced the Maharaj Kumar of Vizianagram, spreading around a 'hello' or two here and there. I put the two newspaper articles alongside each other on the table. I noted to him that in the one on the spot, in Kanpur, he had been full of praise for our sportsmanship, and in the other, up on the border, in the *Northern Indian Patrika*, he had been scathing about our sportsmanship and had said it would be better if we never came back to India. I added that we would need an explanation, and an apology, before he would be welcome again in our dressing-room.

He blustered that some sub-editor had written the article and put his name to it and that I had besmirched his good name. There was plenty more bluster, as though he owned the dressing-room, which on reflection he probably did – ownership of the Cricket Club of India wouldn't be out of the question, and he might even have owned Bombay, which is now known as Mumbai.

We concluded with a compromise: he wasn't welcome in the Australian dressing-room until we received an apology, and he said he wouldn't come back into the dressing-room unless we all, as a team, apologised to him. My suggested compromise worked well!

Sam, after smiling at Karmarkar, the Indian Board secretary, and telling him it was a no pay-no play situation and 'Kar' would be the one who would have to explain that to the 70,000 present at the ground, was given the receipt for the telegraphic transfer and we started on time and played a draw. They were very busy at the ground in the Treasurer's office because a week before the game began every ticket had been sold for every day, a bonanza.

When we first saw the Bombay pitch we had reckoned there was a chance of no result. It looked an absolute belter and proved to be so. It was one of the easiest batting pitches I had seen since last I had played on the same ground three years earlier and the game drifted to a draw. On the other hand, the Madras pitch for the following Test, when we went out to look at it, was as hard as a block of concrete, but felt like a wide strip of sandpaper. We stood at one end for a very long time, trying to work out what was in the surface. Neil Harvey called me up to the other end and for a time neither of us could solve it, then I put my fingernail under a piece of whatever it was, lifted it out and said, 'It's sawdust.'

> 'Out in the field, you haven't got anyone whispering into your ear saying all sorts of things, you've got to do it yourself.'
>
> *RB on captaincy v commentating*

I went over to see the groundsman, smiled at him, shook hands and said, 'Nice pitch, congratulations. What an interesting idea to roll the sawdust in to bind the surface. Who told you to do that?' I was still smiling.

'Thank you for the compliment,' he said. 'The committee told me what to do and how to do it, and they will be very pleased you are so happy.'

Now, casting one eye at offspinner Jasu Patel who had become perfectly fit very quickly having missed the Bombay match, what we really needed was to win the toss and luckily we did. I said to the team I would settle for a first-innings total of 250 and I didn't care how long it took. Time wasn't important in this case because there was no way the game would go the full five days. I reckoned 250 would be plenty.

We were slow, but we did better than I hoped. Les Favell played the innings of his life on the first day, a century out of 183, and Slasher Mackay made a splendid 89 on the second day. The aim was to keep Patel at bay and he certainly spun the *balls* sharply. That plural is correct: a dozen balls were used during the match, with the sawdust surface ripping through the stitching, and in the dressing-room enclosure, with the umpires' agreement, we had sandpapered a box of new balls to remove the shine and threw another one out when the umpires called for it. We bowled India out for 149 and 138, won by an innings and 55 and the game took only three and a bit days. I finished with match figures of 8–86 from 67 overs, which gives an idea of what effect sawdust can have on a pitch, if rolled into the surface.

In the final Test of the series in Calcutta, we were depleted in playing personnel, with Gordon Rorke, Gavin Stevens, Lindsay Kline and Ken Mackay ill. We were so short Mackay had to play, and I had a bout of neuritis in my left arm and a dislocated spinning finger from a knock sustained in Madras. A quick medical finger-pull by Ian McDonald did the trick, but why I should have had neuritis I have no idea, nor could Ian McDonald offer any explanation. In any case he was busy enough with people who were properly ill: he murmured, 'If it's only neuritis and a dislocation you're one of the lucky ones, just get on with it.' The match finished as a draw.

The four NSW members of the team played in the final Sheffield Shield match of the Australian season immediately on returning from India; outright points were vital for the final destination of the Shield. Bob Simpson was in the WA side and made 98 and 161, I took 6–74 in each WA innings and this was the seventh successive Sheffield Shield for NSW.

This had been quite a year – very busy, very successful – and we were looking now at the West Indians touring Australia from October to February. We thought it might be an interesting time, but no one had the slightest idea of what actually lay in store with the Caribbean team.

The Tied Test

West Indies in Australia 1960–61

Richie Benaud, *Over But Not Out*, 2010

The first televised cricket in Australia had been in 1958–59, when the final session of play in Tests could be shown, but this was the season [1960–61] when cricket was to be properly televised by the standards of that time. The Australian Cricket Board came to an agreement with the Australian Broadcasting Commission that Test and first-class matches could be shown on the 'box'. There had been not the slightest interest shown by any commercial television networks.

Before the First Test, which started on 9 December, our usual pre-Test team meeting was prefaced by a talk from Sir Donald Bradman, who, as Chairman of Selectors, had asked if it would be OK to come along and put a point or two to the players. This is commonplace these days, but I can assure you in 1960 it was very unusual. His talk was short and to the point. He said this could be a wonderful year of cricket and that this Australian team in 1960–61 could lead the way to one of the most attractive cricket series seen in

Australia, but that it was totally up to the players, who, in the light of that, paid even closer attention to his next remark.

'The selectors will choose players they believe are playing good cricket, and they will look in kindly fashion on players who play aggressively and are clearly thinking about those who pay their money at the turnstiles. The selectors want you to be winners but not at the cost of making the game unattractive for the cricket follower.'

I can tell you it raised a few eyebrows in the room, and without exception, every player was impressed. Not least because several of us had been together through the 1950s, when we had witnessed a considerable amount of cricket which we wouldn't have wanted to pay our money to watch. This was the start of the 1960s, a chance perhaps for everyone?

In the Test match Sobers played a wonderful innings [of 132], fuelled a little by the newspaper article on the first morning which suggested he might have a few problems with my bowling. He had none. Take my word for that! He played an innings which I put into the top bracket of anything I have seen, an explosive exhibition of strokeplay and power which, in the context of the disappointing tour to that date, was magnificent.

Needing 233 to win on the final day, we were 92–6, and Davo and I, with the pads on, were having a cup of tea when Bradman came down to the dressing-room. He poured himself a cup and said how much he was enjoying the match, and then he asked, 'What are you going for, Richie, a win or a draw?'

I replied, 'We're going for a win, of course.'

All I received was a dry, 'I'm very pleased to hear it . . .'

Our policy after tea that afternoon was to try to rattle the West Indians with our running between the wickets and our selection of shots, carry the attack to them and see if they would crack. They did crack a little, but then so did we under the pressure. Although Joe

Solomon's final throw to hit the stumps and run out Ian Meckiff created the tie and made history, our own effort was rather ordinary, with three wickets lost to run-outs in the last four to fall. If that were to happen to another side these days I would be very critical on television, as I was to Sir Donald when he expressed the view, 'This is the best thing which could possibly have happened for cricket.' Although I agreed with him, as captain I certainly would have preferred that we had played a little better and won. Bradman insisted I would change my mind as the years went on.

It had been a splendid match: some wonderful batting, brilliant bowling, and hour after hour where two teams were striving for the ascendancy rather than seeking to avoid it. There had been such tension in our dressing-room that players didn't remember where their gear was, some wanted to talk, some couldn't.

When the match was finished by that wonderful throw from Solomon, I walked on to the field to greet Worrell and we walked off with our arms around one another's shoulders. The 4,000 spectators came from all parts of the ground to cheer in front of the dressing-rooms and then, eventually, slowly drifted home.

In the dressing-rooms players mingled and drank what they wanted, beer or a soft drink, and the West Indians sang calypsos, in which we joined, though none of us had the ear for music they all possessed. Worrell was exhausted, so was I, and we sat quietly, saying little.

> 'Frank Worrell turned West Indies from being the most magnificent group of individual cricketers in the world into a close-knit team. No one else could have done it.'
>
> *RB on a respected opponent*

Sir Donald Bradman and the other selectors were enthralled by the match, as indeed they were by the summer, and millions of television watchers and radio listeners were captivated by the sequence of events and the climax.

Not everyone felt precisely that way. The Australian Cricket Board at their next meeting passed a motion insisting that 'players should in future be out of the dressing-room within a few minutes of the end of a day's play in a Test match.' The Queensland Cricket Association had complained bitterly to the Board that the night the Tied Test finished, players had stayed in the dressing-rooms far too long. The Board agreed almost wholeheartedly, and eleven of the twelve of them around the rich-red mahogany table enthusiastically outvoted Bradman's solitary dissension! Apart from Bradman, there may have been someone else present who had been in a dressing-room as a first-class player, but they were thin on the ground. The remainder knew little of what happened on a first-class cricket field, and they knew nothing at all of the camaraderie which existed between players and opponents. Nor, I suspect, did they care overmuch.

Sir Donald instigated the Frank Worrell Trophy at the end of the series. Ernie McCormick, the former Australian fast bowler and a Melbourne jeweller, was chosen to design and make the trophy. Frank presented the trophy to me at the end of that final Test, the first such handing over and it was a wonderful occasion. Referring to his scalp, neck and body, Frank as well handed me his cap, tie and blazer as mementoes, bringing laughter from the 25,000 on the ground when he added there was no point in handing over anything to do with his legs, which were, to put it in modern parlance, well past their use-by date.

> 〈 My greatest moment was the speech-making after the last Test . . . Benaud was fluent, with carefully chosen phrases, full of affection and respect for Frank Worrell and the West Indians (and not forgetting his own team); definitely a man of feeling not ashamed or wary of it, but a man seeing the whole of his world and steadily. 〉
>
> *C. L. R. James,* Beyond a Boundary

Stumped in the pavilion!

Richie Benaud, *Way of Cricket*, 1961

The proofs of this book [*Way of Cricket*] were with me when I had the good fortune to play in the finest game of cricket of my life: the tied Test match at Brisbane.

That game was the perfect expression of all those qualities which make cricket still the greatest game in the world.

There could be no better summing-up of all that I have tried to say about the game in this book, so here is what I wrote on December 14th, in the heat of the climax, reproduced verbatim by kind permission of the Sydney *Sun*:

RICHIE BENAUD'S OWN STORY OF THE TEST
STUMPED IN THE PAVILION!

Brisbane, Thursday. Five days of nerve- and body-bruising cricket, five days of razor-edged tension – and no result!

That is how a visitor to the Australian dressing-room summed up the incredible first Test which ended in a history-making tie here yesterday.

The visitor, having a tension-free drink with the two teams, chuckled as he said, 'There's something wrong with you fellows – five days of that for a few bruises and no result!'

How right he was! Never before have I played in a game so full of electrifying thrills, so riddled with periods of nerve-curdling strain.

Disappointment and delight, depending on the side you were on, dominated our feelings in a game of swiftly changing fortune.

This was no Test match. It was a game of cricket full of thrills and dismay.

Combined, these ingredients went to make it the finest game of cricket in which I have ever taken part.

Disappointed? Yes, I'm disappointed we didn't make the extra run that would have given Australia victory after battling for so long.

Thrilled? Yes, I'm thrilled, too, with the magnificent spirit in which the game was played as the West Indies turned impending defeat into an almost blood-curdling tie.

And I'm thrilled, too, with the way our boys fought back in the field with only three bowlers, and the way the batting pulled the match around in the second innings.

Naturally, in a palpitating match such as this, the eventual team efforts will overshadow individual performances, but there were certainly plenty of the latter.

Have you ever seen a better performance than that of Davidson – most wickets ever in a Test match against the West Indies, and those two wonderful batting exhibitions?

Sobers, Worrell, Hall, McDonald, Simpson, O'Neill and Grout all had great individual matches – but who can say their performances were any more valuable than the breathtaking throw from the boundary by Conrad Hunte, or the two sharp-shooting flicks by Joe Solomon to run out Davidson and Meckiff.

Tension – I've never known anything like it!

Everything was fine out in the centre, where both sides thought they had the game under control.

About 5.30 p.m., when we needed 30 in even time, I thought, 'What a hell of a game this is – and what a beauty it would be to win.'

And at ten minutes to six we'd obviously only two overs to go and 10 runs needed. Players in the centre were still cool and reasonably collected, with Frankie Worrell exhorting his boys to 'relax, fellas, and concentrate'.

But in the dressing-rooms and around the ground, other players and spectators were gripped with a frenzy I have never before seen at a cricket match.

Barracking was an effort for spectators, who for days had been tossing their advice to the players.

Spectators screamed, 'Hurry up you logs,' to sightboard attendants, who were moving the screen for Garry Sobers to bowl over the wicket to Davidson.

The moving of the screen took nearly two minutes, and, as the spectators' noise subsided, I called out to Sobers, 'Garry, I'll bet you a quid you're not game to switch to round the wicket now, and have the screen moved back.'

Australians in the dressing-room joined with the West Indian players in shouting or hushing, according to the moment – a moment that invariably changed with the next ball bowled.

In the Australian room, Kline sat at the very back of the dressing-room on the edge of the table, as team-mate Ian Meckiff walked out to bat.

Meckiff missed the second ball from Hall and Grout ran that brilliant single as the ball flew to Alexander.

The keeper hurled the ball to the effervescent Hall, who turned and pelted it at the stumps.

Valentine, at mid-on, just managed to get behind the ball to save four overthrows, as West Indian players on the balcony jumped to their feet in horror.

An Australian player leaned across and asked confidentially, 'What's wrong with Wes out there, he can throw much harder than that.'

Tension broke as 'Mecko' smashed Hall high to the onside boundary, but it returned a thousandfold as Hunte made his fantastic return to Alexander.

And then that last unbelievable throw from Solomon, side-on to the stumps, and needing to hit them to save the game for his country.

It is literally correct to say that neither side won this great match.

The only victor was the game of cricket.

A mentor and a friend

Tony Cozier, ESPN Cricinfo, 2015

IT WAS AN OPPORTUNITY not to be missed.

It was September 2013 and Richie Benaud would be in Barbados for the first time since appropriately delivering the annual Sir Frank Worrell Memorial lecture at the University of the West Indies, Barbados campus, a decade earlier.

At 83, he was unlikely to come again. As it has sadly turned out, it was his last chance to catch up with the five of the West Indian survivors from the unforgettable 1960–61 series in Australia when he, as inventive home captain, and Worrell, his similarly minded West Indies counterpart, influenced their teams into an exuberant approach to the game that revived the fading image of Test cricket.

Immediately sparked by the unprecedented tie first up in Brisbane, the series captured the public's imagination to such an extent that 100,000 thronged the streets of Melbourne to hail their popular visitors at the end. It was a phenomenon unheard of, before or since.

A lunch at one of the island's top restaurants, overlooking the spectacular Rockley beach on Barbados's south coast, seemed the ideal setting for Benaud to be joined by his 1960–61 challengers, Garry Sobers, Wes Hall, Seymour Nurse, Cammie Smith and Peter Lashley. Everton Weekes, then 88 and as effervescent as he is two years on, was also along; he had piled up runs while Benaud twirled his legspin in the 1955 series in the Caribbean. By then, it was Sir Garry, also one of Barbados's ten national heroes, Sir Wes and Sir Everton.

I knew them all as friends, principally from years of covering West Indies wherever they ventured, Benaud from the eight seasons in Australia as part of the Channel Nine panel, learning the intricacies of television, as opposed to radio, commentary under his guidance. In addition, I first met Richie's wife and soulmate, Daphne, when she was secretary to the renowned cricket writer E. W. Swanton.

I was in no doubt they would all be as enthusiastic about the idea as they immediately were. Yet the exercise turned out to be not quite as straightforward as it appeared.

As keen as he was, Richie had one caveat. He was coming for an event unrelated to cricket (it was a special birthday celebration of a close friend of the Benauds, a Trinidadian long since resident in Sydney) and didn't want any diversion from the occasion.

'One possible problem that springs to mind is if media outlets demand access with cameras, tape recorders and notebooks, something which, if it happens, would certainly detract from the idea,' he emailed when I put my lunch proposal to him. He was, after all, then as famous for his second career as television's most authoritative commentator as he was as captain and player.

I nervously assured him that wouldn't be the case, that I had it all under control. So the date was set, the restaurant booked, the local contingent confirmed and sponsorship agreed with the Cricket Legends of Barbados group. I got my son Craig busy designing a four-page menu, entitled 'Remembering the great times', carrying images of the seven players along with the iconic pictures of the final run out of the Tied Test, the summarised scores of the matches and, of course, the menu (Opening Batsmen, starters; Middle Order, main course; Tail-Enders, sweets). Then, suddenly, a setback.

Richie had fallen in the shower at his west coast villa and damaged his ribs. After examination at a nearby clinic, he was transferred to a private hospital on the outskirts of Bridgetown for a couple of days' observation.

Crestfallen, I cancelled the restaurant reservation and advised the others of the situation. Somehow, word got back to Richie. Daphne called to say that whatever I had done I should undo it since Richie was adamant he wasn't going to let a little pain and some tight strapping around his upper body put him off. He would be there at the appointed time.

So the lunch arrangements were restored and, to their shared delight, the invitations to the local contingent reinstated. There was only one anxious moment when Richie arrived at the restaurant; as Wes Hall approached as if to greet him with a hug, he recoiled. 'No hugs today!' he exclaimed, pointing to his ribcage.

The group, including Daphne, Michele Kennedy-Green, the birthday girl from Sydney, and her sister, Patricia, took their seats at a round table at 1.10

p.m. We reluctantly broke up three hours later.

After glasses were raised in memory of those of the 1960–61 team who had passed on – Sir Frank, who died of leukaemia, aged forty-two, Sir Conrad Hunte, Gerry Alexander and Alf Valentine – the banter became increasingly animated, the stories more and more richly embellished, the laughter louder, Cammie Smith's as infectious as ever. It was just what everyone had expected.

His death has thrown a pall of gloom over cricket's global family. West Indians of a certain vintage especially remember his role, along with Worrell, in overseeing as influential a Test series as the game has known. Those of more contemporary generations, who knew him mostly from his reassuring presence on their television screens, appreciated his professionalism, noticed his immaculate dress sense, marvelled at his remarkable cool even in the tensest situations and, above all, valued the absolute impartiality of his measured commentary, a rare attribute at a time of much overt jingoism.

Indulging a hunch
Australia in England 1961
Richie Benaud, *Anything But . . . an Autobiography*, 1998

Later I read a full diagnosis: 'A terrible tear, very extensive, very unusual. The sub-scapularis was torn right down to the capsule that contains the shoulder and, at the start, he couldn't lift his arm above the shoulder without crying out in pain.' They were right about that! It was agony at first and then settled down merely into extreme pain. Dr Bass told me that if I missed the Lord's Test then possibly I would be fit to play at Headingley and certainly at Old Trafford . . . so I missed Lord's. That was heartbreaking.

There are many wonderful things about a tour of England, and for a captain the highlight is to lead the team at Lord's. I confirmed I wasn't a starter for the Test after we had practised the day before the match and were walking back to the dressing-rooms, and passed it on to the media through manager Syd Webb. Neil, as happened right through the tour, did a wonderful job in that Second Test, leading the side with imagination and verve. Although it was tight on the last day when we lost 4–19, he sent Peter Burge out with instructions to get stuck in and the game was won.

Then came the Headingley match, finished in three days on a rubbish pitch – not as bad as the one served up on the same ground in 1972 when 'fusarium' was said to have struck, but rubbish none the less.

At Old Trafford we were in strife for a long time, even though Bill Lawry hit his second century of the series, having already made one at Lord's. On the second-last evening, when we were in a certain amount of trouble, I went across to the Lancashire committee room for an after-match drink.

By chance Ray Lindwall was there, just the man I needed to talk to about the deep footmarks at the Warwick Road End. I asked him about the possibility of bowling around the wicket to the right-handers, recalling Tony Lock coming from a similar angle in Australia at the SCG in 1958, bowling left-arm over the wicket to the right-handers. Lindwall thought it might work but advised me not to stray off line, 'otherwise they'll kill you . . .'

The last day was a real thriller. We were under a lot of pressure because at several points England were clambering all over us. Each time we fought back, and it was one of the more exciting days of cricket in which I had been involved.

We had high hopes of setting England a target of something like 250, thinking at the start of play on the last day that we might add around 100 for the last four wickets. Those hopes disappeared almost immediately as we lost three wickets, but were rekindled by one of the most electrifying partnerships I had seen as a captain, with Davidson and Graham McKenzie adding 98 for the last wicket.

Ted Dexter flayed all our bowlers in a wonderful short innings, and he put England into a clear winning position. I said to Neil that we couldn't save the game, it could only be won or lost. I went around the wicket to bowl into the footmarks, and soon after Dexter was dismissed, though not from a ball pitching in the rough. Brian Close was the danger, and I had him caught at backward square-leg near the umpire, having switched O'Neill to that position to replace the injured Slasher Mackay.

As was often the case in Australian cricket, Slasher did something which had an influence on the saving or the winning of a match. In the course of Dexter's batting savagery, we suffered a cruel blow when Mackay pulled a hamstring whilst turning quickly, possibly when he whipped around to see where Ted had hit him into the stand at the Warwick Road End. He told me about it between overs after Dexter's and May's dismissals and, with Brian Close trying to sweep almost everything, it seemed a good idea not to have Ken fielding near the square-leg umpire. He certainly wouldn't be moving fluently. I quietly swapped him with Norm O'Neill, who had been fielding at cover, and it was O'Neill who caught Close, although Brian has sworn on ten stacks of Bibles for the past thirty-seven years that from the moment he walked on to the Old Trafford ground that afternoon, O'Neill was always the fieldsman near the umpire.

When we went off for tea, with John Murray and Ken Barrington the not-out batsmen, Mackay instantly had the physio, Arthur James, strapping his leg, and he came back out with us after the interval, though I had checked with him as to the state of the injury. 'It's fine,' he said, 'I won't let you down.' He never had done. I reckoned, when we walked out to the centre, that I might as well get what I could out of him before everything started to stiffen up so I gave him the first over, bowled from the Warwick Road End.

Ken Barrington knew, because the first few balls were only gentle medium pace, there was something wrong with Ken, but he didn't know what it was. The next ball was a yard faster and it darted back off the seam and had Kenny plumb lbw. I gave Slash another over and then said 'thanks' and he nodded but refused point blank to go off the field.

'I won't let you down,' he said again.

He never did let me down. The selectors knew what I thought about him, and I knew what they thought about him after he justified their faith in choosing him as Ron Archer's replacement to South Africa. In the 1962–63 series, having made Mackay twelfth man at the SCG in the Third Test match, they quite deliberately chose him in the twelve for the final Test in Sydney, knowing they were to make him drinks waiter on the morning of the match.

Some say selectors can be heartless at times, but the good ones I knew, like Bradman, Ryder and Seddon, had another dimension to them. They knew they were probably about to end Mackay's Test career and they cared. Ken had many friends in cricket and the three selectors already knew that two of his best friends, Neil Harvey and Alan Davidson, were retiring of their own volition after the 1963 match. They reckoned he deserved to be in the nominated twelve and that it would be nice for him to go out at the same time as Harvey and Davidson, rather than be in Perth playing in a Sheffield Shield game against Western Australia.

At the same time, they started Ken's replacement, Neil Hawke, on his 27-Test match and 91-Test wicket career. It was a brilliant yet somewhat controversial choice, and they did it so that if Hawke had a poor year in 1963–64, they could still take him to England, as he would have had one Test to his name on selection day in February 1964.

Ken Mackay carried the drinks out to us in his final Test and looked after us in the dressing-room, no less enthusiastic a cricketer than when he had started with Queensland seventeen years earlier.

At tea, it was 93 to win for England, five wickets to win for us and 85 minutes still to play. With twenty minutes to go, Alan Davidson knocked Brian Statham's off stump out of the ground and the Ashes were ours, the first time Australia had won a Test at Old Trafford since 1902.

There was plenty of jubilation in our dressing-room but I suspect England felt as though they had been sandbagged. It was a feeling that had come my way on many occasions playing against England over the years. Bowling around the wicket into the footmarks was something new in those days and it won a Test match. In 1998, the ICC is suggesting the tactic might be banned. They are thirty-eight years too late!

7
Legspin

❝You must always look where you want to land it. If I offered you 10,000 dollars to hit a tin can, you'd never take your eyes off it.❞

Richie Benaud on focusing the mind

Words of advice
Richie Benaud, *Over But Not Out*, 2010

Cricket is a straightforward game, and everything to do with it should be kept as simple as possible, therefore I have written only two pages on the subject of bowling, particularly legspin bowling. I believe the advice is good and uncomplicated. It could be extended into 200 pages or even a book, but that would mean the youngster wanting to learn to be a legspinner would be wasting a couple of hours of valuable practice time.

For over-the-wrist spin, grip the ball so that the seam runs across the first joint of the index finger and the first joint of the third finger. For the leg-break, and the overspinner or topspinner, the ball is spun off the third finger. The wrist is cocked, but *definitely not* stiffly cocked, which would prevent flexibility and, in delivery, would give you the feeling the ball was simply falling out of your fingers. In delivering the ball, you look at the spot on the pitch on which you want the ball to land, your bowling hand starts level with your face and then describes what could loosely be termed an anti-clockwise circle to the point of delivery.

The position of the bowling hand dictates in which direction the ball will spin.

At the moment of delivery the positioning of the hand is as follows: *Leg-break*: in delivery, the back of the hand is facing your face. (The ball will spin out with the seam rotating in an anti-clockwise direction towards slip.) *Overspinner or topspinner*: in delivery, the back of the hand is facing the sky and then the batsman. (The ball will spin out with the seam rotating in an anti-clockwise direction and towards the batsman.) *Wrong'un*: in delivery, the back of the hand is first facing the sky and then the ground. (The ball will spin out with the seam rotating in an anti-clockwise direction towards fine-leg.) You should be side-on to the batsman and looking over your front shoulder as you deliver the ball. A good guide for a right-hand bowler is that *in delivery stride to a right-hand batsman, your front arm should be in line with fine-leg so you are, in effect, looking 'outside' that front arm*. In 'following through' your bowling hand will finish up going past your front thigh.

This means, if you have done it correctly, your body, at the finish, will have pivoted and rotated anti-clockwise. This 'pivot' is of *great* importance. If you bowl a ball that is too short, you can be almost certain it happened because you were chest-on to the batsman, rather than side-on, and you dragged the ball down into the pitch.

When you are bowling in a net, make a white shoe-cleaner mark the size of a large coin on what seems to you to be a good length: that is, with the ball landing where, if you were batting against a legspinner, *you* would *not* like it to pitch. In your net practice, make sure you bowl against the tail-enders as well as the top-class batsmen. The position of your arm in delivery is of the utmost importance. *Think of looking at a clock face*. Look at the area from nine o'clock to midnight. Nine o'clock is 'round arm', *ten o'clock to eleven o'clock is the perfect position*, between eleven o'clock and midnight is potentially very dangerous, past that perpendicular point is completely useless.

At Scarborough (UK), at the conclusion of the 1953 tour, I had dinner with Bill O'Reilly. It was the evening of Thursday, 9 September, the night before the Australians beat T. N. Pearce's XI by two wickets after three wonderful days of cricket. I distinguished myself with the bat but not the ball, and the latter was the purpose of the dinner. Throughout the tour Bill was unhappy with my bowling and he could see that I was just as unhappy. Over the two hours he listed six things for me to do if I were to become a good bowler. He added that it would take me four years to get it right, and he was correct, 1953 to 1957. In 1957, by using O'Reilly's advice during the Australian tour of South Africa, I took more first-class wickets in that season than any other bowler had done before or since. Below are O'Reilly's six points from 1953.*

1. **Plan:** don't bowl six different balls in an over in a desperate bid to claim a wicket so the captain won't take you off. Develop the ability to land a hard-spun leg-break on the *chosen* spot on the pitch, ball after ball.

2. **Patience:** bowling is a tough game and you will need to work on a batsman with your stock ball, sometimes for several overs, before executing your plan. It may not work the first time or even the second.

   If you take a wicket on average every nine overs in Test cricket, you will have a better strike-rate than any of Warne, O'Reilly, Grimmett and Benaud. If you take a wicket on average every seven overs, you could have the best strike-rate of any modern-day Test bowler, fast or slow.

* Unsurprisingly, RB expanded and adapted this list over the years.

3. **Concentration:** this must be 100 per cent when you are running in to bowl. The spot on the pitch where you want the ball to land (judged by looking from the *middle* stump at the bowling end to the *middle* stump at the batting end) should be the most important thing in your mind from the moment you turn at your bowling mark. Clarrie Grimmett was the first to use and advise this.

   If someone offered you $10,000 if you could bowl a ball and hit an object nineteen paces away, in trying to win the money, would you, as you were bowling, look at the wicketkeeper, the stumps or a batsman's feet?

4. **Economy:** this game is a war between you and the batsmen.

   Is there some very good reason you want to allow him more than two runs an over, thus possibly giving your captain the idea you should be taken off?

5. **Attitude:** calm, purposeful aggression and a clear mind are needed, plus a steely resolve that no batsman will get the better of you over a long period of time. Always remember as well that cricket is a game to be enjoyed and that you are responsible at all times for ensuring play is conducted within the Spirit of the game, as well as within the Laws.

   In other walks of life you will want to be mentally strong and on top of the opposition. Is there some particular reason why, within the Spirit of the game, this should not be the case in your battle with the batsmen?

6. **Practice:** all practice should be undertaken with a purpose.

   You think hard before doing most other important things in life, why should you allow cricket practice to be dull and boring?

Good luck, and enjoy your cricket.

Shane Warne
Richie Benaud, *Over But Not Out*, 2010

Cricket can be a lot of things to a lot of people as a sport, but never lose sight of the fact that luck plays a great part, and not merely on the field. Take Shane Warne as an example.

I first heard of Warne when he went to the West Indies in August 1990. Brian Taber, the coach, told me over lunch that he had seen an interesting young legspinner who had been at the Adelaide Academy, had experienced a few disciplinary problems but then had come through the Caribbean tour in excellent style. The report from tour manager Steve Bernard to the Australian selectors gave Warne a big wrap. It was Taber who with his knowledge of people had given Warne positions of responsibility on that youth tour and Warne had responded magnificently to the gesture.

Later in that Australian season he made his Sheffield Shield debut, against Western Australia in Melbourne, but didn't do much. I then went to England to cover the West Indies tour, and at the final Test at The Oval, Brendan McArdle, who played Sheffield Shield for Victoria, sent up a message to the commentary box asking if he and young Shane Warne could come up. Warne was playing with Accrington at the time, in the Lancashire League, and little snippets were reaching London that he was going OK.

We only had time for a short chat, but it was long enough for him, as a Victorian, to ask some advice on whether or not he should take a very good offer to move interstate. My advice to him was to stay with Victoria, purely because my old-fashioned instincts on the Sheffield Shield would not have allowed me to play other than for NSW, unless I had been forcibly moved by business to another state.

'Make a success of the important thing first, learn to bowl well before you start thinking about going anywhere,' I advised him.

My brother, who was a national selector at the time, was in charge of a team captained by Mark Taylor touring Zimbabwe, and Warne was included. He then made his Test debut against India, took a belting from Ravi Shastri and Sachin Tendulkar but at the same time showed plenty of the attributes which were to take him to the top almost without an apprenticeship.

Towards the end of the summer Bill Lawry asked me if I would come to Melbourne for a special golf day he was arranging for the Victorian players and sponsors. It was a delightful day, almost as though Bill had specially turned on the Melbourne weather, and we had an excellent barbecue lunch, chatting with the sponsors and the cricketers.

When they announced the tee-times I walked with Shane across to the first tee, and in the course of the stroll he asked me if there was anything I could offer by way of advice. All I offered was that he should keep it simple and develop a fiercely spun leg-break as a stock ball. A ball which he could pitch perfectly at will, and which could therefore be used as both an attacking and a defensive weapon. I warned him it would take *four* years to do it properly. Like all champions he made a nonsense of such strictures and did it, 'on his ear', in *two*!

A month later Warne took 3–0 from 13 balls against Sri Lanka in the first Test in Colombo and the game was won by Border's team. It was an extraordinary victory. I was at Lord's at the time and the Texaco game between England and Pakistan was delayed by rain. The packed house was being kept up to date with the match in Colombo and there was continual high delight as the news came through that the Australians were being crushed, with Sri Lanka needing only 54 from 24 overs with eight wickets in hand. The final PA announcement was terse and to the point. 'Australia have won the Test in Colombo by 16 runs.' It was greeted with gloom, disbelief and muted applause.

Since that 3–0 Warne has done some wonderful things with the ball for Australia, none more so than dismissing Mike Gatting in 1993 at Old Trafford. It is rare for one ball to have such an effect on a Test series, particularly at the start of the five matches. Some have been so carried away by the delivery they say it spun a yard and was therefore unplayable. In fact, it spun about 14 inches and was almost unplayable. The real problem it posed for Gatting was that it moved as well, starting on middle and off and then swerving to a spot just outside leg stump before spinning back and hitting the off bail.

> ❝He's done it. He's started off with the most beautiful delivery. Gatting has absolutely no idea what has happened to it. Still doesn't know. He asked Kenny Palmer on the way out. Kenny Palmer just gave him a raised eyebrow and a little nod.❞
>
> *RB on the Ball of the Century*

A dismissal I particularly enjoyed was the one with which he took the wicket of Shivnarine Chanderpaul at the SCG in 1996–97. The West Indians were right on target for a possible win or, at worst, a face-saving draw and Chanderpaul was batting beautifully. Immediately before lunch Warne bowled him a ball which did spin a yard. It was so wide that had it been a topspinner it would have been called wide, but instead, landing in the rough, it spun back and hit middle and off. It was close to the unplayable delivery and it snapped the West Indian resistance.

There have been other stand-outs in Warne's career. Richie Richardson was one in Melbourne in the 1992–93 series in Australia when Warne dismissed him with a flipper which won the match, also Alec Stewart at the 'Gabba in 1994–95 when Shane had him with a slightly slower flipper which completely deceived the batsman. It was wonderful bowling.

Warne had Graham Gooch at Edgbaston in 1993 with a ball that pitched two feet wide of the leg stump, quite deliberately bowled at that spot, and whipped behind Gooch to hit leg stump. Gooch played Warne as well as anyone I have seen and he says the swerve Warne imparted to the ball was a big factor in the difficulty batsmen had in playing him, particularly as he had the ability to swerve the ball a lot or a little. The other aspect Gooch talked about when I spoke to him some years ago was the difficulty in getting down the pitch to him because of the amount of side-spin he imparted to the ball.

There have been many theories about how best to play him, others on the matter of how he shouldn't be played. Above all he had control of that basic legspinner, the one that most of the time drifts towards the right-hander's pads and then spins from leg to off. The thing about Warne was that he would still have been difficult to play even if that had been the only ball in his armoury, but he had many others. Some he might not have possessed, but the batsman thought he had them, or at least couldn't be totally certain that he didn't have them. This in turn led to even more confusion and Warne did nothing to assist the opposition, nor should he have done.

If you want to be a good legspinner then concentrate on what Warne did and perfect that leg-break. That's not to say you will become as good as Warne, but you will improve and you could become a good bowler. What used to be a trickle of correspondence asking how to bowl leg-breaks became a flood when Warne began to captivate the watching audiences at the ground and the millions who watch on television. Even Warne, who was the best of his type to play the game and who did some things differently, adhered to many of the old-fashioned traits. Shane was an orthodox legspin bowler. He was, though, something else as well. He was an orthodox legspin bowler who combined a fiercely spun leg-break with wonderful accuracy.

Comparisons are popular these days, and if you want to know how the respective merits of Warne and Benaud compare in regard to bowling, then you need look no further than one statistic. When Warne reached his 300th Test wicket he was playing in his 63rd Test, the same number I played in my whole career to take 248. Statistics sometimes lie, but definitely not this one: he is that much better than I was – and he went on to a total of 708 Test wickets. I had batting and fielding and captaincy to help me in any all-round ratings, but Warne is the best of his kind I've ever seen.

The earlier notes I have made about when I met Warne, and the other sidelights, lead me to emphasise that I am in the very good position of never having had anything to do with coaching him. The only times I offered him any advice were on the occasions when he asked, and fortunately he was so good that those occasions were rare. This stems from my determination when I retired never again to go into a dressing-room, on the basis that this area belongs to the players, which was exactly as I felt when I was playing. I have rarely departed from this, although one occasion was when Dennis Lillee broke my Australian Test wicket-taking record and I took a magnum of champagne in to him.

The night before the Lord's Test in 1997, Daphne and I had a delightful meal with Shane and his parents, Brigitte and Keith, together with Allan Border and Austin Robertson, Shane's manager and a good friend. We walked around the corner from the Montcalm to Il Barbino, a small and delightful Italian restaurant, where I found it fascinating listening, and contributing a little, to a discussion between Warne and Border on various field-placings for batsmen and how Shane could improve on what had definitely been a below-par performance at Edgbaston. The Portuguese waiter at Il Barbino was one of the most avid followers of cricket in the United Kingdom, and was fascinated by the group and the shuffling of salt and pepper shakers and wine glasses to denote batsmen and fieldsmen.

On the occasions Shane did call to discuss a possible problem, or to check how he was bowling, I always tried to avoid a coaching answer in suggesting what, if anything, he should do. Instead I tried to pose him a question which would make him think about why the problem might exist. He has a sharp mind and he never missed coming up with the right answer to the few questions I posed. To me this approach is far preferable to providing a long, involved coaching answer. The important thing is that the player must be able to think and solve the problem for himself – there is no coach standing by your side in the centre of the ground if things aren't going right. The same arrangement existed between Dennis Lillee and me: I was always available to discuss a problem and be of assistance.

From the batsman's point of view, if you want to be able to play legspin well, then perfect your footwork. A leaden-footed batsman is manna from the cricket ground in the sky for a good over-the-wrist spinner, but you need good judgement as well. There have been many ideas floated about how best to play Warne and, as mentioned earlier, some of them have worked, some haven't. Poor footwork, however, means oblivion. One of the reasons Sachin Tendulkar has played so well against Warne and other bowlers is that his footwork is close to flawless.

The best players of slow bowling in my playing time were Neil Harvey and Arthur Morris. Being left-handers did them no harm against legspin bowling, but they were also wonderful players of offspin and any other type of spin. Harvey was brilliant against medium pace and fast bowling, his only detectable weakness was claimed to be that he was too attacking a player, that he didn't concentrate enough on grinding the opposition into the dust, and that he tried to score from many balls which could have been left alone. Precisely. Harvey was one of the greatest crowd-pleasers the cricket world has known.

It's my view that, in general terms of players I have seen since 1948, only batsmen like Harvey, Morris, or Sachin Tendulkar, Garry Sobers and Brian Lara, Mark Waugh and the Chappell brothers, Gooch and a few others would be equipped consistently to deal with a fully fit Warne. Others could do it on a piecemeal basis, and in fact have done so, and centuries were scored against him, some of them in attractive fashion but, to be able to do it consistently *and attractively*, is another thing.

I saw Harvey play some wonderful innings against spinners on pitches sometimes designed to favour spin, I felt the force of Garry Sobers' bat and brilliant skills, and I bowled against Ian Chappell in his early days. The others, Tendulkar, Lara, Mark Waugh, Gooch and Greg Chappell, I have watched, and they all had several angles to the fact they were fine players, but the most important was that their footwork, playing either back or forward or dancing down the pitch, was close to perfect.

There have been over-the-wrist spin bowlers who have turned the ball more than Warne – David Sincock for example, and Peter Philpott spun the ball a lot – but I have never seen anyone combine the amount of legspin achieved by Warne with such a degree of accuracy. It's not merely that he ran up and dropped it on the spot all the time: the spot varied with each batsman, but the result was the same, the ball dropped on the spot but it was the one worked out by Warne for each individual. That is the aim of every spin bowler who has walked on to a field, but very few have been able to achieve it.

Warne developed a number of variation balls, some for publicity, some for the more direct business of knocking batsmen over, and one of his skills seen in more recent times on spin-vision cameras and lenses was to vary the type of spin from side-spin to horizontal-spin, which is with the seam of the ball going towards the batsman in a flatter style.

On spin-vision cameras this delivery appears to be something *like* a leg-break; to the batsman it looks very much like one and it still drifts in the air from off to leg for the right-hander. However, it then skids straight on rather than spins as the leg-break does.

From all that I have read of the times around the late 1920s and early 1930s and from everything I have been told by those who knew him, Bradman was unique as a batsman and as a publicist for the game of cricket. This is no effort to compare Warne with him, but in Australia Warne had an extraordinary effect on the game of cricket. Warne was good for the game because he rejuvenated what was becoming a lost art, and most important he lifted the spirits of those who watch at the grounds and on television.

Dear Richie
Shane Warne, Instagram, 2015

I've known you & Daphne for close to 30 years & to everyone you were a legend on all levels & rightly so too. As a cricketer, commentator & as a person, you were the best there's ever been & to top it off, an absolute gentleman . . . For me it was an honour & a privilege to call you a close friend & mentor, we had so many wonderful times together, talking cricket & in particular, our love & passion of leg spin bowling. I will cherish our entertaining dinners & all the fun times we shared over a long period of time. I would also like to thank you & Daphne for all your support & time you made for me as a young cricketer & leg spin bowler trying to make his way as an 18 year old, your tips & advice along the journey meant so much!!! Richie, you were loved by everyone, not just the cricket family, you were the godfather of cricket & you will be missed by all . . . R.I.P. my friend #hero #BowledRichie

Richie Benaud – career playing statistics
Benedict Bermange, 2015

Test batting

Overall record	M	Inns	NO	Runs	HS	Avge	100	50	0
Test matches	63	97	7	2201	122	24.45	3	9	8

By opponent	M	Inns	NO	Runs	HS	Avge	100	50	0
v England	27	41	2	767	97	19.66	0	4	6
v India	8	12	2	144	25	14.40	0	0	1
v Pakistan	4	6	1	144	56	28.80	0	1	0
v South Africa	13	21	2	684	122	36.00	2	1	1
v West Indies	11	17	0	462	121	27.17	1	3	0

By country	M	Inns	NO	Runs	HS	Avge	100	50	0
In Australia	29	46	1	1078	90	23.95	0	6	2
In England	12	20	2	260	97	14.44	0	1	5
In India	8	12	2	144	25	14.40	0	0	1
In Pakistan	4	6	1	144	56	28.80	0	1	0
In South Africa	5	7	1	329	122	54.83	2	0	0
In West Indies	5	6	0	246	121	41.00	1	1	0

By continent	M	Inns	NO	Runs	HS	Avge	100	50	0
In Africa	5	7	1	329	122	54.83	2	0	0
In Americas	5	6	0	246	121	41.00	1	1	0
In Asia	12	18	3	288	56	19.20	0	1	1
In Europe	12	20	2	260	97	14.44	0	1	5
In Oceania	29	46	1	1078	90	23.95	0	6	2

Home and away	M	Inns	NO	Runs	HS	Avge	100	50	0
Home	29	46	1	1078	90	23.95	0	6	2
Away	34	51	6	1123	122	24.95	3	3	6

By year	M	Inns	NO	Runs	HS	Avge	100	50	0
1952	2	4	0	72	45	18.00	0	0	0
1953	6	10	1	89	30	9.88	0	0	3
1954	3	5	0	103	34	20.60	0	0	0
1955	7	10	0	291	121	29.10	1	1	0
1956	9	15	1	313	97	22.35	0	2	1
1957	2	2	0	155	122	77.50	1	0	0

	M	Inns	NO	Runs	HS	Avge	100	50	0
1958	5	7	1	190	100	31.66	1	0	1
1959	8	10	1	227	64	25.22	0	1	1
1960	5	8	2	128	52	21.33	0	1	0
1961	7	12	1	175	77	15.90	0	1	2
1962	2	3	0	91	51	30.33	0	1	0
1963	4	5	0	179	57	35.80	0	1	0
1964	3	6	9	188	90	31.33	0	1	0

By captain	M	Inns	NO	Runs	HS	Avge	100	50	0
R. Benaud	28	40	4	816	77	22.66	0	5	4
I. D. Craig	5	7	1	329	122	54.83	2	0	0
A. L Hassett	8	14	1	161	45	12.38	0	0	3
I. W. G. Johnson	17	27	1	673	121	25.88	1	3	1
R. R. Lindwall	1	1	0	2	2	2.00	0	0	0
A. R. Morris	1	2	0	32	20	16.00	0	0	0
R. B. Simpson	3	6	0	188	90	31.33	0	1	0

Captain/ not captain	M	Inns	NO	Runs	HS	Avge	100	50	0
Captain	28	40	4	816	77	22.66	0	5	4
Not captain	35	57	3	1385	122	25.64	3	4	4

Test bowling

Overall record	M	Balls	Runs	Wkts	BBI	Avge	Econ	SR	5	10
Test matches	63	19108	6704	248	7–72	27.03	2.10	77.00	16	1

By opponent	M	Balls	Runs	Wkts	BBI	Avge	Econ	SR	5	10
v England	27	7284	2641	83	6–70	31.81	2.17	87.7	4	0
v India	8	2953	956	52	7–72	18.38	1.94	56.7	5	1
v Pakistan	4	1446	416	19	5–93	21.89	1.72	76.1	1	0
v South Africa	13	4136	1413	52	5–49	27.17	2.04	79.5	5	0
v West Indies	11	3289	1278	42	5–96	30.42	2.33	78.3	1	0

By country	M	Balls	Runs	Wkts	BBI	Avge	Econ	SR	5	10
In Australia	29	9044	3197	104	6–115	30.74	2.12	86.9	5	0
In England	12	2619	992	25	6–70	39.68	2.27	104.7	1	0
In India	8	2953	956	52	7–72	18.38	1.94	56.7	5	1
In Pakistan	4	1446	416	19	5–93	21.89	1.72	76.1	1	0
In South Africa	5	1937	658	30	5–49	21.93	2.03	64.5	4	0
In West Indies	5	1109	485	18	4–15	26.94	2.62	61.6	0	0

By continent	M	Balls	Runs	Wkts	BBI	Avge	Econ	SR	5	10
In Africa	5	1937	658	30	5–49	21.93	2.03	64.5	4	0
In Americas	5	1109	485	18	4–15	26.94	2.62	61.6	0	0
In Asia	12	4399	1372	71	7–72	19.32	1.87	61.9	6	1
In Europe	12	2619	992	25	6–70	39.68	2.27	104.7	1	0
In Oceania	29	9044	3197	104	6–115	30.74	2.12	86.9	5	0

Home and away	M	Balls	Runs	Wkts	BBI	Avge	Econ	SR	5	10
Home	29	9044	3197	104	6–115	30.74	2.12	86.9	5	0
Away	34	10064	3507	144	7–72	24.35	2.09	69.8	11	1

By year	M	Balls	Runs	Wkts	BBI	Avge	Econ	SR	5	10
1952	2	137	57	3	2–20	19.00	2.49	45.6	0	0
1953	6	1152	437	10	4–118	43.70	2.27	115.2	0	0
1954	3	433	168	5	3–43	33.60	2.32	86.6	0	0
1955	7	1611	694	23	4–15	30.17	2.58	70	0	0
1956	9	2045	754	32	7–72	23.56	2.21	63.9	3	1
1957	2	680	274	10	5–49	27.40	2.41	68	1	0
1958	5	1959	561	28	5–82	20.03	1.71	69.9	3	0
1959	8	3184	1007	54	5–76	18.64	1.89	58.9	4	0
1960	5	2076	617	21	5–43	29.38	1.78	98.8	1	0
1961	7	2614	998	33	6–70	30.24	2.29	79.2	2	0
1962	2	808	337	8	6–115	42.12	2.50	101	1	0
1963	4	1336	423	14	5–68	30.21	1.89	95.4	1	0
1964	3	1073	377	7	4–118	53.85	2.10	153.2	0	0

By captain	M	Balls	Runs	Wkts	BBI	Avge	Econ	SR	5	10
R. Benaud	28	10720	3559	138	6–70	25.78	1.99	77.6	9	0
I. D. Craig	5	1937	658	30	5–49	21.93	2.03	64.5	4	0
A. L. Hassett	8	1289	494	13	4–118	38.00	2.29	99.1	0	0
I. W. G. Johnson	17	3535	1422	55	7–72	25.85	2.41	64.2	3	1
R. R. Lindwall	1	402	152	4	2–54	38.00	2.26	100.5	0	0
A. R. Morris	1	152	42	1	1–42	42.00	1.65	152	0	0
R. B. Simpson	3	1073	377	7	4–118	53.85	2.10	153.2	0	0

Captain/ not captain	M	Balls	Runs	Wkts	BBI	Avge	Econ	SR	5	10
As captain	28	10720	3559	138	6–70	25.78	1.99	77.6	9	0
Not as captain	35	8388	3145	110	7–72	28.59	2.24	76.2	7	1

Series by series

	M	Inns	NO	Runs	HS	Avge	100	50	Ct	Balls	Runs	Wkts	Avge	BB
v West Indies in Australia 1951–52	1	2	0	22	19	11.00	0	0	0	35	14	1	14.00	1–14
v South Africa in Australia 1952–53	4	7	1	124	45	20.66	0	0	4	846	306	10	30.60	4–118
v England in England 1953	3	5	0	15	7	3.00	0	0	5	408	174	2	87.00	1–51
v England in Australia 1954–55	5	9	0	148	34	16.44	0	0	3	935	377	10	37.70	4–120
v West Indies in West Indies 1954–55	5	6	0	246	121	41.00	1	1	8	1109	485	18	26.94	4–15
v England in England 1956	5	9	1	200	97	25.00	0	1	3	924	330	8	41.25	3–89
v Pakistan in Pakistan 1956–57	1	2	0	60	56	30.00	0	1	0	102	36	1	36.00	1–36
v India in India 1956–57	3	4	0	53	24	13.25	0	0	0	1019	388	23	16.86	7–72
v South Africa in South Africa 1957–58	5	7	1	329	122	54.83	2	0	5	1937	658	30	21.93	5–49
v England in Australia 1958–59	5	5	0	132	64	26.40	0	1	8	1866	584	31	18.83	5–83
v Pakistan in Pakistan 1959–60	3	4	1	84	29	28.00	0	0	2	1344	380	18	21.11	5–93
v India in India 1959–60	5	8	2	91	25	15.16	0	0	5	1934	568	29	19.58	5–43
v West Indies in Australia 1960–61	5	9	0	194	77	21.55	0	2	3	2145	779	23	33.86	5–96
v England in England 1961	4	6	1	45	36*	9.00	0	0	4	1287	488	15	32.53	6–70
v England in Australia 1962–63	5	7	0	227	57	32.42	0	2	9	1864	688	17	40.47	6–115
v South Africa in Australia 1963–64	4	7	0	231	90	33.00	0	1	6	1353	449	12	37.41	5–68

How he was dismissed in Test cricket

	Times	Percentage
Bowled	35	38.89
Caught by fielder	37	41.11
Caught by 'keeper	6	6.67
lbw	12	13.33
Total	**90**	**100.00**

Bowlers dismissing him

	Times	M
J. C. Laker	6	10
F. S. Trueman	6	13
R. Appleyard	4	5
H. J. Tayfield	4	9
J. B. Statham	4	21
D. A. Allen	3	5
W. W. Hall	3	5
F. H. Tyson	3	8
A. L. Valentine	3	9
T. L. Goddard	3	9

How he took his wickets

	Times	Percentage
Bowled	42	16.94
Caught by fielder	136	54.84
Caught by 'keeper	28	11.29
Hit wicket	2	0.81
lbw	26	10.48
Stumped	14	5.64
Total	**248**	**100.00**

Batsmen he dismissed

	Times	M
P. B. H. May	8	19
M. C. Cowdrey	8	23
E. R. Dexter	7	11
N. J. Contractor	6	6
F. S. Trueman	6	13
P. S. Heine	5	4
G. S. Ramchand	5	8
P. E. Richardson	5	9
T. L. Goddard	5	9
M. H. Mankad	4	3
V. L. Manjrekar	4	3
N. S. Tamhane	4	4
J. S. Solomon	4	5
R. B. Kanhai	4	5
E. D. Weekes	4	6
F. H. Tyson	4	8
Pankaj Roy	4	8
K. J. Funston	4	9
W. R. Endean	4	9
G. A. R. Lock	4	11
J. H. B. Waite	4	12
J. B. Statham	4	21
Israr Ali	3	2
R. B. Desai	3	3
C. B. van Ryneveld	3	4
C. G. Borde	3	5
J. T. Murray	3	5
C. L. Walcott	3	6
D. S. Sheppard	3	7
S. Ramadhin	3	7
R. A. McLean	3	8
K. F. Barrington	3	9
F. M. M. Worrell	3	10
J. C. Laker	3	10
T. G. Evans	3	15

Scores of fifty or more in Test cricket

	Opponent	Venue	Season	Fours	Sixes
122	South Africa	Johannesburg	1957–58	20	0
121	West Indies	Kingston	1954–55	18	2
100	South Africa	Johannesburg	1957–58	9	1
97	England	Lord's	1956	14	1
90	South Africa	Sydney	1963–64	5	0
77	West Indies	Adelaide	1960–61	7	0
68	West Indies	Georgetown	1954–55	8	2
64	England	Melbourne	1958–59	7	0
57	England	Sydney	1962–63	7	0
56	Pakistan	Karachi	1956–57	6	0
52	West Indies	Brisbane	1960–61	6	0
51	England	Brisbane	1962–63	7	0

Five or more wickets in an innings in Test cricket

	Opponent	Venue	Season
7–72	India	Madras	1956–57
6–52	India	Calcutta	1956–57
6–70	England	Manchester	1961
6–115	England	Brisbane	1962–63
5–43	India	Madras	1959–60
5–49	South Africa	Cape Town	1957–58
5–53	India	Calcutta	1956–57
5–68	South Africa	Brisbane	1963–64
5–76	India	Delhi	1959–60
5–82	South Africa	Port Elizabeth	1957–58
5–83	England	Sydney	1958–59
5–84	South Africa	Johannesburg	1957–58
5–91	England	Adelaide	1958–59
5–93	Pakistan	Karachi	1959–60
5–96	West Indies	Adelaide	1960–61
5–114	South Africa	Durban	1957–58

Tests – match by match

Start date	Opponent	Venue	Batting	Bowling	Catches
25/1/1952	West Indies	Sydney	3 & 19	dnb & 1–14	0
24/12/1952	South Africa	Melbourne	5 & 45	2–20 & 0–23	1
9/1/1953	South Africa	Sydney	0	dnb & 2–21	1
24/1/1953	South Africa	Adelaide	6 & 18*	4–118 & 1–28	1
6/2/1953	South Africa	Melbourne	20 & 30	0–55 & 1–41	1
11/6/1953	England	Nottingham	3 & 0	dnb & 0–15	2
25/6/1953	England	Lord's	0 & 5	1–70 & 1–51	1
23/7/1953	England	Leeds	7	0–12 & 0–26	2
26/11/1954	England	Brisbane	34	0–28 & 3–43	0
17/12/1954	England	Sydney	20 & 12	dnb & 1–42	2
31/12/1954	England	Melbourne	15 & 22	0–30 & 1–25	1
28/1/1955	England	Adelaide	15 & 1	4–120 & 0–10	0
25/2/1955	England	Sydney	7 & 22	1–79	0
26/3/1955	West Indies	Kingston	46	0–29 & 2–44	4
11/4/1955	West Indies	Port-of-Spain	5	3–43 & 0–52	1
26/4/1955	West Indies	Georgetown	68	4–15 & 1–43	0
14/5/1955	West Indies	Bridgetown	1 & 5	3–73 & 1–35	1
11/6/1955	West Indies	Kingston	121	1–75 & 3–76	2
7/6/1956	England	Nottingham	17	dnb & 0–41	0
21/6/1956	England	Lord's	5 & 97	2–19 & 1–27	2
12/7/1956	England	Leeds	30 & 1	3–89	0
26/7/1956	England	Manchester	0 & 18	2–123	0
23/8/1956	England	The Oval	32 & 0*	0–21 & 0–10	1
11/10/1956	Pakistan	Karachi	4 & 56	1–36	0
19/10/1956	India	Madras	6	7–72 & 1–59	0
26/10/1956	India	Bombay	2	2–54 & 2–98	0
2/11/1956	India	Calcutta	24 & 21	6–52 & 5–53	0
23/12/1957	South Africa	Johannesburg	122	1–115 & 0–15	0
31/12/1957	South Africa	Cape Town	33	4–95 & 5–49	4
24/1/1958	South Africa	Durban	5 & 20	5–114	0
7/2/1958	South Africa	Johannesburg	100	4–70 & 5–84	1
28/2/1958	South Africa	Port Elizabeth	43 & 6*	1–34 & 5–82	0
5/12/1958	England	Brisbane	16	3–46 & 4–66	1
31/12/1958	England	Melbourne	0	1–61 & 0–4	1
9/1/1959	England	Sydney	6	5–83 & 4–94	0
30/1/1959	England	Adelaide	46	5–91 & 4–82	3
13/2/1959	England	Melbourne	64	4–43 & 1–14	3
13/11/1959	Pakistan	Dacca	16	4–69 & 4–42	1
21/11/1959	Pakistan	Lahore	29 & 21*	2–36 & 2–92	0
4/12/1959	Pakistan	Karachi	18	5–93 & 1–48	1
12/12/1959	India	Delhi	20	3–0 & 5–76	1
19/12/1959	India	Kanpur	7 & 0	4–63 & 1–81	1
1/1/1960	India	Bombay	14 & 12*	1–64 & 0–36	2

Start date	Opponent	Venue	Batting	Bowling	Catches
13/1/1960	India	Madras	25	5–43 & 3–43	0
23/1/1960	India	Calcutta	3 & 10*	3–59 & 4–103	1
9/12/1960	West Indies	Brisbane	10 & 52	0–93 & 1–69	1
30/12/1960	West Indies	Melbourne	2	2–58 & 2–49	0
13/1/1961	West Indies	Sydney	3 & 24	4–86 & 4–113	0
27/1/1961	West Indies	Adelaide	77 & 17	5–96 & 2–107	2
10/2/1961	West Indies	Melbourne	3 & 6	2–55 & 1–53	0
8/6/1961	England	Birmingham	36*	3–15 & 0–67	0
6/7/1961	England	Leeds	0 & 0	1–86 & 1–22	0
27/7/1961	England	Manchester	2 & 1	0–80 & 6–70	1
17/8/1961	England	The Oval	6	1–35 & 3–113	3
30/11/1962	England	Brisbane	51	6–115 & 1–71	3
29/12/1962	England	Melbourne	36 & 4	1–82 & 0–69	1
11/1/1963	England	Sydney	15	1–60 & 1–29	2
25/1/1963	England	Adelaide	16 & 48	1–82 & 1–38	1
15/2/1963	England	Sydney	57	2–71 & 3–71	2
v6/12/1963	South Africa	Brisbane	43	5–68 & 0–4	1
10/1/1964	South Africa	Sydney	43 & 90	3–55 & 0–61	1
24/1/1964	South Africa	Adelaide	7 & 34	0–101 & 0–17	2
7/2/1964	South Africa	Sydney	11 & 3	4–118 & 0–25	2

Batting partners in Test cricket

	Inns	Unb	Runs	Best	Avge	100	50
K. D. Mackay	15	0	536	117	35.73	1	4
A. K. Davidson	18	0	382	134	21.22	1	1
A. T. W. Grout	12	2	343	115	34.30	1	1
N. C. L. O'Neill	9	1	275	75	34.37	0	2
B. C. Booth	5	0	273	102	54.60	2	0
K. R. Miller	9	1	268	73	33.50	0	2
R. N. Harvey	11	0	227	59	20.63	0	1
J. W. Burke	2	0	207	158	103.50	1	0
G. D. McKenzie	5	0	191	160	38.20	1	0
R. R. Lindwall	8	0	190	81	23.75	0	1
R. G. Archer	9	0	176	64	19.55	0	1
I. W. G. Johnson	3	0	168	137	56.00	1	0
G. B. Hole	8	1	160	39	22.85	0	0
B. K. Shepherd	4	0	139	91	34.75	0	1
P. J. P. Burge	8	0	130	35	16.25	0	0
C. C. McDonald	4	0	124	71	31.00	0	2
D. T. Ring	3	0	92	61	30.66	0	1
D. E. Hoare	1	0	85	85	85.00	0	1
R. B. Simpson	3	0	59	26	19.66	0	0
G. R. A. Langley	3	0	57	35	19.00	0	0
L. E. Favell	2	1	51	34	51.00	0	0

	Inns	Unb	Runs	Best	Avge	100	50
N. J. N. Hawke	1	0	44	44	44.00	0	0
I. Meckiff	3	0	44	42	14.66	0	0
I. D. Craig	1	0	23	23	23.00	0	0
G. F. Rorke	1	0	22	22	22.00	0	0
J. W. Martin	3	0	17	10	5.66	0	0
A. L. Hassett	1	0	7	7	7.00	0	0
L. V. Maddocks	2	0	6	5	3.00	0	0
A. R. Morris	1	0	4	4	4.00	0	0
W. A. Johnston	1	0	2	2	2.00	0	0
L. F. Kline	1	0	0	0	0.00	0	0
F. M. Misson	1	0	0	0	0.00	0	0

All his matches as captain

Start date	Opponent	Venue	Toss	Decision	Result
5/12/1958	England	Brisbane	Lost	Bat	Won
31/12/1958	England	Melbourne	Lost	Bat	Won
9/1/1959	England	Sydney	Lost	Bat	Drawn
30/1/1959	England	Adelaide	Lost	Bowl	Won
13/2/1959	England	Melbourne	Won	Bowl	Won
13/11/1959	Pakistan	Dacca	Won	Bowl	Won
21/11/1959	Pakistan	Lahore	Lost	Bat	Won
4/12/1959	Pakistan	Karachi	Lost	Bat	Drawn
12/12/1959	India	Delhi	Lost	Bat	Won
19/12/1959	India	Kanpur	Lost	Bat	Lost
1/1/1960	India	Bombay	Lost	Bat	Drawn
13/1/1960	India	Madras	Won	Bat	Won
23/1/1960	India	Calcutta	Lost	Bat	Drawn
9/12/1960	West Indies	Brisbane	Lost	Bat	Tied
30/12/1960	West Indies	Melbourne	Won	Bat	Won
13/1/1961	West Indies	Sydney	Lost	Bat	Lost
27/1/1961	West Indies	Adelaide	Lost	Bat	Drawn
10/2/1961	West Indies	Melbourne	Won	Bowl	Won
8/6/1961	England	Birmingham	Lost	Bat	Drawn
6/7/1961	England	Leeds	Won	Bat	Lost
27/7/1961	England	Manchester	Won	Bat	Won
17/8/1961	England	The Oval	Lost	Bat	Drawn
30/11/1962	England	Brisbane	Won	Bat	Drawn
29/12/1962	England	Melbourne	Won	Bat	Lost
11/1/1963	England	Sydney	Lost	Bat	Won
25/1/1963	England	Adelaide	Won	Bat	Drawn
15/2/1963	England	Sydney	Lost	Bat	Drawn
6/12/1963	South Africa	Brisbane	Won	Bat	Drawn

Captaincy summary

Played	Won	Lost	Drawn	Tied	Toss Won	Toss Lost
28	12	4	11	1	11	17

Test cricket double

Allrounders who have achieved the Test double of 2,000 runs and 200 wickets.

	Name	Test No	Date
1.	Richie Benaud	548	December 1963
2.	Garry Sobers	685	April 1971
3.	Ian Botham	911	November 1981
4.	Kapil Dev	952	March 1983
5.	Imran Khan	973	December 1983
6.	Richard Hadlee	1013	September 1985
7.	Wasim Akram	1406	March 1998
8.	Shaun Pollock	1544	April 2001
9.	Shane Warne	1593	March 2002
10.	Chris Cairns	1689	March 2004
11.	Chaminda Vaas	1719	October 2004
12.	Daniel Vettori	1798	April 2006
13.	Jacques Kallis	1800	April 2006
14.	Anil Kumble	1808	June 2006
15.	Andrew Flintoff	1883	July 2008
16.	Harbhajan Singh	1988	January 2011
17.	Stuart Broad	2113	January 2014

Sheffield Shield double

Allrounders who have achieved the Sheffield Shield double of 2,000 runs and 200 wickets.

	Name	SS No	Date
1.	Richie Benaud	598	December 1961
2.	Alan Davidson	607	February 1962
3.	Johnny Martin	662	January 1965
4.	Terry Jenner	855	November 1974
5.	Ray Bright	1119	February 1985
6.	Peter Sleep	1226	November 1988
7.	Ken MacLeay	1277	March 1990
8.	Greg Matthews	1323	December 1991
9.	Tony Dodemaide	1340	February 1992
10.	Brendon Julian	1498	March 1997
11.	Tom Moody	1560	March 1999
12.	Shaun Young	1618	March 2001
13.	Andy Bichel	1754	November 2005
14.	Ashley Noffke	1820	November 2007
15.	Damien Wright	1849	November 2008
16.	Luke Butterworth	1991	March 2013
17.	James Hopes	1993	March 2013

Other notable facts and figures

- RB scored 121 between lunch and tea against West Indies at Kingston in 1955.

- In that innings, his century came from about 75 deliveries in just 78 minutes – the third fastest in terms of minutes in Test history.

- He captained six series, winning five and drawing one.

- It is a pity about that draw: Australia would probably have won the series if he had chosen to chase a straightforward target of 242 off about 90 overs in the final Test of 1962–63.

- Against Pakistan at Lahore in 1959 he took the final wicket for his team and then scored the winning run.

- Against England at Melbourne in 1959 he faced 29 successive deliveries without giving up the strike.

- Against South Africa at Johannesburg in 1958 he top-scored in Australia's first innings and had the best bowling figures in both of South Africa's innings.

- Against West Indies at Sydney in 1961 he bowled 72 consecutive deliveries without conceding a run.

II
THE OBSERVER

'He has been an amazing influence for all those people who have followed the game and loved it for a long while because he always spoke with authority, a gentle authority, and with an understated humour. He loved being on the television, but his best work was probably when he was not actually saying that much, because he was one of those television commentators who knew that the picture told the story, and if you didn't have anything to add to it, don't say anything. He waited for the crowd, waited for the moment and then dropped in a word or a line or some drollery that added so much more weight to what everyone had seen.'

Jim Maxwell, The Times

8
Journalism

❛In his early days on the Sydney *Sun* he worked as a crime reporter and suchlike. To make things look as effortless as he did takes hard work. Working in Australia during our winters and in England during our summers, and with jobs as a writer and broadcaster, he was so thoroughly involved in the game that he was a master of his subject. He probably watched or played in more Tests than anybody else. He also possessed a very good memory for events and conversations that had taken place many years earlier – an invaluable asset for a broadcaster. He had a wealth of stories. His vast experience served him well when a big story broke. He was far too shrewd to rush into a judgement that he might swiftly have regretted as events continued to unfold.❜

David Gower, *Sunday Times*

A foot in the door
Richie Benaud, *Anything But . . . an Autobiography*, 1998

When January 1950 arrived my salary at the accountancy firm moved up to the princely sum of three pounds a week and I was promptly put off. Although I was disappointed at the time, it turned out to be a good and thoroughly sensible thing for both employer and me. From my employer's point of view, he could put on another youngster at a pound a week as an articled clerk, and be guaranteed far more regular attendance, with no cricket practices and matches intervening. It was hardly a workable proposition to have someone putting green ticks on a page and then being away from the office for a week. From my point of view, I was about to experience the delights or otherwise of being on the open employment market, so the first thing I did was look through the jobs vacant section of the newspapers.

Sometimes luck plays a part in life, and I had a stroke of good fortune which had a wonderful effect on my cricket career. One advertisement to catch my eye was for a position at the *Sun* newspaper, in the counting house, acting as a clerk, no grading necessary with a starting salary listed at six pounds a week. Six pounds a week! I had just finished one job at three pounds a week and now there was a chance that, aged twenty, I might be able to double that figure if only I could obtain the job.

I was interviewed by the head accountant, a Mr Scotford, a cricket fan who had heard of me, which did me no harm at all. It was agreed I would be given time off for cricket practice as long as I tried to make up the lost hours by various rostering methods. Bert Scotford was one of the finest men I have met. He died a few years ago, and in all the time I knew him he never changed, a gentle but firm man, married to a delightful lady, Jessie, and with two children, Tony and Narelle. Bert was one of the reasons I was able to perform as well as I did in the early days of my cricket career.

Jack Fearnside was in charge of the section to which I was first allocated at the *Sun*; I made good friends in the six years I worked in various sections of the accounts department of what was a splendid newspaper. It was produced in the morning, with the first edition coming out to hit the streets around eleven o'clock. I was able to obtain the late final extra when dashing for the train to Parramatta late in the day. When I started I was vaguely aware that Keith Miller worked in the building on a publication called *Sporting Life*, having transferred from Melbourne at the start of the 1947–48 season. Dick Whitington worked there as well, as did Johnnie Moyes, a fine attacking batsman and a highly respected commentator, and 'Ginty' Lush, who had played in the first Sheffield Shield match I ever watched.

It was a wonderful privilege to be able to slip up to the *Sporting Life* offices occasionally and listen to some of the opinions on the game and its various players. Miller was as forthright in his conversation as he was on the field, and there seemed little that was defensive about his attitude to life, which was hardly surprising I suppose when you consider the things he and others had gone through during the war. Ginty Lush was a wonderful, swashbuckling character and a fine cricketer who had played for Sir Julien Cahn's team in England. As captain of the Gordon club in Sydney, he was always one to champion the cause of young cricketers.

Johnnie Moyes, the editor of *Sporting Life*, was a good enough cricketer to be chosen for the Australian tour of South Africa in 1914, the tour cancelled because of the First World War. He wrote one biography and called it *Bradman*; he wrote another in 1962, a year before his death, and titled it *Benaud*. In it he said of my Melbourne head injury:

> When years later I watched Benaud hooking Tyson and Wesley Hall I marvelled at his courage. That tremendous blow, received at the beginning of his career, might well have caused him to flinch when the ball was dropped short – or at least it could have ended any desire he had to play the hook stroke. It didn't. He continued to hook – Tyson, Trueman, Hall and others – and to hit the ball with tremendous power. A man who will do that has a fighting heart, real personal courage, and indeed, audacity.

It never occurred to me there was anything more brave in *my* doing it, or attempting to do it, against fast bowlers than would be the case with a batsman who hadn't had his skull badly fractured.

Police rounds
Richie Benaud, *Anything But . . . an Autobiography*, 1998

After the 1956 tour I went in to see Lindsay Clinch, the Editor of
the *Sun* newspaper, to pursue our earlier conversation that I should
talk to him after the tour about a transfer to the editorial department.
At the time there was no better or tougher editor in Australian
newspapers, and I haven't heard of anyone better since then. He said
he had decided to approve a transfer for me and that he wanted me
to write a sports column, which someone could ghost for me if
necessary. That wasn't what I wanted at all and I said to him I wanted
to work on News and Police Rounds if possible, to learn about
newspapers and how to write for them.

'OK, go and see Jack Toohey the news editor,' he said. When I was
at the door his quiet voice came from behind me, 'He's expecting you!'

Jack Toohey greeted me with, 'Good to see you, Richie. Lindsay
told me you'd be in and we've organised that you'll be working under
Noel Bailey in Police Rounds.'

This was a very lucky break for me: Bailey was a magnificent
journalist who had some legendary battles with another very good
Police Roundsman, Bill Jenkings of the *Daily Mirror*. In those days
the afternoon newspapers in Sydney and other states had police
rounds as the hub of the news section.

These days motorcar accidents, murders and assaults are so
commonplace that they may not be reported, or they could be lumped
together on a page where a running total is kept. Back in 1956, whilst
not rare they were certainly newsworthy, and cases like the one involving
the murder of a prison warder and the subsequent manhunt for two
chaps called Simmonds and Newcombe kept us all on our toes.

Building up contacts in the police force was quite important for a
young reporter, but the finest training of all was to trail on the

coat-tails of Noel Bailey. It was wonderful to see and hear him in action, phoning stories to catch an edition. There were no mobile phones in those days: you needed to find a public telephone, and sometimes this would happen, with your pocket stuffed with shorthand notes, about five minutes before the edition was due to run. If it were a big story and they were holding the front page with say twenty-five paragraphs, about 600 words for Bailey, it was an education to see the way he went about it. He adlibbed everything. His eyes would flick to the relevant notes, some in shorthand, some scribbled, and he would always remain perfectly calm, no matter what the pressure of the clock ticking down, or the editor back in the office grabbing the copytaker's headset and barking in his ear.

I was never able to do any of this as well as Bailey, nor would I expect to, but it taught me how to dictate my own stories against time and against space. I didn't know it at the time, but there has been nothing I have done in life which has proved more valuable in presentation on television. Because of Bailey's training I have been able to teach myself to finish on zero when the count is being made in my ear at the end of a cricket telecast, a very valuable attribute when you know that if you over-run by five or ten seconds, that has to be made up in some manner in the studio if the six o'clock news is to start on time.

It was a varied life on the *Sun*. Being in the Police Rounds section meant there was plenty of excitement, and not always to do with police matters. Once, when a USA fly-by-night promoter was trying to sign the great Australian athlete Herb Elliott to run professionally. I had a successful but also hilarious night tracking down the American, who had flown secretly into Sydney on a cargo plane. Lindsay Clinch also called me in one day to say the directors, particularly Vincent Fairfax, wanted me to cover the Billy Graham Crusade when it came to Sydney. One of the more interesting aspects of this assignment was when I arranged, through his PR people, to play golf with him at Royal Sydney. It was a success and a front-page story.

The assignment came to an end when, after writing along the same lines most days about people making their way to the stage and to Billy Graham, my final paragraph mentioned the 'sound of the wind soughing in the trees'. Lindsay Clinch called me in and said, 'Nice final paragraph – I think we understand you're all written out. Take a day off and we'll find someone else!'

Shaping a new career
Richie Benaud, *Over But Not Out*, 2010

Nineteen sixty was a watershed year for me. Whilst I was in India and Pakistan, a very good friend, Ron Roberts, sent me a message concerning a friend of his, George Greenfield, who was the head of a firm of literary agents, John Farquharson Ltd. Would I like to write a book, working title *World of Cricket**, embodying coaching sections and a variety of opinions on world cricket, and have it published around April 1961 before the start of the Australian tour of England; it was assumed I would be captaining that side.

I was starting to consider my future, life after twelve years of cricket, so to speak. There was enjoyment to be had playing the game, more so if you were winning rather than losing, but there was absolutely no chance of any financial security. There were long absences from home, I had my wife and two children aged five and two who had to put up with being on their own, and it was time to start looking at media work, not just in Sydney, but on a larger scale. The book would be a start. A following offer arrived through George Greenfield to go to England in 1960 to cover the South African tour of that country for BBC Radio and a newspaper.

---

* RB's first book was published in 1961, with the title *Way of Cricket*.

Ron Roberts himself decided to take another combined team, known as 'the Cavaliers', to Rhodesia and South Africa. He had already managed one such team to South Africa the previous summer. I informed the Australian Cricket Board of the Roberts tour and asked permission to go, and also informed the Board that, as part of my work as a journalist, I was going to England to cover the South African tour.

At the same time as we were in the middle of our tour of Pakistan and India, the England team set out on a tour of the West Indies. It was to turn out to be a significant event for a number of reasons, not least that it was something of a new-look England side. We had beaten them four-nil in Australia, they then returned the compliment to India, who toured England in 1959, by beating them five-nil.

In the series against India, and then in the Caribbean, only seven of the players who toured Australia were retained, and it was clear the England selectors were looking to the series against West Indies in 1959–60, and against South Africa in 1960, to build up for the Ashes battle in 1961. That had become the stated policy of the new England selection committee of Gubby Allen, Herbert Sutcliffe and Doug Insole, that they were embarking, in 1959, on a three-year plan 'so as to provide a side worthy of challenging Australia for the Ashes in 1961'. Some of those to disappear included Peter Richardson, Tom Graveney, Willie Watson, Arthur Milton, Trevor Bailey, Godfrey Evans, Jim Laker and Tony Lock.

Some never made it back, but Tom Graveney did, being recalled for the opening Test against Pakistan at Edgbaston in 1962. He made 97 and 153 in the Second Test and followed that with 37 and 114 before they dropped him again for the Fifth Test of the series. Probably 'rested' is a more appropriate word! In fact, from the time he was recalled, he played another thirty-one times for England, even captaining his country when Colin Cowdrey pulled out of the Headingley Test in 1968. Tom was an outstanding batsman, a good player of spin and pace and a very elegant stroke-maker. I was pleased he came back, because Australians always had a very high regard for his ability – we wouldn't have left him out even for one game, let alone for twenty-eight!

Visiting England in 1960 was a great opportunity for me to have a look at what they had to offer in their cricket resurgence, with an eye to the 1961 Australian tour. As it turned out, there were many other things happening, including a throwing controversy, and it was an educational five months working for the BBC, *News of the World* and the Sydney *Sun*.

As I arrived in England in 1960 I was saddened to hear Alec Skelding had passed away. He was a delightful chap and a very unorthodox umpire who had been a useful cricketer with Leicestershire. He was, to my eyes, an unusual figure when I first came across him, because he was the only umpire I had seen in England who wore white boots or shoes. These were worn in Australia by umpires, but in England it was brown brogues, or occasionally, in dry conditions, brown or navy suede. Umpires often wore brown felt hats as well.

Alec stood in some of our matches in 1953 and 1956, but the only time I played in a game when he was officiating was when we met Essex at Southend, in 1953, and he was very amusing as well as seeming a good umpire, and not solely because he gave Doug Insole out lbw to my topspinner. There was never a dull moment from a man who was highly respected by every cricketer who knew him and it was a treat to hear, 'And that, gentlemen, concludes the entertainment for the morning . . .'

By the time I was on my way to England, Peter May's side had returned with their first-ever victory in a Test series in the West Indies but there had been some contentious items on the agenda with time-wasting, throwing and short-pitched bowling heading the list. When May's side had been in Australia, in 1958–59, there had been many problems about bowling actions and dragging. That controversy had continued after the tour with the Imperial Cricket Conference, as it was in those days, stepping in to say they were working towards finding a proper definition of the throwing Law.

In Australia there had been several players under scrutiny. Ian Meckiff had been the one most mentioned, and I said at the time I had looked at Meckiff from different parts of the field and, like the umpires, was satisfied his action conformed with the laws formulated by MCC. I added that he had bowled in New Zealand, South Africa and Australia and had never been called. The same question was asked in Pakistan and India and I gave the same answer.

That criticism of Australia's bowlers in 1958–59 was now followed by further criticism of the West Indian bowlers, of whom it was said there were at least six, two of them playing in the Tests, who had suspect actions. That was receiving considerable publicity, but so too was another matter which was important to me. In the Caribbean, from where May's team had just returned, there was a real push to have the West Indian captain, Gerry Alexander, removed and Frank Worrell made captain instead for the tour of Australia.

Sir Donald Bradman, who was to take over as Chairman of the Australian Board in late 1960, was working hard to come up with some form of agreement on the question of doubtful bowling actions, though he was careful to emphasise the difficulties in arriving at a definition. I was in England and, having summed up the mood and the general situation, started writing a series of articles to the effect that this, in my opinion, was for Australia the most important ICC meeting of all time.

❛It defies description – the feeling that hits players when there is a no-ball called for throwing . . . The game was carried on by instinct for a while, for the Australian players were not "with it" .❜

RB describes the Australian team after Meckiff was called for throwing

I stressed that, instead of using the Board's representative in England, or it being a trip for a couple of ordinary administrators, the Australian Board must send Bradman and, as their second representative, Chairman Bill Dowling. The habit was that the Board's representative in England would attend ICC meetings and the various social engagements and then report back to the Board in writing about what had eventuated. This was going to be completely useless now because I could see there were tough discussions ahead. I hammered the point that it was essential Bradman appear as one of Australia's representatives, and as chairman, Dowling should accompany him. Bradman and Dowling duly arrived for the conference which began on 14 July.

In England, MCC had stated they would be providing full support for any umpires who might feel the need to 'call' bowlers with suspect actions. The problem was, would the definition stand up when they finally came up with a new wording? In the 1959 season in England there had been several bowlers no-balled for throwing, including Tony Lock, who had worked on remodelling his suspect bowling action after being shown some movie films taken by Harry Cave in New Zealand at the conclusion of the tour to Australia in 1958–59. The same kind of thing was being done in Australia, where the word 'jerk' had also been removed from the throwing definition.

In the history of Australian cricket there had been twenty-three occasions when an Australian bowler had been called for throwing and that list had involved eighteen bowlers up to 1960.

Before Bradman and Dowling arrived in England there had been some no-balling of South African Geoff Griffin. The first time this happened he was merely called for dragging, by Paul Gibb standing in the match Derbyshire against the touring side. Griffin had already been called for throwing in South Africa in February and March 1959, when he was playing for Natal.

One of England's best umpires, Syd Buller, had officiated in South Africa's opening game against Worcestershire when Griffin didn't play. When the South Africans journeyed to Lord's in late May to play MCC, two other good umpires, Frank Lee and John Langridge, stood. Lee called Griffin once and then Langridge called him twice for throwing, and once he was called simultaneously for both throwing and dragging. At a meeting at the end of the match, the umpires said his basic action was OK but that he threw the ball on the occasions he was called. When Griffin was called eight times for throwing against Nottinghamshire, the team management said he would be sent to Alf Gover's cricket school for remedial treatment.

By the time Bradman and Dowling returned to Australia from the London conference, and there had been much correspondence between the two Boards, as well as other cricket Boards around the world, considerable progress had been made. It had been made, however, in a slightly odd fashion, with the compromise between England and Australia being that during the first five weeks of the Ashes tour, when I was likely to be captain, umpires would not call, on the field of play, any bowler thought to be throwing, but would complete a confidential report and submit it to Lord's and to the Australian team.

In addition to the decisions on throwing in 1960, the ICC brought four major issues under scrutiny:

1. *Time-wasting was criticised.* At last cricket administrators decided this aspect of play and captaincy was to the detriment of the game.
2. *Drag was under notice.* Umpires were trying to work off the front foot and one of the officials concerned in the Griffin throwing incidents, Syd Buller, an outstanding umpire, was to be a key man in that aspect of the game when we toured England in 1961.
3. *Pitches should not be damaged by bowlers in their follow-through* was another recommendation. Correct. We had already seen to our detriment in Australia, in 1958, what damage could be done, and we were about to see it very much to our advantage in 1961.
4. *Batsmen using their pads instead of their bat* came under fire, as should have been the case many years earlier. There was

thought given to bringing in a Law that a batsman could be out lbw not playing a stroke, even if the ball pitched outside off stump.

This was a very important ICC meeting in 1960, and it did more for the game than had been done in the previous fifty-one years of the ICC's existence. I'm certain one of the main reasons for its success was that Australia, for the first time, had sent two top-class administrators and negotiators to England.

It was useful to have the Australian captain there keeping an eye on things as well, and I was able to steer Sir Donald and Bill Dowling in the right direction a few times, once in selfish mode when I persuaded them that, in addition to the bedrooms, for the first time an Australian team should have a team-room at the Waldorf Hotel in London, where we were to spend most of our time during the 1961 tour. They examined the room suggested by the hotel management, studied the proposition, agreed, and then persuaded the Board in Australia it should be done.

> ❛Even after Richie had stopped broadcasting in England, he would be stationed in good time in the press box on every Saturday of a Test match to write for the *News of the World*, an association that lasted for half a century. He was meticulous and utterly committed to the end. Indeed Benaud was in print the last time the *News of the World* went to press, on 10 July 2011. "Each evening Daphne and I raise a glass and offer a toast to someone," he wrote. "Last night it was: 'To the old *News of the World*'." ❜
>
> *Vic Marks,* Guardian

At this time I was also doing some work in the London office of John Fairfax Ltd, who published the *Sun* newspaper. It was a good time to be there, sub-editing and also writing my own stories back to Australia. It was the time of the Rome Olympics when Herb Elliott won the 1,500 metres, one of the finest sports performances I have seen from an Australian in any area.

I thoroughly enjoyed my time with the *News of the World* as a feature writer on cricket, working with the regular cricket writer, seeking and filing my own stories and liaising with the sports editor, Frank Butler. Frank was my first of only a handful of sports editors there and I have been with the paper now for fifty years.

Scoop!

Richie Benaud, *Anything But . . . an Autobiography*, 1998

I was happy enough with my own performances in 1961–62, heading the first-class wicket-takers and the averages with 47 at 17.97.

As soon as the season was over, I was on my way to New Zealand with Ron Roberts's international team and I managed to hold my form with bat and ball and also captaincy. Matches were played in Rhodesia, where the tour began in Bulawayo, then Dacca, as it was still known, in East Pakistan, followed by two games in New Zealand, two in Hong Kong and two in Bombay and Karachi.

Ron Roberts was a very good journalist and a fine cricketing man, and while he had organised several tours in his time, this was by far the most ambitious. The team covered more than 40,000 miles and twenty-five players took part, with some joining and others dropping off at different times. Before I joined the tour Ray Lindwall and Everton Weekes shared the captaincy, then I took over for the second half. Everton Weekes and Roy Marshall were the West Indian representatives, Neil Adcock and Roy McLean were the players from South Africa, and there were several from England, including Tom Graveney and Harold 'Dusty' Rhodes, the fast bowler.

The Hong Kong match gave rise to the statement concerning the luck which often came my way as a captain, and the play on words of the old phrase about diamonds being a girl's best friend. In that game, a one-day affair, after fiddling about a bit, we suddenly needed to take the last three wickets in one over and they required only two runs for victory. Dusty Rhodes, as he walked past me, smiled and said, 'I'm going to enjoy this, Richie, let's see you get out of this one.'

I called up Neil Adcock and he took a hat-trick, two of which I caught at second slip. As we walked off the field laughing, Dusty came up shaking his head and saying ruefully, 'Skip, if you put your head into a bucket of slops you'd come up with a mouthful of diamonds.'

When we were in New Zealand, Doug Ford, from New South Wales, was our wicketkeeper, but Harold Stephenson of Somerset was due to rejoin the side for the Hong Kong games. Doug was well liked, and so he might continue the tour, we endeavoured to find a way to pay his air fares up to Hong Kong. The only way we could manage this was to back a winner at the races. Everyone in the team put in a tenner and we consulted the best judges of trotting in Auckland, where the meeting was to be held.

They came up with what they said was a conveyance with good form, ability and was at a good enough price, 11–2, which would give us the £500 needed in those days for a return air ticket to Hong Kong. The fairy story would have been that it won and everyone had a splendid time in HK. In fact, it ran second by three long lengths, and all the good intentions disappeared into the bags of the satchel-swingers.

The final game of that tour was against the Pakistan Board XI team, which was very close to the side which toured England three weeks later. I went straight back to Australia after this and set myself to have a little rest and recreation, with England due to arrive in Australia in October 1962.

It looked from what happened in the series in England between Pakistan and England as though David Sheppard might well captain the team to Australia but, in fact, on 19 July came the announcement that Ted Dexter had the job and, a week later, that the Duke of Norfolk would be the manager of the team. This was an interesting appointment, which was said to have come about because of the inability of the MCC Committee to make a decision. The Duke apparently went home from the meeting at Lord's and, in conversation with the Duchess of Norfolk, she is said to have expressed the view that he should do it himself. I was on the sub-editor's desk in the Sydney *Sun* at the time the story came through, and it was my job to write the front-page story about Bernard Marmaduke Fitzalan Howard, the Sixteenth Duke of Norfolk, being appointed as manager.

At the start of the season I took the opportunity to go to Perth to cover the opening match of the MCC tour for the Sydney *Sun*. I travelled to Perth with Bob Gray, a good mate and my opposition cricket writer on the Sydney *Mirror*. We stayed at the John Barleycorn Hotel, and on the Wednesday night, we decided to have a look at Perth's nightspots, which in those days were few in number. My, how time flies when you're having fun. We arrived back at the John Barleycorn at 4 a.m. in only reasonably good order, though I was certainly in better shape than Gray. That point was driven home to me when he went to sleep the instant his head hit the pillow and nothing I tried would wake him.

I adlibbed my story to the Sydney *Sun* and then picked up the phone and called Gray's *Daily Mirror*, gave his name and adlibbed a story for him to the copy-taker. His sports editor rang him later in the morning with profuse congratulations. My sports editor telephoned me after the first edition to say I'd made a bad start to the tour because Bob Gray had scooped me in the *Mirror* with a good story about Graham McKenzie. There wasn't much I could say other than, in future, I would try harder. Gray, when he awoke, thought it very amusing.

Mentor, inspiration and friend

Justin Langer, *Sunday Times*, 2015

RICHIE BENAUD WAS the voice of our Australian summers. Like everybody else in the country, I grew up watching and listening to him, but for me personally he became a bit of a mentor, although not so much with regard to playing the game of cricket as writing about the game.

> ❝He's not quite got hold of that one. If he had, it would have gone for nine.❞
>
> *RB on a Justin Langer six*

In 1997, I had become quite keen on writing and was producing a regular column for the BBC website. While Australia were playing a Test match against England at Headingley, I decided to approach Richie, feeling a bit like a young kid going up to his hero and asking him for an autograph.

I asked him if he would have a look at a piece that I had written and tell me what he thought about it.

He looked me up and down and said: 'So you're interested in journalism, are you?' I said that I was.

'Okay, leave it with me and I'll get back to you when I have read it.' Next day he came and knocked on the door of the Australian changing room. This was very unlike Richie. I never saw him there before or after that. He handed me back my piece of work.

It had scribbles all over it, snippets of advice scattered here and there. He'd basically edited my piece for me. He said something along the lines of: 'You're a good writer, keep it up.' He nodded and walked off.

A night or two later a little package arrived at my hotel. It contained a small book called *The Elements of Style*. It was a handbook about grammar. With it was a beautifully written note from Richie in which he said that he hoped the book would serve me as well as it had him. I have kept it with me ever since and it sits on my desk for when I need it.

Every time I saw him after that he would ask after my family and my writing. He was the consummate gentleman. Like all wise men he often used few words. I never heard him criticise anyone. Yes, he had strong opinions but he made his points in a humorous way or with a well-chosen comment. He always gave people the benefit of the doubt, which is a rare and wonderful trait.

9
Broadcasting

'The fact that Australia never lost a series under his captaincy says so much and those standards were just as high when he turned his attention to calling the game. We loved listening to him commentate when the team was together in the dressing room. When he was on air, we always had the TV volume turned up because his comments were so insightful. He spent a lot of time talking to players of all ages, passing on his great knowledge and love of the game. What stood out more than anything about Richie is that he always put the game first. There will only ever be one Richie Benaud.'

Darren Lehmann, *Daily Mail*

Training at the BBC, 1956
Richie Benaud, *Over But Not Out*, 2010

There is something slightly offbeat, even bizarre, about battling for the Ashes in England, going through a hectic three-week television course, flying to Rome to have dinner, then from Ciampano airport to Pakistan and India, to play four Test matches. All the boys were in good spirits on 8 October when I met them after their three-week break, and so was I. I had been working so hard on a BBC TV course, I hadn't had time to think much about cricket. The course had been arranged for me by Tom Sloan, BBC's Head of Light Entertainment at that time. I worked from 11 a.m. to midnight almost every day of the three weeks. It was wonderful! The purpose was to try to find out something about television, other than in watching it, because this was the year the medium began in Australia.

Channel Nine was first on the air in Australia, and I had no idea at the time that twenty years later I would be working for them and would continue to do so for another thirty years; nor did I have plans at that stage to work for the BBC for almost forty years, but I suppose the course was just one of those things that seemed a good idea at the time. I wasn't trying to learn about the finer points of production and directing, but to give myself a general knowledge of what happened each time a television programme went to air, from everyone's point of view. It would be accurate to say that my main desire was to look at it more from the commentator's point of view than anything else.

> ❛My mantra is: put your brain into gear and if you can add to what's on the screen, then do it; otherwise, shut up.❜
>
> *RB on commentating*

In retrospect I suppose all the production assistants, and the producers as well, slumped their shoulders a little when the news came through that this guy Benaud was coming along as an observer, just to have a look and to try to learn something for Australian television. Whatever they might have thought, however, they were all great; nothing was too much trouble; particularly as I seem to recall the occasional question about what I was doing in television in Australia, and I replied each time that I didn't do anything!

I sat with producers, in directors' vans, with the audience on some occasions, at the side of a stage, talked with Denis Monger the producer and trailed behind Peter O'Sullevan at Newbury races and watched how he prepared so meticulously for his job. I watched what Alec Weeks did at the speedway races at Wembley and how the commentators reacted to everything that went right and wrong.

We might not have done all that well with the cricket, but 1956 was very much a year for Australia in other sports which had an influence on my career in television.

While the Tests were being played, Wimbledon was on as well, and I watched and listened to Dan Maskell as he commentated in his inimitable style on Hoad beating Rosewall in four sets in the men's singles final, and when Peter Thomson won the 1956 Open Championship at Hoylake, Henry Longhurst was the commentator who caught my ear. I didn't meet either of them for many years, but what I saw and heard from those two, and O'Sullevan, has stayed with me over the years.

Tales from the commentary box
Richie Benaud, *The Appeal of Cricket*, 1995

Television takes us to some strange places, to some wonderful ones as well, and there is always the chance to meet interesting people, whether they be strangers who are viewers, strangers who know nothing about cricket or television, or sportsmen and women who make their names in other jobs, pastimes or professions.

One of the more interesting aspects of those lives of international sports people is what they do away from the playing arena. In cricket it used to be that every Australian cricketer had a profession. I was a journalist, having started on police rounds in the mid-1950s and worked through various other areas until lack of time, and being constantly on the move with cricket, meant I became a full-time sports journalist, something I had been doing part-time since 1956 along with the police-rounds job. Starting off as a journalist of the print variety, with the need to write 250 words to fill a space, has been of great value to me in television. No point in writing 400 words if the space only takes 250. It was a great lesson in putting as much as possible into the shortest time, or smallest space. Others in the cricket team worked as salesmen or clerks, and some had interesting hobbies as well, like Bill Lawry, who took up pigeon racing at a very early age.

Tastes in the arts were varied. Neil Harvey took me to watch Dame Margot Fonteyn dance at Covent Garden the first week we were in London, in 1953, and it was one of the greatest things I had ever seen. Classical music was as popular with me as whatever might have been the equivalent of the Top 20 of the day. Opera? Well, not quite as popular, though I did make the effort to listen. It was a bit much for me then but listening to great opera singers provides pleasure these days, far more on CD though than on stage. So too does playing as much golf as possible, though time restraints, and a change of focus in business, mean there is never quite enough time available. My wife Daphne and I covered the Masters Tournament at Augusta over a fourteen-year period for newspapers, radio and, if needed, as a presenter for Channel Nine television.

Sometimes though, because of the time difference, as the event was beamed back to Australia, our job was more likely to be a straightforward pick-up from CBS: 'And now we take you to the thirteenth fairway, where your commentator is . . .' The Masters was always one of our hardest jobs, with the conclusion of the tournament, 5–6 p.m. in Augusta, coinciding with edition times of the *Melbourne Herald* and morning drive-time for Radio 2UE in Sydney.

After the daily work was done there was the chance to relax and each year during the tournament Mark McCormack* put on a splendid party which started in the early evening and could go late. It was always delightful conjecture to see which of Mark's many clients and business associates outside golf would be there and it was

---

* The sports agent and founder of IMG, whose clients included Arnold Palmer, Jack Nicklaus and Gary Player.

nice to be able to talk with the golfers, if they wanted to talk about golf, and to catch up on any other things they might be doing. In 1992 I was chatting with Irishman David Feherty, each of us with a glass in hand, and he knew he probably needed to shoot no worse than a par seventy-two the following day to have a chance of making the cut. David was slightly on edge musing about the morrow, so thinking it might help a little, I asked about operas he had seen lately, knowing there is no keener opera buff in the golfing world, and few in the real world. He hadn't had much time to see anything because of practising for the Masters and other golfing events but he had spent many hours listening to CDs, some featuring Dame Kiri Te Kanawa. Kiri may have greater fans in the world than David Feherty but I doubt it. She and husband Desmond Park are also two of the keenest golfers you would find anywhere. I was just starting to say, 'Well, David, there's a chance at a McCormack party . . .' when his eyes widened and, although the rest of the room still buzzed, he didn't. He was looking past my left shoulder and had stopped talking. I turned around and Kiri was threading her way across the patio towards us.

'Richie,' she said.

'Hi, Kiri, how are you? Meet David Feherty.'

I chatted for a few moments and then left them to it, David asking about opera, Kiri wanting advice on the short chip from alongside the green when the putting surfaces are like lightning. I don't think I have ever seen a sportsman from one area more excited to meet a great performer from another.

Did David make the cut? He certainly did and shot his par seventy-two to make it by a shot, knowing he had to have a par four on the very difficult eighteenth to have a chance to play the last two days. It might, in the event, have had something to do with the refresher course on chipping he gave Kiri the previous evening!

*　　*　　*

It was at Augusta I had one of my best moments in sport. You know how it is to be able to say, 'I was there.' Well, I was there [in 1986] when Jack Nicklaus pulled off one of the greatest-ever sporting victories. I've seen many other wonderful happenings in various sports, and played in one of them in the Tied Test in Brisbane in 1960. I've met 80,000 people who talk as though they were there at the 'Gabba that day although, in fact, the actual crowd was 4,100. I've been very grateful to have had the opportunity to be a part of those matters but, in golf, the Nicklaus one was special.

It was the usual wonderful finish to four great days at Augusta and, out on the course, I was mentally tearing up several intros for radio and newspapers back in Australia. Daphne and I had followed Greg Norman at the start of the final round and he was playing with Nick Price of Zimbabwe. We had already experienced all the thrills of Price's course-record sixty-three the previous day where, because of his first two rounds, he was off the first tee before midday and played in front of a remarkably small gallery and took only thirty shots on the back nine. Now here we were watching him again but the adrenalin wasn't quite flowing on the final day, nor was it for anyone else for that matter. Norman, leader by one stroke at the start of the day, quickened our heartbeats on the first, second and fourth holes by sinking putts to save par; Seve Ballesteros played the first nine well enough, but no one was really on fire.

One of the many great features of the Masters Tournament is the brilliant work done on the scoreboards around the course, and the clarity of the scoreboards themselves. They still showed Norman in the lead, then suddenly Ballesteros eagled the eighth and went one ahead of Norman. New intro! Up ahead Nicklaus sank a putt for birdie that started his charge. Four groups behind Nicklaus we were watching Norman and Price and, as the scoreboards changed, so did the intros; Nicklaus was just getting into gear for an eagle and other birdies.

Meanwhile, we watched Norman double-bogey the tenth, having seen him four-putt the same hole on the second day of the tournament. Now it was close to decision time for me, for there were editions to be caught back in Australia and, as the enormous roar signalled Nicklaus's birdie on the sixteenth, we decided Daphne would continue with Norman and Price, who had just putted out on the fourteenth, and I would wait for Nicklaus to come up the seventeenth, the green of which is close by the fourteenth.

I wasn't the only one to leave the pair. One moment Norman and Price had hundreds clambering all over one another to get a glimpse of them, the next something like forty people remained, one of whom was Daphne, walking just behind them as hundreds raced for the Nicklaus–Ballesteros pairing. She got the quote and I missed it. It was a little like Merlin waving his magic wand and the crowd disappearing, and a moment later Greg said tersely to Price, 'Come on, Nicky, let's show these people we can bloody well play golf,' and they strode off to the fifteenth tee. Because Nicklaus was two holes ahead, I positioned myself at the back of the seventeenth green and purely by chance, when he putted, the hole was perfectly placed between him and me so I saw every inch of the twelve-foot putt which broke to my left and then to my right before going into the centre of the hole. I was there!

Relatively it brought one of the greatest sporting roars I have ever heard, bearing in mind you can only get so many people around a golf green even when there is a great spectator mound as well. We caught all our editions, the newspaper one by three minutes, and I used Daphne's exclusive Norman quote in my intro. When I phoned the subs' desk a little later to enquire if all was OK, the sub-editor told me everything had gone in as written, except the Norman quote.

He said he had changed it to: 'Forty-six-year-old Jack Nicklaus won the Masters Tournament at Augusta today, defeating Greg

Norman by a stroke.' Never argue with a sub is a good rule but I did think Daphne's on-the-spot exclusive would have had just a little more oomph!

Television is a very interesting and challenging medium and the commentary box requires intense concentration. There is never a shortage of little glitches through the wires which transport the sound and pictures from the producer's van. It is astonishing though that there are so few of them in either Australia with Channel Nine or in the UK with the BBC. In England, the BBC's Keith Mackenzie is the Executive Producer, a man who learnt his cricket in Australia and knows many other sports as well. He produces the Grand National, used to produce the Cheltenham Gold Cup Festival until Channel 4 gained the rights, has handled the snooker production for a considerable time and is a highly regarded producer in the line of those who have handled cricket for the BBC over the years.

Alan Griffiths is Welsh, and would love to see Glamorgan win any of the cricket championships, cups or trophies, or all of them for that matter. He is a cricket and rugby man and, like other BBC producers, can produce or direct anything. There are times when, sitting back in your living-rooms, you might think from the slight rise in tone in the commentator's voice that he is excited, or, without you knowing it, it could be that one of those little glitches has appeared. It might be that a camera has 'gone' just at a crucial moment, or a cameraman has been defeated by an on-drive that goes past point, something to do with sound, or someone may have pressed an unusual button somewhere in the world. It might be something to do with the commentator, it could be something to do with production at the ground, and on the rare occasion the latter might occur, I have been known to say softly into the 'lazy mike', 'Everything all right down there . . .?'

Just after the England versus New Zealand Test at Old Trafford in 1994 we went to Headingley to cover the NatWest match between Yorkshire and Somerset. Alan Griffiths was on his own as the main producer, though John Shrewsbury was also there to lend a hand on what turned out to be a rain-marred day.

Because of the rain, the commentators' roster turned into a dog's breakfast with additions, deletions and initials everywhere and Tony Lewis, as presenter, was doing another brilliant job of providing interviews, detail and all other things necessary when nothing at all is happening on the field. Coming up to what would have been tea-time, I knew that I, in the commentary box, needed to keep an eye on things for Jack Bannister, who was on air in the studio with Tony and Geoff Boycott, but, for some reason, I put my brain into Plan B mode and settled down at the small table in the even smaller commentary box, earpiece in my ear, and started on a sandwich and a cup of tea. I was able to hear the interesting discussion between Tony, Jack and Geoff and see it on the monitor at the side of the commentary box. Suddenly there was a frenzied shout from the van and in my ear because Tony had said, 'And now to Richie Benaud in the commentary box.' Plan B changed to Plan A in an instant. I moved at considerable speed and the following ensued.

I dropped the sandwich on the floor and banged my right knee hard on the side of the chair. With the pain from that, I dropped my binoculars on the chair and my earpiece, which was connecting me with the shouts from the van, became tangled in the connecting wires. When I joined it all together, I found the plug was out of, instead of in, the sound box.

Eventually, while everyone else in the commentary box was hysterically helpless, I was able to say in a suitably calm voice, with only a slight edge to it, 'Now that you've had time to study the scorecard at your leisure . . .!'

In my ear there came an equally calm Welsh voice, but with a definite hint of laughter about it: 'Everything all right up there . . .?'

It was the ultimate Welsh '*touché*'.

The perils in being the senior commentator are those associated with the name itself, which might be an indication of being more aged and infirm than your colleagues. Occasionally, senior or junior, things go to air and you wish they had not, but it is difficult to pull them back as they are leaving your mouth. Sometimes though the position produces some interesting and amusing situations, one of which occurred at Brian Lara's home ground, Queen's Park Oval in Trinidad, during the Third Test of that 1991 Australia versus West Indies series. The first day was washed out at 2.50 p.m., and on the second morning I did the usual in-vision presentation in front of a grandstand in the outer.

Throughout the Caribbean this was the equivalent of making one's way from the Channel Nine commentary box in the Bradman Stand at the SCG to a spot five metres from the front row of a packed Hill. For Channel Nine in the Caribbean no luxuries such as air-conditioned studios and commentary boxes. On my way to this open-air, in-vision position, I walked past the armed guard at the entrance to the playing area and we exchanged a civil 'good morning'. Twenty minutes later, when I returned, my very good friend, the armed guard, had been joined by what was either a dog or possibly a large wolf, an animal approximately two metres long and a metre tall, and made of an extraordinary number of muscles and teeth. It was the original steroid dog. It was a Dobermann. Common sense dictated that I stop, and there was a very good reason for this: the Dobermann was standing between me and the entrance, or, as it was now, the exit.

We looked at one another for a considerable time. When he drew back his lips and smiled and then barked I leapt only nine inches or a foot in the air, but quickly adopted Plan B. This involved saying nothing and locking eyes with the armed guard rather than the dog. After a minute or two it worked. The guard said nothing but stood up, led the dog out on to the playing field and I made for the exit with calm assurance.

It was then I noticed several Trinidadians helpless on the asphalt, rolling around, overcome by laughter. They are nothing if not resilient in moments of comical stress, however, and one of them recovered fast enough to shout, to the delight of the stand, 'Hey man, you face Wesley Hall, what for now you take a backward step? That puppy's teeth only made of rubber . . .'

One of the problems which was around when I still played cricket was the matter of common ground between media and players on the question of how much each knows about the other's job. The media know that some players flounder when asked questions; they know that some players, even captains, can be like time bombs if you allow enough silence after an answer. The media is also well aware that, given the task of writing an account of a day's play, a player might hardly be able to put thirty words together for the intro and, if he did, it would take him an hour and the edition would be gone. Some players, astonishingly, are too lazy even to write their own copy, but they are certainly agile enough to pick up the cheque.

Alongside that is the question of what cricket the media man has played, if he has played any at all, if he just likes the game and has always had an ambition to write about it, or if his father owns the newspaper. If a newspaperman, or a television commentator, is writing or talking about the game at Test level, and he has never risen above a village or an outback match, then a player might have some difficulty with the reports about his perceived lack of technique in a Test match against the ball which swings out and then cuts back between bat and pad before taking the leg bail. This is the most contentious cricket media question, without answer, that I have found over the past forty years.

These days millions of viewers of the TV screen have a first-hand sighting of what goes on, and consider they have every right to be experts on all aspects of cricket and to offer their opinions – and do so. They all have good memories for everything that happens on the field, though that has been a trait of cricket followers the world over in the past fifty years. Some cricket spectators in fact have *very* long memories. A few are brilliant with their repartee, and when they marry that with their memory, the effect can be devastating.

Forty years ago, I toured the West Indies and played in all five Tests. Led by Ian Johnson, Australia won the First Test by nine wickets, drew the Second and won the Third in Georgetown by eight wickets in only four days. When we played the Fourth, in Barbados, we made 668 and had them in all kinds of trouble at 147–6 on the third evening. The next day, the overnight not-out batsmen, Denis Atkinson and Clairmonte Depeiza, batted throughout the five hours' play. The following morning, I bowled Depeiza straight away with one that ran along the ground.

In 1991, I was in Barbados and just about to host the Channel Nine 'intro' to the one-day game eventually won by the Australians. The crowd was in high good humour at Kensington Oval and some, pre-match, were even celebrating their anticipated victory. Loudly! In my earpiece the voice of director Geoff Morris said, 'Fifteen seconds to on-air' and, at the same time, the ground went quiet.

Then, 'Hey, Sir Richard Benaud. You the son of that guy who couldn't get out Atkinson and Depeiza all the fourth day in 1955?'

Right match, wrong family connection.

'If you couldn't bowl them out, you do right to take up television, man,' he continued, just as I began my into.

'Good morning and welcome to this delightful island of the

Caribbean.' I said it through my own laughter and that of hundreds of spectators in the Kensington Stand right behind me.

You need to keep your sense of humour on television and to bear in mind a few little things to help you through commentaries. I'm often asked for advice on how to commentate, but simply copying someone else never works. You must be an individual and there are a few little notes I keep which are of some benefit in my own commentaries and general organisation. They would not suit other commentators but might or might not be of some assistance, in a general sense, to any younger people who are thinking of moving into the commentary position. In my general organisation, working in the office and in business, the approach to a day, a week and a year of work, I try to bear in mind:

- Do your best, never give up.
- Golf course behaviour mirrors business behaviour.
- The same error twice is only one mistake, but a very big one.
- Make your own luck, keep two overs ahead of the play.
- Mediocrity is contagious.
- Silence can be your greatest weapon.

Then, in the television commentary box, there are many aspects of discipline to be observed; it is necessary to be organised, particularly if you also have other media work to do, as happens with me. My freelance work includes television commentaries, writing for newspapers, working for radio, writing feature and special articles and doing interviews.

> The *Titanic* was a tragedy, the Ethiopian drought a disaster, and neither bears any relation to a dropped catch.
>
> *RB on maintaining a sense of perspective*

There are literally hundreds of things which might be said by a commentator which should not be said. Some of them find their way into journals like *Private Eye*, and some are imprinted on the minds of those who have heard and now cherish them. Some will never be forgotten by the commentator who uttered them. They are inscribed on his or her mind for ever.

These are the ones I try to avoid. Even so they will slip through occasionally although it is a matter of lack of concentration if they do. It doesn't make me feel any better when it happens and it's then a matter of concentrating harder and trying to make certain it doesn't occur again:

- Put your brain into gear before opening your mouth. Try not to allow past your lips:

    He is a doyen, a guru or an icon . . .

    He gives 120 per cent, or 150 per cent, or even 200 per cent . . .

    At this point in time . . .

    Of course . . .

    You know . . .

    Well, yes, you know, I mean . . .

    To be perfectly honest . . .

    Really and truly . . .

    I really must say . . .

    I must ask you . . .

    As you can see on the screen . . .

    Have a look at *this* . . .

    The corridor of uncertainty . . .

    That's a tragedy . . . or a disaster.
- Don't take yourself too seriously!

This very short list needs to be read in conjunction with the amount of concentration needed to be a commentator: it is fierce, the same as applies to successful players and captains. One or two people I know say working on television is a 'doddle'. Not for me it isn't. If you're not prepared to concentrate and to work as hard as is required, then you are better off in another job.

But, above all, remember a job as a cricketer or a TV commentator might need fierce concentration but, just as important, you also must have a bit of fun, otherwise it just turns into an ulcer-making dirge!

One thing of which you can be certain about television commentary is the advice noted earlier, that silence is your greatest weapon. Timing is another. It is no use talking about something, making comment on a happening, if there is nothing to do with that on the screen.

We were covering a Test match at Lord's five or six years ago when there was a commotion of sorts on top of a building on the eastern side of the ground. There was a small group of people having a barbecue on top of one of the rooftops and along just a little further was a lady who, even without the benefit of binoculars, I could see was dressed in slightly eccentric fashion. What there was of her garb seemed to be black. Closer examination showed it to be filmy black, possibly lace. She was standing in front of some lettering but I didn't have time to pay attention to that because the bowler was coming in at the Nursery End.

In between balls there were murmurs from the crowd, who by now were paying as much attention to the lady on the roof as they were to the game. Keith Mackenzie, our producer/director, said into my earpiece, 'I'm going to have to show what's happening if nothing comes from the next ball.' I said, 'OK,' and then made a comment about the quick single that had been taken. Keith cut to the roof across the road and there she was, looking different now she was much closer on the screen from the way she did to the very naked eye. The lady, clad in black fishnet stockings and with a thick piece of string across her frontage, was draped over a well-lettered, well-planned and painted sign advertising vodka. It proclaimed, 'Fiona Vladivar loves Richie Benaud.' I said, 'And just think, that's only her mother.'

Peter Alliss of the modern-day commentators is outstanding and is a master of the pause and build-up. He was responsible for one of the best pieces of sports television commentary I have heard. It was during the Dunhill Masters at Woburn several years ago when Seve Ballesteros was playing the eighteenth, which is normally the first hole for club members. It was very late in the tournament and Seve had slightly pulled his tee shot to within a yard or two of the fence alongside the road. He had been saved from being out of bounds by the ball brushing the gorse but his stance was still going to be impeded by some more gorse. Seve gave it everything when he arrived down there. He took his stance then he changed it, then he put on his waterproofs and took them off and all the time there was the camera behind him at ground level and Alliss, after telling the viewers what kind of shot Seve might be able to fashion from virtually nothing, remained quiet. There was plenty going on for the viewers to see, which is what television is all about, but there are some commentators who would have been chatting away and describing what the viewers could see for themselves. When Seve finally settled into the gorse again and wriggled around several times with a very pained expression on his face as his buttocks were scratched and torn, Alliss finally used just one sentence to add to the picture and the viewers' enjoyment. 'Ah yes,' he said, 'but how will be explain all that to his wife when he gets home!'

In 1994, Channel Nine organised a special match for Allan Border at the 'Gabba. It was a tribute to a great cricketer and the personnel taking part varied from current players to those out of the game some years, and then to one or two showbusiness personalities and footballers. It was a 16,000 all-ticket sell-out and was very successful, something which doesn't always happen with matches of that kind. They have to be done very carefully or they will quickly become run-of-the-mill. Channel Nine did it well and used a variety of experiments, with microphones on players and umpires and various other little touches, in a match which lent itself to entertainment. At the end of the game when I was racing for a taxi for the airport, with little time to spare, I was bailed up by a cricket fan who had been watching the game on television in the Queensland Cricketers' Club next door. 'Been watching all that stuff you've been doing with the microphones on the players, talking to one another and being quizzed out on the field by the commentators. Bet you're cranky you weren't able to do that in your day?'

Just shows nothing is new under the sun, because back in 1963 I played in a Lord's Taverners match at Lord's with Denis Compton and others and Brian Johnston was the BBC Television presenter for the day. He did a three-way conversation with me and with Compton, in which I was

> **❛**There was a slight interruption there for athletics.**❜**
>
> *RB on an invading streaker*

describing what I would bowl, Compton was commenting, and then, for variety, we did it with communication to Johnston and the viewers, but not between ourselves. It was said at the time by those watching the television that, 'it was wonderful to watch, great to listen to and close to unbelievable the things that can be done with modern communications.' Little did they know.

There is no doubt one of Channel Nine's strengths is that its commentators, whether they be ex-captains of national teams or ex-Test or first-class players, have the necessary experience to talk about a particular situation in the centre of the ground. Viewers sometimes have a problem with accepting a firm opinion if it is not based on experience. For example, much as I love golf and enjoy the golf work I have done, I am not prepared to offer, on television, an opinion as to why a top-class professional golfer, say Greg Norman, has pushed a ball to the right of the eighteenth green at Augusta. I'm quite prepared to say he *has* done it and describe what happened, because that is fact.

I am a reasonably solid eleven-handicapper at the Australian Golf Club in Sydney, and I have tried to learn as much as possible about the game and the rules, but for me to add for millions of viewers that Norman hit the ball to the right of the green because his set-up was faulty, perhaps an inch or two too far to the left, he came off the ball a little, or he didn't allow for the slightly sidehill lie, would be, in my view, ridiculous. I would certainly ask Jack Newton, Peter Thomson or Clive Clark the reason and I might find out that, in fact, it was Norman's grip which was slightly faulty.

> ❛What I want most from being a television commentator is to be able to feel that, when I say something, I am talking to friends.❜
>
> *RB on commentating*

I might be prepared to offer expert golf commentary if later this year I were to pass all the PGA coaching certificate examinations, and if I managed to play as an amateur in some big tournament events so I could sample the intense pressure these players are under over the last nine holes on the final day, with a bunched leader-board and a first prize for the professionals of $200,000. Until that time, and without that expertise, I wouldn't do it.

I am quite prepared though to offer praise or criticism of Mark Taylor's or Michael Atherton's Test match captaincy, Mark Waugh's cover-drive for four or dismissal, or why Craig McDermott was slanting the ball towards the batsman's pads. That's because I've been there.

It's been absolutely marvellous
England v Australia at The Oval, 2005
Richie Benaud's final words on British TV

We've had all sorts of music here today – *Land of Hope and Glory*, the National Anthem, *Jerusalem* before we started. I always carry a lot of music around with me, and one of the great ones for me is Andre Bocelli and Sarah Brightman singing that duet, that wonderful duet, *Time to Say Goodbye*. And that's what it is, so far as I'm concerned – time to say goodbye. Add to that, thank you for having me. It's been absolutely marvellous for forty-two years. I've loved every moment of it, and it's been a privilege to go into everyone's living-room throughout that time. What's even better, it's been a great deal of fun ... but not so for the batsman – McGrath has picked him up. Late in the day, he's got a beauty through Kevin Pietersen; 308–8 now. Pietersen will receive a standing ovation. He gets one from Shane Warne at the moment. And there is the roar to end all roars. A standing ovation from the moment he started to walk off the crease. The wicket too late for Australia, but perfectly timed so far as England is concerned. Pietersen 158; 308–8 England. [Watching replay] Beautifully bowled. McGrath gets his man, and we've got our two men in the commentary box now – Mark Nicholas and Tony Greig.

Richie pitches it just right

Ian Wooldridge, *Searching for Heroes*, 2007*

So IT IS FAREWELL, then, to the Master of Measured Words. Richie Benaud will not be returning to England next summer to sustain his pre-eminence as cricket's finest television commentator.

That is not merely my judgement. A recent poll by *The Wisden Cricketer* magazine attracted an astonishing 12,000 votes. Precisely 10,128 of them nominated Benaud as the best.

Fortunately, he does not leave us without a word or several of advice to those who seek to emulate his success, particularly retired players whose agents deem them instantly equipped to pick up a microphone and irritate us with an effluent of Tower of Babel verbiage.

He does so in a valedictory book [*My Spin on Cricket*], of which more later. It is an encyclopaedia of broadcasting wisdom.

He names no names. He is too polite for that. Nor is there a hint of the tetchiness that occasionally afflicts icons in their pensionable years.

At 74, Benaud is still as fit as a flea, the result of a lifestyle as measured as his commentating. Yes, there are rare occasions when he will let down his hair with the rest of us, but when serious business is afoot he will rise from an increasingly raucous dinner party, check his watch that it is exactly 10 p.m. and announce: 'Thank you very much. We're off.'

At sunrise next morning, he and Daphne, his elegant and unfailingly supportive English wife, will be striding out on their three-mile constitutional.

He is meticulous in all things. On TV commentary days even Daphne is not allowed to iron his shirts. He presses them himself. He is a food faddist, preparing his Test match lunch boxes at home to be certain of what he is eating. Once he took a week-long course in Italy to learn how to cook pasta to perfection.

* This piece by RB's friend Ian Wooldridge was originally published in the *Daily Mail* in August 2005 before being included in *Searching for Heroes*, a collection of his articles

His desks at his homes in London, south of France and Sydney are polished plateaux of precision, his reference-book shelves indexed for instant reach.

It is this unrelenting self-discipline, instilled by a schoolmaster and great club cricketer father and a lovely mother — there is a gorgeous picture of her celebrating her 100th birthday with Richie and his Test cricketer brother John in the book — that launched him into his dual career life.

The first, of course, was in cricket, where to haul oneself from school to club, to State, the Australian team and then its captaincy, was a classic climb. Benaud led his country in 28 of his 63 Tests and never lost a series. Such was his cunning as a wrist-spinner that his batsmanship was often overlooked.

In fact, he became the first, in an era when far fewer Tests were played, to scale the double of 200 wickets and 2,000 runs.

But what next? All of seven years before he retired from cricket, Benaud wondered if there could be a distant future in the communications industry. There was little doubt about that since he had been a young crime reporter on a Sydney newspaper, where sub-editors ruthlessly deleted from his copy any flowery phrases which he thought rather good but were irrelevant to the story. It was an important lesson.

Then a curious opportunity, which couldn't happen in today's schedules, presented itself. At the end of Australia's 1956 tour to England, all their players were given three weeks off to enjoy such fleshpots of relaxation as they could discover in the British Isles.

Benaud proceeded otherwise. At his own expense he moved from the Kensington Palace Hotel into a cramped lower ground room in the RAC club in Pall Mall and took a BBC television training course, watching alongside directors, commentators, even audiences, to learn how television worked.

He trailed Peter O'Sullevan at Newbury and he studied the commentating techniques of Henry Longhurst on golf and Dan Maskell on tennis. All three had their idiosyncrasies, but one thing they had in common.

O'Sullevan, voice rising to overdrive at the climax of a horse race, was circumspect about collateral chatter just as Longhurst and 'Oh I say' Maskell knew the value of golden silence. Indeed, one of Longhurst's silences was so long that his director asked over the private intercom: 'Excuse me, Henry, but are you still alive?'

Benaud now says: 'I didn't know if I had a future in broadcasting. If I hadn't done that BBC course my life would have been very different, even though I had to wait for seven years for my chance. The key feature it taught me was the economy of words. Never insult the viewers by telling them what they have seen perfectly clearly themselves. Only add to it if you had something pertinent to say.'

These days, if only.

Has he ever made a bloomer? Of course, like all of us, he has. On one celebrated occasion, handing over from a Test match for a news update from Moira Stuart, he called her Moira Shearer, the celebrated ballerina who had starred in an acclaimed film.

When Moira Stuart handed back he said: 'Thanks, Moira, our newsreader wearing Red Shoes.'

Many, who had not heard his initial blunder, wondered what on earth he was on about.

'At the time,' he recalls, 'I thought it was a pretty clever remark, but many tuning in at that moment had no idea what it meant. It taught me never to be such a smart-arse again.'

Laconic, economic, massively instructive and with a dry impartial wit about whoever is getting the upper hand in a Test match, I wonder if we shall ever hear his like again on television?

Many are called and surprisingly many are given the opportunity behind the microphone. Very few have served the slogging apprenticeship that makes a master cricket commentator.

10
World Series Cricket

❝He was an important influence in the formation of Kerry Packer's World Series Cricket in 1977, a climactic event at the time but one which has left a lasting, positive influence on the game.❞

Wally Edwards, Chairman of Cricket Australia

The origins of WSC
Richie Benaud, *My Spin on Cricket*, 2005

In the early 'fifties and 'sixties, television was slightly primitive compared with today. Television didn't begin in Australia until 1956, Channel Nine was the first to go to air and the first presenter on Sunday, 16 September 1956, was Bruce Gyngell. This was on the day after the Australian cricket tour of England finished with the match against Scotland at Aberdeen. We had all been given a three-week break at the end of the tour of England and each player had made his own decision on what he would do during that break. The team travelled by train from Aberdeen to London to pack and on Monday, 17 September, I moved from the Kensington Palace Hotel to the Royal Automobile Club. The team during the tour had been honorary members of that club and I had organised my accommodation in a tiny room on the lower ground floor which was going to suit me as I was paying all my own expenses for that three-week period. My decision of what to do in the break was to attend a specially arranged BBC Television training course.

There was a small story in a couple of London newspapers stating that television had begun in Sydney, but it was of no real importance in London because the medium had been going there for a considerable number of years.

If I hadn't done the BBC course in 1956 my life would have been very different. It was a most fortunate experience, even though I had to wait seven years for my chance actually to find any work on television as a sports commentator. In 1960 I worked on BBC Radio but up to the First Test, England v West Indies at Lord's in 1963, I had never done anything on television other than be interviewed. This was when I was captain of the Australian team and during that 1960 English summer I was several times interviewed by Brian Johnston and Peter West. It was great experience.

I had watched and listened to Henry Longhurst and Dan Maskell in the 1953, 1956, 1960 and 1961 English summers and had trailed around behind Peter O'Sullevan at Newbury for two days during the 1956 BBC course. The key feature with all of them seemed to be economy of words, even Peter, who had to describe the races with a running commentary. It was natural for me to follow the same path, at least until I was shown, or told, this was not the way to go. It isn't easy being a summariser on television and at the same time being economical with words but, on the BBC, it was mandatory there would be comments made at the end of each over, even if nothing much had happened. It was important to be able sensibly to fill that gap between overs.

I knew none of the work I had done in the BBC training course would be of direct use to me on arrival back in Australia. I looked on it though as a form of insurance if I were, for example, to be interviewed on television. At least I would know what was going on. With TV in its infancy in Australia, the two channels available for viewing had their own schedules worked out, as well as their own commentators and stars. Any work coming my way would be well in the future, if at all, and I was more concerned with doing well in the Australian summer with bat and ball and then making it into the Australian team for the short and unofficial tour of New Zealand, also the major one against South Africa which was scheduled to start at the beginning of October 1957.

Lord's 1956 was a turning point for me in my cricket career. I didn't know it then but I was approximately halfway through the sixteen-year span of breaking into first-class cricket in 1948–49 and retiring in 1963–64. If Lord's was a turning point, then the South African tour was vital because it was there I managed to make a mark as a Test match cricketer, in the main due to the extra responsibility I was given.

Scheduling of Australian tours of England was strange in those days. The sequence was 1948–1953–1956 and then 1961. That was one reason it was such a good idea to begin what might be termed a proper job at the newspaper and try to build a career in writing, which I enjoyed anyway. It was around this time that television networks and the Australian Board of Control started talking about the televising of cricket, albeit in an extremely low-key manner. No one at this stage had the slightest idea of the impact television would have on sport, or sport on television, almost fifty years on.

One of the great ironies of the administrators' dipping-a-toe-in-the-water approach around this time was that the first match they allowed to be televised was sensibly chosen because they decided the two strongest teams in Sheffield Shield Cricket, New South Wales and Victoria, should provide the entertainment. And it was played at the suburban St Kilda ground in Melbourne in 1956–57 because the MCG was out of action for cricket, being listed as the main stadium for the 1956 Olympic Games, which were to be held from 27 November to 8 December. The television people didn't properly realise the significance of the match; they were far too busy putting together all their outside broadcast equipment and making certain a signal was getting as far as the city of Melbourne up the road and possibly to the whole of the metropolitan area.

What made it even more unusual was that the game was played over six days, though only four of them were actual playing days. It started on Saturday, 22 December. There was no cricket then on Sundays, so that took out the 23rd, we played on the 24th, but not on Christmas Day, the 25th. The game then continued on Boxing Day and came to its gripping climax late in the afternoon of Thursday, the 27th. The crowd paying their money on the last day totalled 7,092 through the turnstiles, but quite a few of them had gone home to watch on television by the time the final wicket was taken by Ian Meckiff for the match to be tied.

It was the beginning of what for me is a rather unusual record in that I have seen three ties in Australian cricket, that one at St Kilda, then the Tied Test at the 'Gabba when I was captain against the West Indies in 1960, and the one in Adelaide, South Australia v Queensland in early February 1977, just before the Centenary Test at the MCG. There were three run-outs in the final over of the Queensland second innings, Phil Carlson, Malcolm Francke and Col Cooke. It was not dissimilar to the final over Australia had gone through seventeen years earlier at the 'Gabba. One thing we did know after the Victoria v NSW match in 1956 was that the television people went home happy because there had been some excitement to show the viewers. At least it showed both cricket administrators and television networks that there might be something in this cricket business, though the general feeling in Australia was that it was all a bit too drawn out to be able to hold the attention of viewers over four or five days.

The good news for them was that it didn't cost much. The television network had to pay £50 apiece to the NSW Cricket Association and the Victorian Cricket Association.

Later relaying cricket telecasts became very important. When, on 9 January 1959, Australia played England at the SCG in the third match of the Ashes battle, the final two hours of play each day were relayed from Sydney to Melbourne. This in a sense was an experiment, but it worked, and it was the basis of more televised cricket when the West Indian side came to Australia under Frank Worrell's captaincy in 1960–61. In fact, that Tied Test series was the catalyst for televised sport in Australia, so exciting were the matches and so captivating the thought for viewers that they would be able to watch the action at no cost from an armchair in their living-room. Television had only been a factor in Australian life for a relatively short time at this stage, something around four years, and it was only the linking of ground-based relay stations between Melbourne and Sydney that allowed a complete telecast of the final Test in Melbourne in February 1961. The series at that stage stood at 1–1 following the 'Gabba tie. Between the first and last matches of the series Sydney viewers had been able to watch the last couple of hours of Australia winning the Second Test played in Melbourne. Additionally, at the end of the Adelaide Test, the Fourth, one of the biggest viewing audiences to watch television to that time in Australia tuned in to see 'Slasher' Mackay and Lindsay Kline save the match for Australia in dramatic fashion. It was the kind of audience that in 1961 could only ever be obtained by an extraordinary prime-time evening show or a special event.

The introduction of satellite technology meant that in 1970–71, when Ray Illingworth brought the England team to Australia, the whole of the country was able to watch the Test series on television. This, purely by coincidence, turned out to be one of the more important happenings for cricket because, when the first three days of the 1970–71 Melbourne Test were completely washed out on 31 December and 1 and 2 January, the cricket authorities from both countries tried to find something to interest an irritated and frustrated Melbourne cricket public and they arranged a one-day match with a maximum of 40 eight-ball overs each side. This was slightly more than the 50 overs of six balls that apply to all one-day

Internationals these days. It was an instant success. No one had really bothered to tell the players what was going on, or what was about to go on, nor had anyone asked them if they wanted to play a one-day match. There was some one-day cricket being played between the Australian states at that time and I had watched and been part of television in England one-day cricket for the previous ten years. That began in England with Rothmans Sunday matches, then the 'Cup' started in England in 1963 with 65 overs maximum for each team, and, extraordinarily, with no sponsor, though later Gillette came in as the first sponsor of that facet of the game.

The match at the MCG in 1971 drew a crowd of 46,000. It was a splendid game and ABC Television had great ratings, though in those days they spurned ratings as being something invented by the devils of commercial television. How times change! In 1972 the whole of the final day of the Oval Test was telecast by satellite to Australia on the ABC and then the introduction of colour television on 5 March 1975 further lifted audience interest. Hundreds of thousands stayed up through the night to watch the 1975 World Cup final telecast from Lord's and this match also alerted the minds of Australian government ministers to the fact that legislation was necessary to ensure the type of programmes which would be shown at certain times during a 24-hour period.

The Australian Broadcasting Control Board decreed that from six o'clock in the morning through to midnight at least half the programmes shown had to be Australian in origin. Until this legislation was enforced, most sports broadcasts were handled by the Australian Broadcasting Commission, serving not only the capital cities but also far-flung country areas. It was certainly free-to-air. The attention of commercial networks was drawn to the possibility of covering cricket once colour was introduced and it was the following year that Channel Nine lodged with the Australian Board of Control a bid for the exclusive rights to televise cricket.

The bid was something that should have caught the attention of the Australian cricket authorities because it was A$500,000 a season for three seasons, compared with the A$70,000 a season being offered by the Australian Broadcasting Commission. The Cricket Board at that time had Bob Parish as chairman and Kerry Packer had been trying for several months to arrange a meeting with him to discuss the matter of exclusive rights. At the 1977 High Court hearing before Mr Justice Slade, Mr Packer testified that he had failed to organise that meeting and then later was very quickly told, when he walked into the Board's meeting, that they were declining his offer because the rights had already been granted to the ABC. Mr Packer in the witness box added his opinion that the Board's lament that they weren't able to pay the cricketers more money could have been solved instantly by accepting Channel Nine's bid. The Board's miserly payment of players was quickly to be a factor in the greatest change ever to take place in cricket.

When Channel Nine decided on their tactics regarding ratings in the year of 1977 it was a coincidence that one of the people Mr Packer talked to on a personal basis was John Cornell, who was the manager of Australian television star Paul Hogan. At the same time, one of John Cornell's friends, Austin Robertson, a former Australian Rules footballer, talked to him about his knowledge of serious player unrest over the fact that the Australian Cricket Board were paying the players as little as possible in match fees. Also that there were similar difficulties in other countries over the fact that administrators wouldn't listen to the players on the subject of higher payments.

From that came World Series Cricket and for two years Channel Nine televised their own matches while the ABC televised the Australian Board matches. It was Mr Packer who tabled the idea of playing day-night games with the grounds floodlit for the second half of the matches, as in American baseball, with spectators able to leave their place of work and go to the grounds to see a result. Television coverage also changed. To that time a cricket match had been covered with the minimum number of cameras, now Channel Nine started using eight cameras and coverage in WSC matches was from both ends so that viewers would no longer see the backside of the wicketkeeper, just in front of that the backside of the batsman, then the bowler in the distance running towards the camera and therefore the front of both the above-mentioned players.

One of the reasons commercial television began to be interested in cricket coverage was certainly the Australian content provision for programming, but equally the fact that the Australian population was increasingly interested in buying television sets.

‘Richie Benaud's passing has robbed us not only of a national treasure but a lovely man. Richie earned the profound and lasting respect of everyone across the world of cricket and beyond. First as an outstanding player and captain, then as an incomparable commentator and through it all, as a wonderful human being.’

David Gyngell, Nine Network CEO

The advent of colour TV made a big impact on sales in various retail outlets and although, in that, there was no direct benefit to the television networks, there definitely was the dramatic indirect benefit that more television sets around the country meant the possibility of more advertising and a vastly expanded market. This market involved an increase in television being watched in homes around Australia from 58 per cent to 80 per cent. As is the case with all sport from the moment television took hold, the watching audience paying their money at the turnstiles was a small number compared with those who might choose to watch it in their own homes. A Test at the SCG for example could cater in a day for 35,000 to 40,000 paying spectators, whereas the same play could be televised throughout the country to more than two million people.

The aim over the past twenty-eight years in Australia, as far as Channel Nine are concerned, has been and remains to provide viewers with the best seat in the house. Mr Packer and David Hill, the producer, revolutionised the way cricket was telecast and things which were innovative in the early years are now regarded as commonplace. When Hill and Brian Morelli, the senior director, at a cricket match in Perth in the early 1980s invented the moving scorecard, the 'ticker' in the top left-hand corner of the screen, it was regarded as an extraordinary breakthrough. Now it is taken for granted, no sports telecast would be without it and it is being adapted in new ways every year.

A proposition from Kerry Packer
Richie Benaud, *Anything But . . . an Autobiography*, 1998

It was Monday, 5 January 1998, when Shane Warne took his 300th wicket in Test cricket at the SCG, having started his career, almost to the day, six years earlier. This was a momentous occasion: a wonderful talent had been on show, and the ball with which he dismissed Jacques Kallis was worthy of the congratulations and the adulation which followed. It was especially pleasing to me that Warne should have achieved this milestone on the ground where I had played all my home cricket and, as a sideline, a ground which in the previous twelve months had improved immeasurably as regards pitch and outfield condition.

Pleased as I was for Warne, I was even more delighted by one other aspect of the game, which was that it had finished at 7.09 p.m. in conditions poor enough that the lights had been turned on by the umpires under the new playing condition passed by the International Cricket Council. Test cricket under lights – who would have believed it twenty years before that moment? Certainly not the Australian Cricket Board when they were at loggerheads with World Series Cricket. This was the ground where, at the beginning of Kerry Packer's WSC, there had been so much trouble with the installation of the lights. The Establishment, knowing they were a key ingredient, fought hard to stop them being put up, but WSC, with NSW State Government intervention, finally saw them installed.

On 28 November 1978, I was present at the inaugural [WSC] match between Australia and the West Indies. I arrived at the ground two hours before the start of play scheduled for 2.15 p.m., anticipating, because reserved ticket sales had been outstanding, that there could be a problem with traffic, even over the couple of miles between Coogee where we live and Moore Park where the SCG is situated. By one o'clock, traffic jams were building up on all the roads leading to Moore Park and enquiries established that this was not due to any roadwork problems or accidents, but simply to hundreds of cars, all of them aiming for Moore Park and the SCG.

Nowadays there is a ceiling crowd figure of 40,000 at the SCG, but that didn't apply in 1978, and by the time we were moving towards the tea, or, as it became known in WSC, the dinner interval, there was a crowd of around 25,000 actually in the ground, thousands more were clamouring to be let in and traffic by now was really banking up on the feeder roads and the lights were beginning to take effect. Mr Packer arrived before the dinner interval and instead of the normal situation where ground authorities would close the gates for a sell-out crowd, he instructed they be opened to the public and we were estimating up in the television box that around 50,000 people were in the ground. The Hill was packed, the outer was packed, the Members' Stands were packed and it was one of the most wonderful sights I have seen.

The match itself was a low-scoring one. West Indies were slaughtered for only 128, Australia made the runs without any great difficulty, and seven hours after the first ball had been bowled, the winning run was hit.

The attraction of the day-night match, the excitement of the lights and the wonderful atmosphere combined to make it an evening I'll never forget, and after I had finished wrapping up the television commentary and the highlights, I walked around the back of the Noble Stand and into the Old Members, up the stairs and into the NSWCA Executive Room, where Daphne had already arrived.

I poured a couple of glasses of white Burgundy and we took them over to the corner where Kerry Packer was standing. The atmosphere was calm, even reflective.

'What did you think?' he said quietly to us.

We each raised our glass in a silent toast. The gesture covered 632 days of excitement and problems, strain and pleasure, and now a win as conclusive as that shortly before achieved by Australia.

We had first heard about World Series Cricket on 6 April 1977, a week after I had bumped into Kerry Packer at the Australian Golf Club where we were both members. He was in conversation with Mark McCormack, whom I had known for many years.

The ideas for World Series Cricket were put to me at a meeting at Australian Consolidated Press a week later; I said I found the concept extremely interesting, possibly exciting, that it ran alongside my ideas about Australian cricketers currently being paid far too little and having virtually no input into the game in Australia. I added to Mr Packer that I would go back and discuss the proposition with my wife and let him have an answer the next day. He reminded me that at the start of the discussion I had agreed the matter would be completely confidential and that was the way it must remain – no discussion with anyone, wife included. Daphne and I worked together in the consultancy business, so I told Kerry we would make the decision together and that I would come back to him the next day with the answer, which I did.

The answer was yes and we were looking forward to being part of it. I also gave him some notes which, in retrospect, turned out to be spot on for accuracy concerning the administrators who ran Australian cricket at that time, and listing Bradman, Steele and Parish as outstanding. As well, I mentioned the type of reaction which could be expected from the Australian Board and the type of letter which should be written to them to apprise them of what was happening.

As I was going out of the door Mr Packer's voice followed me: 'Excuse me, you haven't said what your fee will be . . .'

Although I knew Australian players at this time were financially treated poorly by the Australian Cricket Board, I hadn't actually realised the extent of their dissatisfaction. Apparently it had come to a head eight years earlier when Australia had toured India and South Africa, and although there was a profit to the Board of more than a quarter of a million dollars, the players received paltry amounts. They weren't alone. In England just prior to the start of World Series Cricket, a county player earned less than the average wage. West Indies cricketers were paid poorly, as were the stars of what was then the subcontinent.

Between saying yes to the WSC proposal and the start of the next season there were many things to do, one of which was to cover the Australian cricket tour of England for the BBC and various newspapers and magazines whilst running our own sports consultancy. Daphne and I arrived in England in late April, stayed with the Morleys in Knightsbridge and kept a close eye on various happenings in the cricket world. We were very busy.

Much has been chronicled concerning the lead-up to the announcement of World Series Cricket, and it appears to have been a combined breaking story between journalists Peter McFarline and Alan Shiell. However, the first intimation I had that the story was to hit the streets was when the English sports writer, Ian Wooldridge, phoned me at the Morleys'. He said he was about to publish a big story in the London *Daily Mail* concerning a breakaway cricket movement, and did I have any information on it. I told him I'd ring him back as I was a bit busy at that moment. I didn't know about McFarline and Shiell then, and Wooldridge seemed to be the one with the story: the facts he had listed over the phone were substantially correct, although there were some minor omissions.

That 1977 summer in England revolved as much around the High Court as the cricket field. Justice Slade's judgment when handed down was not unexpected to me after I had listened to the background of other court cases. A precedent had been set twelve years earlier with the case of Florence Nagle, the would-be racehorse trainer, asking for the right to work; in 1963 there was the landmark George Eastham restraint of trade case; and, a year prior to that, a natural justice verdict to do with decisions concerning the suspensions of players by sporting clubs. In the light of those matters it would have been unusual if the plaintiffs, Tony Greig, Mike Procter and John Snow, had not won their case against defendants, the Test and County Cricket Board and Doug Insole. They do say, though, that you should assume nothing in legal matters.

A lot of people will tell you courtroom battles are boring, and I suppose some might be, but not this one, with Robert Alexander and Andrew Morritt as Counsel for the plaintiffs. It provided me with some most interesting insights and every night I took home the transcripts of the day and studied them. When I saw anything that didn't seem to gel, I made a note and brought it up with Robert Alexander and the instructing solicitors the next morning at the pre-court conference. Some were small matters, others more important, and finally we even finished up with the exact number of people present at the meeting in the Long Room at Lord's, and which of them were visible and what they were doing. Unfortunately, I had to leave before the Slade verdict was delivered in order to sort out with Lynton Taylor the matter of the pitches and grounds in the various states in Australia.

Daphne had returned to Australia at this stage, and with Barbara Loois, Irene Cave and others was setting up the complex but small staffed and very efficient WSC administration office which turned out to be a vital part of the organisation's success.

That success was elusive in the first year of WSC, but as the day-night matches gathered pace, and spectator numbers rose and television ratings soared, things started to move very quickly.

Twenty-one years after WSC, there is an astonishing increase in interest in the game, despite intense competition from other sports.

Coaching of the game has intensified, in general terms in a good fashion, but sometimes along the lines of it becoming an industry. New sponsors have realised, as a direct off-shoot of WSC, that cricket is a game with which they should be involved. The judgment in the WSC court case was a direct reflection on the fact that monopolies were good neither for the game nor the players, and the latter are much better off now that the old-style relationship has, to a certain extent, been changed. Players are no longer precluded from pursuing a professional livelihood in a proper fashion, a situation different from those employer–employee relationships in existence pre-1977. They are also flexing a few muscles, not without argument from administrators, but that is nothing new.

The best result from WSC came from the fact that if they are good enough, players are able to secure regular employment at higher standards of remuneration, and that the best players, the stars, are better off. Many players now, depending on their form and the choices of the selectors, will stay on longer in the game. Selection will always be the final arbiter, but there were many good players lost to the game pre-1977 because they simply couldn't afford to keep playing.

11
The Spirit of the Game

'He's an amazing example to a lot of sportsmen. I think all of us look up to Richie . . . He was a great player and a great captain, a wonderful leader of men, and I think he's continued that off the field. He sets a great example, he's a gentleman, he played the game in the right spirit. He loved winning and he helped the Australian team have that attitude that they wanted to win, but he played the game the right way.'

Michael Clarke, *Daily Mail*

Fifty-two years with Benords
Ian Chappell, ESPN Cricinfo, 2015

'AFTER YOU, IAN.' They were the first words spoken to me by Richie Benaud.

It was 1962 and South Australia had just enjoyed a rare victory over a star-studded New South Wales line-up. Benaud, as the not-out batsman, magnanimously stood back to allow Les Favell's team to walk off the Adelaide Oval first. I was on the field as twelfth man and wasn't about to leave ahead of the Australian captain and a man whose leadership style I'd admired from afar, but he insisted.

That story is indicative of Benaud. He was a thorough gentleman and meticulous in his preparation – I was staggered he knew my name.

He was also a generous man. Not long after the Adelaide Oval experience, a Gray-Nicolls bat arrived in the post while I was playing in the Lancashire League. It was from Richie, and so began a relationship that only ended after fifty-two rewarding years with his sad passing on Friday.

I say rewarding; that was

from my perspective, but I'm not sure what Benords received in return. Often when I spoke to him or called, he had a helpful suggestion, which emanated from a mind that was regularly in lateral-thinking mode.

As a young man he advised me: 'Ian, it's a simple game. The simpler you keep it the better off you'll be.'

When I became captain I called to explain how a mate had said: 'You've got the field in the wrong place for Sobers.'

He laughed. 'There's no right place for the field when Sobers is going,' he explained. 'All I'd say is you're wasting a fieldsman putting someone in the gully. He hits the ball in the air in that direction, but it's six inches off the ground and going like a bullet. No one can catch it.'

When I retired and turned my hand to writing and television, he organised for me to commentate on the BBC – with whom he'd trained in 1956 – during the 1977 Ashes. He also suggested (Richie rarely advised) I become a member of the Australian Journalists Association so there would be no objection to me writing columns.

He did offer me advice once. It was the 1976–77 season and we were commentating on the 0/10 network. Over a drink he told me: 'Ian, there's a better way.' I was eagerly awaiting his thoughts on how I could improve my commentary, when he expanded: 'You don't have to tell every pest to p--- off. There is a better way.'

He listed some options but I don't think they registered, as I replied, 'But sometimes I get a lot of satisfaction from telling someone to p--- off, Benords.'

The very next day a strange thing happened. I accepted an invitation to lunch with cricket officials, where there was an even stranger occurrence. I told a former schoolmaster of mine who had recently written me a scathing letter that I'd enjoyed reading his missive.

I walked away feeling buoyant and thinking, 'Benords is right: there is a better way.'

When I happily related the incident, he looked at me quizzically and said: 'Then how do you explain what happened to me after play?'

Richie had met a mate in the bar at the cricket ground and no sooner had he enjoyed his first sip of wine than a guy marched over to him and said: 'You don't remember me, do you?'

A pause, another sip of wine, and then Benaud responded: 'Don't tell me. Just give me a few seconds and I'll get the name.'

After a couple of exchanges the guy couldn't contain himself and blurted out his name. 'Well, p--- off then,' was Benaud's response.

For a man who lived up to his 'keep the game simple' advice on the cricket field, he had a propensity for complicating golf. I remember when he proudly announced he'd bought an odometer so he could measure courses and distances. I was quick to remind him that his good friend and five times British Open champion Peter Thomson always said: 'It's a hand and eye game.'

However, he did live up to his 'keep it simple' advice as a television commentator and presenter. 'Don't say anything unless you can add to the pictures,' was his mantra as a commentator.

As a presenter, he had that marvellous ability to make it look like everything was progressing without a wrinkle, when in reality all hell was breaking loose in the studio. In the early days of *Wide World of Sports*, he was opening the telecast at the 'Gabba when the set fell forward on to the back of his head. Without breaking sentence he slowly pushed back with his shoulders to move the set off his head. At that precise moment his watch alarm started buzzing. Maintaining his composure while issuing a perfect sentence, he surreptitiously reached under his cuff and turned off the alarm.

He was the game's great salesman but he could be hard-hitting when he felt the need. When Greg Chappell ordered brother Trevor to deliver the underarm against New Zealand he was quite critical of the move in his after-match summary.

❛I think it was a disgraceful performance from a captain who got his sums wrong today, and I think it should never be permitted to happen again. We keep reading and hearing that the players are under a lot of pressure, and that they're tired and jaded and perhaps their judgement and their skill is blunted. Well, perhaps they might advance that as an excuse for what happened out there today. Not with me they don't. I think it was a very poor performance – one of the worst things I have ever seen done on a cricket field.❜

RB on the 1981 Trevor Chappell underarm incident

It was illuminating to hear people's comments on Benaud. Occasionally they would say, 'I love Richie's commentary but it's a pity he hasn't got a sense of humour.' I felt like replying, 'So you watch television but you don't listen to it.'

His was a droll sense of humour and at times it could border on wicked.

We were discussing the unwritten rule of fast bowlers not bouncing fellow speedsters on air when I brought up an incident where Ray Lindwall hit Englishman Frank 'Typhoon' Tyson on the head at the SCG in 1954–55.

Tyson had taken a pounding in the first Test at the 'Gabba as Australia thrashed England. However, the roles were quickly reversed when Tyson took ten wickets at the SCG after being hit on the head by Lindwall.

In conclusion I said, 'But you were playing at the SCG that day, Richie, what happened?' He slowly picked up the microphone and said: 'It was a mistake,' then gently rested it back on his knee. I was still laughing when, uncharacteristically, he raised his microphone again. 'I'll rephrase that,' he said, 'it was a very big mistake.'

Sledging
Richie Benaud, *My Spin on Cricket*, 2005

Sledging has become so fashionable in modern-day cricket that it even makes it into the *Collins Concise Dictionary* (Third Australian Edition): **sledge** (sledʒ) vb. **sledges, sledging, sledged**. (tr) *Austral.* to bait (an opponent, esp. a **batsman** in cricket) in order to upset his concentration. (*from?*)

That '(*from?*)' refers to the fact that apparently no one at dictionary level knows the derivation of the word. There's no problem with that. It happened many years ago at a party in Adelaide, in November 1967, and had nothing at all to do with anything that had occurred on a cricket field, or has happened on a cricket field since that evening. The New South Wales team threw the party but a couple of players had to leave to attend another function. When they arrived back at the party room it was to find a waitress, carrying a tray of drinks, knocking on the same door. The door was opened to display an almost empty room apart from a couple of players, one of whom, Graham Corling, who was at the time nicknamed *'I'll be'*, looked past the waitress at his two team-mates and said, using a well known four-letter expletive, that the party was over. Another player, embarrassed at the swearing in front of a lady, said: 'Aw *I'll be*, that's as subtle as a *sledgehammer*.' In the way of Australian cricketers' use of nicknames, Corling instantly became known as 'Percy' because at that time the big song in the hit parade was 'When a Man Loves a Woman' and the singer was Percy Sledge. From that moment anyone in Australian cricket who swore in front of a lady was said to have been guilty of *sledging*.

It is a complete mystery how the media managed, in such extraordinary and convoluted fashion, to transpose that to fieldsmen or bowlers who back-chat batsmen in the centre of a cricket ground.

I played within a stretch of fifteen years in first-class cricket and hardly ever had anything derogatory said to me on the field, except in NSW–Victoria Sheffield Shield matches, probably from Jack 'Snarler' Hill, but I can guarantee you I wasn't in the habit of saying anything derogatory to any opposition players. The closest I reckon I got to experiencing sledging was in Jim Laker's Old Trafford extravaganza in 1956. There were some very unhappy Australians in that match, in the main because we had the feeling we were playing on a rather unusual pitch, and we were looking at defeat, which never actually makes one happy.

Well, you would be unhappy too if you were thrashed, one of the opposition bowlers took nineteen wickets in the match and the ball turned square for much of the game. Additionally, the rain fell on either side of the ground on the last day, but none fell on it. You would also be unhappy if you were the bowler who only took one wicket of the twenty little Australians to fall. Jim Burke was the generous batsman who was the victim of Tony Lock.

On the final afternoon I was engaged in some prudent 'gardening' against 'Lockie', patting down the pitch, sometimes not quite ready to face up, so much so that one prominent English administrator, sitting alongside a very prominent Australian administrator, said grimly that, because of the gardening, I should never at any time in the future hold a position of responsibility in an Australian team.

Out in the centre at Old Trafford, Colin McDonald and I were battling our way through to the tea interval and, in the last over, Tony bowled from what was then the Warwick Road End. I played forward firmly to a half-volley and it went to the bowler's left hand. Great fielder, 'Lockie', and a very good and accurate throwing arm in either the infield or further out. He gathered this ball and it rocketed into Godfrey Evans's left glove, alongside my left ear, and 'Tap that one down, you little bastard' came floating down the pitch.

Godfrey and I burst out laughing, it was an amusing interlude and I forgot about it the moment I turned to walk back to the dressing-room. However, the late Rev. David Sheppard had been fielding at short-leg and he was into our dressing-room very quickly to apologise for the profanity on the field. I didn't say to him I'd encountered much worse than that in my short career, particularly in New South Wales–Victoria matches, but I did have a chuckle and tell him it wasn't a problem. I added, as well, that I didn't blame 'Lockie' one little bit.

Sledging always seems to me to be such a waste of time. I came up through the game concentrating on my bowling, trying to land the ball on the right spot, endeavouring to be one step ahead of the batsman with bowling skills, trying to bowl him out rather than talk him to death. Fred Trueman had a good line in letting the batsman know he was an attacking bowler and there were others, generally fast bowlers, whose chat was occasionally interesting, though mostly boring. I can't believe, with the best will in the world, that fast bowlers of today are any more intelligent than fifty years ago. Some may be very clever bowlers on the basis of how to dismiss a batsman, though most of the time in the modern era it seems to be more a case of organising the media to do the work for them. A bowler goes out of his way to tell a media interviewer which method he intends to use to dismiss a batsman. It may have no relevance at all, it could be the direct opposite of what he actually intends to do, and the media seem quite happy to do the work for the bowler.

Far more dangerous though is when a batsman announces he intends to knock a bowler out of the attack, possibly out of the team and therefore, if followed to a logical conclusion, end that player's career. It might produce a headline of 'It's him or me' but it seems to me to be a very dangerous thing to do. You could for example do it with an athlete if you know you can always run or swim faster than the other person. It's easy enough to announce you will win tomorrow's race. But cricket is such a game of chance that once you have stated you intend to hit a bowler out of the attack, it only needs one little piece of ill-luck for you and suddenly you are mentally in trouble. A fielder dives two yards to take a miraculous catch, you slip on some greenish grass, can't regain your ground and are run out. The faintest inside edge on to your pad in successive innings and the umpire gives you out. Suddenly the media and general public are, if not baying for your body, certainly not patting you on the back and saying everything will be OK.

Early in 2005 one of the great sledgers of all time passed on to the sledging ground in the sky, or wherever it might be located. Peter Heine, the South African fast bowler, was never short of a word, or two or three, but he could bowl as well. He wasn't just all talk. Fast and furious, and with a very big heart, he bowled in partnership with Neil Adcock in the 1950s, having made his debut at Lord's in

1955, taking five wickets in England's first innings. Then he took eight in the next Test at Old Trafford and already his name was being mentioned in dispatches as a good bowler with plenty of chat. South Africa drew both Test series against England in 1955 and then in 1956–57, the year before we went to play SA in 1957–58, they were ready for us because they had been successful and England had made a mess of us in 1956. Peter took six wickets in an innings twice against us in 1957–58, in the First and Fourth Tests played at Wanderers' in Johannesburg; I made a century in the first innings of each match. Rule 1: Make sure your hook and pull shots were working well because the short ball and the very occasional yorker were definitely the preferred deliveries.

Heine wasn't quite as fast as Adcock but he didn't like to see anyone play him off the front foot. His follow-through was down the offside of the pitch, but then he had the ability to veer towards your left ear, all the better to enable you to hear the advice he was offering. I found the best way to counter this was to decline to catch his eye, turn my back on him and shuffle around the crease so that, from the grandstand, it might have appeared we were a couple of ballet dancers in a *pas de deux* routine. No stump microphones and no television in those days, which was probably a good idea because he was asking personal questions about my mother and father and I was offering him advice that would have made him a gold medallist in the sexual Olympic Games.

Repartee is good if it is also funny. Some of the things credited to Fred Trueman portray good Yorkshire humour, some are simply things thought up by media who regarded them as a good idea at the time. I liked Colin Cowdrey being flown to Australia as an additional player in 1974 when Dennis Amiss and John Edrich suffered broken bones in the First Test in Brisbane. In the Second Test at the WACA in Perth, Cowdrey batted number three and went in after Brian

Luckhurst was caught by Ashley Mallett in the gully off Max Walker for 27, with the score 44. It was a perfect day and 16,000 spectators watched Cowdrey walk to the centre. The crowd were lively because they were watching some very fast bowling from Jeff Thomson and Dennis Lillee. No one said a word to Colin. After a couple of overs, as 'Thommo' was walking back past the non-striker's end, Colin took a pace towards him, smiled and said, 'Good morning, my name's Cowdrey.' The ultimate disarming remark!

Sometimes you need a sense of humour. In the same game David Lloyd made 49 in the first innings and announced to his fellow players that he could play Thomson with his prick. In the second innings he had made 17 when 'Thommo' got one to rear and the ball smashed his protective box to pieces. When they had air-lifted him back to the England dressing-room his first agonising words through gritted teeth to solicitous team-mates were, 'See, told you I could.'

For straightforward repartee I've always liked David Steele, who Tony Greig brought into the England team in 1975 after he took over the captaincy from Mike Denness. When, in the first innings, Barry Wood was lbw to Dennis Lillee with the score at ten, and the very grey-haired right-hander from Northamptonshire arrived in the centre, it was to hear someone chiding Dennis for not having mentioned his father was playing in the match. It is said Steele looked straight past Rodney Marsh and muttered, 'Take a good look at this arse of mine; you'll see plenty of it this summer.'

Walking, or not walking

Richie Benaud, *My Spin on Cricket*, 2005

In 2003, at the World Cup, Adam Gilchrist walked without waiting for the umpire's decision. Basically that is only a moderate news story but, in this case, it was one which ran, and ran . . . and continues to run.

The New Zealanders toured Australia in 2004 to play two Test matches because the West Indians had reneged on an agreement with Cricket Australia to play three Tests, with Pakistan playing another three. This would make up a normal Australian programme where either five Tests or six would be played in the early part of the summer. Australia won both matches against New Zealand quite easily and the latter part of the match at the 'Gabba was remarkable only for the altercation between Gilchrist and Craig McMillan when the latter was caught behind off a very thin inside edge and waited for the umpire's decision, which was 'not out'. McMillan was out lbw next ball and whatever words were exchanged between the pair then continued to the edge of the boundary at the end of the game, when the teams were smiling and laughing, thanking one another and saying what a great time they'd had over the few days. It turned out later that McMillan had told Gilchrist he was a player who waited for the umpire's decision and then obeyed it. He was not a walker.

I thought the New Zealand captain Stephen Fleming had it right when he said at his press conference that there are a few guys on a walking crusade, but that was unlikely to change the ways of 95 per cent of other cricketers around the world. Fleming said, 'It's still an individual decision. We all like to see the game played in the right spirit but if individuals choose to look at the umpire and have him make the decision, and it's their right to do so, it has to be respected either way.'

Australian captain Ricky Ponting was of the opinion that Gilchrist's walking decisions and opinions didn't put pressure on his own team-mates or on the opposition players. Ponting said, 'Adam doesn't expect any Australian player to walk, so he can't expect it of any of the opposition players either. They've got to make up their own minds if they're going to walk or not and do what they think is best for them and their team.'

It's nothing new for walking to be a contentious subject in cricket.

Walking, or not walking, has been around as long as the game of cricket has existed. So too has been the stricture, sometimes disregarded, that no one should ever do anything on the field that could in any way be derogatory to an umpire. Of those two aspects of the modern-day argument, I strongly favour the latter. It's a question of how you were brought up by parents, mentors, captains or advisers. My upbringing was always to respect the umpires and to do exactly as they said, whether it was out or not out.

My father instilled in me that if I were batting, and there was an appeal made against me, the first thing I had to do, instantly, was look at the umpire whose job it was to make the decision. Then obey instantly whatever decision had been given. No hesitation and certainly nothing that might in any way allow the spectators to believe the umpire could have made a mistake.

Walking was very much an English thing and part of it was that umpires in England, standing in county matches, were almost always ex-players. They knew those taking part in the matches through having played with or against them in previous times and a batsman who didn't walk was soon known around the circuit in that regard.

Australians tended to remain of the view that they should obey whatever the umpire said and that generally decisions evened up over a time. The argument has often been produced by batsmen that they have been on the end of poor decisions; sometimes say three on the trot. Two of those might have been inside edges on to the pad and the umpire's finger was raised for lbw and the batsman had to go. Then next time at bat he was given out caught down the legside when in fact the ball had flicked his thigh pad and there had been no bat contact. The argument went on that if, in his next innings, he feathered a ball outside off stump and to a half-hearted appeal was given not out, should he have walked?

In 1961 I captained the Australian team to England and walking was a public issue. Would the Australians walk was one of the many questions at the commencement of the tour which took place immediately after the Tied Test series in Australia. When Neil Harvey (vice-captain), Colin McDonald (third selector) and I had a meeting on board the ship a few days out of England, we decided there were in fact far more important things than the walking question to be put at the top of our agenda.

At the press conference on arrival I stressed the team would be endeavouring to play the most attractive cricket possible for the spectators at the ground, television viewers, radio listeners and readers of newspapers. We would try to do this by bowling our overs as quickly as possible, moving smartly between overs and not wasting any time. If we batted first in the games against the counties we would be trying to close our innings on the first evening, we hoped to be able to set challenges for the opposition and receive challenges from them. We would not be worried about losing any of those matches and we would definitely not be using the lead-up games to the Test simply for practice, as had been done in 1956.

On walking, it would be a matter for each individual in the team to make up his own mind. I said some of the team had decided to walk; others had been brought up to wait for the umpire's decision and accept it without demur. We did stress, and it was noted in *Wisden* 1962 in the summing up of the tour, that on controversial issues we intended to leave matters entirely in the hands of the umpires. Additionally *Wisden* said, 'Encouraged by Benaud, the Australians never queried an umpire's decision and, at times, when they knew they had touched a ball, did not wait to be given out but went their way, as did the England players. Moreover the Australians formed a high opinion of the ability of the English umpires, especially J. S. Buller.'

For my part, I had made up my mind to walk. When we played Sussex at Hove just before the First Test I was out for a duck in the first innings, caught at short backward-square off medium-pacer Ian Thomson. On the last day we had an exciting contest going, with Colin McDonald making runs and looking for victory when I went out to bat. Ronnie Bell was bowling; he was a left-arm orthodox spinner and was bowling into the rough and spinning away to slip. I tried to drive him and the ball landed in the rough and spun to Alan Oakman, who dived to his left and caught it amid shouts of joy from the fielders. Instinctively, on the shouts, I had turned and taken a pace to the pavilion when suddenly I thought, 'Hell, I didn't hit that.' I also thought instantly of the headlines had the Australian captain turned and walked back to the crease. So I kept walking, out for a pair, but not out and unable to do anything about it.

We managed an exciting draw, one wicket in hand, Norman O'Neill unable to bat, nine runs needed and Colin McDonald 116 not out. Half an hour later the players of the two teams were having a drink at the bar before we caught the train to Birmingham and the Sussex chaps were laughing their heads off asking why I had walked when the ball had clearly missed the bat by inches. All I could do was laugh with them, say it was a long story and would they like another beer?

The crunch question of walking really comes down to a scenario of Australia in possession of the Ashes. One match all in the last of the five matches in the series. Australia, deep in trouble, have lost nine second-innings wickets and the final over of the match is being bowled with fieldsmen crouched around the defending batsman. If England take a wicket the Ashes are theirs after eighteen years. The Australian batsman plays a flurried defensive stroke, he knows there was the faintest feather touch on his glove, but no one else does and there is only a very half-hearted appeal from one close-in fieldsman when the ball is caught via the pad. The umpire takes his time. Does the batsman walk?

I know that is a difficult question but it is also a perfect scenario to use as an example in these days when technology plays such a big part in decision-making in the commentary boxes. There will be different opinions on the answer to the question posed. Whether technology can ever be geared to be completely accurate and provide extremely fast decision is another matter, as is the question of walking.

The Spirit of Cricket in Australia
Richie Benaud, *My Spin on Cricket*, 2005

Much has been achieved between Australian administrators and cricketers in the past ten years. These days there is a good blend of knowledge of what is needed to run the game in businesslike fashion and mix it with a good knowledge of what goes on in the centre of the ground.

Having seen cricket administration in Australia over fifty-seven years, the improvement is dramatic and more than welcome, as is the fact that Cricket Australia and the Australian Cricketers' Association have also taken a constructive path with the Spirit of Cricket.

The Spirit of Cricket is an initiative which started in England when Colin Cowdrey and Ted Dexter in the late 1990s were trying to find a method of reminding the players that the game had twofold aims involving playing to the Laws and also the Spirit of Cricket. I was asked to deliver the first UK Spirit of Cricket Cowdrey Lecture at Lord's in 2001. I'm in good company because the next three years saw Barry Richards, Sunil Gavaskar and Clive Lloyd deliver the lectures, with Geoff Boycott listed for 2005.

Cricket Australia followed the UK lead and instituted the Benaud Spirit of Cricket Awards in Australia. Around the cricket world there are many more famous cricket families but none who loved the game more, nor were more pleased to be associated with it. My father, Lou, was a fine cricketer at country and then Central Cumberland first-grade club level, my brother John played for Cumberland, NSW, then captained NSW and played Test cricket, hitting a century in his last Test in Australia. I had thirteen years at Test level and fifteen in the first-class game.

Cricket Australia in their announcement said:

Teams adjudged by the umpires as having best displayed the true spirit, traditions and values associated with cricket are recognised each season in Australia with the Benaud Spirit of Cricket Awards. The awards were first handed down in 2003–04 to reflect the influence and stature of the Benaud family in Australian cricket, and they underline Cricket Australia's commitment to the spirit of cricket, a concept outlined in the recently drafted preamble to the Laws of Cricket.

In 2003 Cricket Australia's contracted players wrote a code that represents the spirit in which they seek to play the game. It reads:

As cricketers who represent Australia we acknowledge and embrace 'The Spirit of Cricket' and the Laws of our game.

This Players' Spirit of Australian Cricket serves as a guide to the shared standards of behaviour that we expect of ourselves and the values we hold.

Our on-field behaviour –

We play our cricket hard but fair and accept all umpiring decisions as a mark of respect for our opponents, the umpires, ourselves and the game.

We view positive play, pressure, body language and banter between opponents and ourselves as legitimate tactics and integral parts of the competitive nature of cricket.

We do not condone or engage in sledging or any other conduct that constitutes personal abuse.

We encourage the display of passion and emotion as a sign of our enjoyment and pride in the game, as a celebration of our achievements and as a sign of respect for our opponents.

Our off-field behaviour –

It is acknowledged that we have a private life to lead but understand our off-field conduct has the potential to reflect either positively or adversely on us as individuals and also on the game of cricket.

We consider off-field conduct that may be likely to warrant legitimate public criticism to be unacceptable conduct.

Our team –

We take pride in our sense of the importance of the team and acknowledge the role of the team captain and our direct support staff. We demonstrate this by displaying loyalty and compassion to each other, by accepting our role as mentors and by supporting each other to abide by these values.

We value honesty and accept that every member of the team has a role to play in shaping, and abiding by our shared standards and expectations.

We strive to be regarded as the best team in the world. We measure this by our on-field achievements and by exploring ways in which we might continue to 'raise the bar' in respect of our own professionalism.

We acknowledge and follow the traditions of our game while encouraging and accepting experimentation that will enable us to create our own traditions and history. We do this in the expectation that we will leave the game in a better shape than it was before we arrived.

Our opponents –

We acknowledge and respect that our opponents may hold different cultural values and beliefs from our own, and value the diversity and richness this adds to the game.

By treating our opponents with dignity and forging bonds of mutual respect, we will overcome any cultural barriers.

Our supporters –

We value our supporters and acknowledge those who support our opponents and the game of cricket. We demonstrate commitment to our supporters by always giving our best and demonstrating leadership in everything we do.

Our family –

We value the contribution and sacrifices of our families that enable us to meet these expectations.

Respect –

We respect the governing bodies of the game, our support teams in every capacity and our players' association. We demonstrate this respect by seeking and offering frank and open communication in accordance with the Players' Spirit of Australian Cricket.

No place for violence
Richie Benaud, *Over But Not Out*, 2010

Finally, a gentle reminder concerning the Spirit of Cricket.

The Laws of Cricket have been around a long time. They are occasionally changed, most times for the better, occasionally not so.

When Ted Dexter and Colin Cowdrey started talking about a Preamble to the Laws of Cricket, to be named 'The Preamble – The

Spirit of Cricket', their determination was to keep it as simple as possible. That is one reason the Preamble is fewer than 500 words.

Although the whole of the Preamble is important, I have always said that the most important aspects come in Paragraph 1 and Paragraph 6.

Paragraph 1 reads:

Responsibility of captains

The captains are responsible at all times for ensuring that play is conducted within the Spirit of the Game as well as within the Laws.

Paragraph 6 reads:

Violence

There is no place for any act of violence on the field of play.

In my view, if there is any form of violence on the field of play or the laying of a hand by one player on another, the player or players responsible for this should be fined double their relevant match fee and suspended for four matches in the same type of match in which the offence occurred. The captains of the suspended players should be suspended for two matches in the same type of match in which the offence occurred.

Having a look for myself
Richie Benaud, *Over But Not Out*, 2010

In 1975 I was approached, at the conclusion of the World Cup and the four Tests between England and Australia in England, to see if I would be prepared to play in or take part in a private tour of South

Africa. Playing was out of the question because of a bad back and a determination to retire completely from that side of the game, and I had always sworn, having been a player and seen what troubles and stress they cause managers, that I would never, under any circumstances, become a manager, so I sensibly declined the offer. However, with two distinct areas of pressure being applied to me, I began to have second thoughts. One pressure group was constantly telling me South Africa were doing *all* the right things, which was rubbish; the other group told me only critical things about the country. I decided to have a look for myself and make up my own mind.

I laid down various conditions before I would finally accept the invitation. I stipulated that, except in members' stands at the various grounds, audiences must be allowed to mix freely and that bars, other than in the members' stand, must be open to all. I insisted on complete freedom to meet any non-white cricket officials I wished whilst in the country, and told the organisers of the tour I would be the sole selector of the International Wanderers team. I added a little rider as well: every time a South African opposition team walked on to the field, there were to be three non-white players included. The latter proviso could easily have been a problem, not for the obvious reason, but because everyone at the time was talking about selection on merit. The difference was that, even though on the surface there were no Basil D'Oliveiras hidden away ready to be selected on merit, I was interested to see if we might unearth one or two. There was an additional note that if the conditions weren't adhered to, we would all make our various ways home!

There were two occasions when I had to make it clear that these conditions would be invoked unless certain matters were attended to. They both took place in Port Elizabeth but were of completely different character and concerned both black and white. The first was on the morning of a one-day match, when one of the local black administrators came to see me to say he had been refused service at the bar at the back of the stand. I had an agreement with those running the tour that if anyone had trouble of this kind they would find me and let me have the details.

I went to look for the local officials in charge of the match, and together we went to find the chief of police who had created the problem. Built like a country barn, his opening remark was that he didn't care what I thought and he would continue doing exactly as he wished. However, after a short discussion during which I told him he could either be amenable or famous, he said he would reconsider and could definitely make the necessary arrangements.

I thanked him and mentioned he had instantly reduced to zero the chance of me and all my players catching the following day's plane out of Johannesburg for points east or west.

> ❝My every waking moment was spent working out how to win cricket matches. Now I suddenly find that around the cricket world there are b------- who spend every waking moment working out how to lose cricket matches.❞
>
> *RB on the Hansie Cronje match-fixing scandal*

The same night, at a post-match reception at the ground, one of the white South African selectors, smarting bitterly under the defeat of the day, told the world that it was the last bloody time they would allow themselves to be forced into choosing three non-white players. In future it was going to be a test of strength. When the teams got to Johannesburg, South Africa would have their best possible team in the field and they would carve up bloody Lillee and stuff the rest of them, including me.

It only took moments to sort that out, with the same wording as the morning misunderstanding, but I waited until the right moment in Jo'burg to let Dennis know about it. He took 7–27 against the South African XI and gave the crowd a rare moment of cricketing joy with some of the finest fast bowling seen at the Wanderers. It would have been better had he been able to bowl out the little dark-haired batsman who showed enormous courage against him and refused to give an inch. This was Tieffie Barnes and he showed a rare brand of fight in combating Lillee and the other International Wanderers bowlers. I saw Tieffie again in 1994 when Channel Nine covered the Australian tour in South Africa. He looked very well and still plays a part in cricket in South Africa these days.

One of the best efforts on the tour came from left-arm spin bowler Baboo Ebrahim. The Wanderers were set 348 to make in the last innings of the Durban match and he bowled superbly as South Africa charged to victory by a margin of 122 runs.

Not the least interesting of the off-field confrontations was the meeting mentioned earlier with Prime Minister Vorster, Dr Piet Koornhof and Joe Pamensky in Parliament House, Cape Town, during our stay in that city. It would be an exaggeration to say, because of his general bonhomie and goodwill, Mr Vorster made a lasting impression on me, though he did deliver a speech, as though on the hustings, to let me know visitors to South Africa were expected to conform to the laws of the land. All I could do was reply that if I found any of my pre-tour conditions were not being adhered to, then I would remember his thoughts on the laws of his land and go home, and my players would go with me.

He heard it, but I doubt if it registered. It was an interesting experience to have someone talking *at* you, rather than *to* you, verbally poking you in the chest whilst never able to bring himself to catch your eye.

12
Limited-Overs Cricket

If any form of game can pull 20,000 spectators into a game of cricket, it's great for the sport. I think it's wonderful.

Richie Benaud on Twenty20

The long and the short of it
Richie Benaud, *Anything But . . . an Autobiography*, 1998

Right from the time I saw my first proper limited-overs competition I loved the style of game. I have been accused in recent years of being too supportive of the modern game and its players, and particularly of one-day cricket, a criticism I regard as nonsense. Cricket means only one thing to those who deeply and desperately hate the one-day game: that matches must be played over a long period, as has been the case since Test matches began.

It has been put to me by cricketing zealots that the only way to save the game is for those who care about cricket and its rich tradition to join in depriving others of the chance to watch the shortened version. This attitude is perfectly straightforward and patronising, suggesting that one group of people knows what is best for another group. Their belief is that, if most limited-overs matches were removed from the cricket calendar, the cricket-watching public would eventually abandon limited-overs cricket, restoring Test cricket to its sole dominant place in the game.

Well, I won't have a bar of that. I believe Test cricket is the best form of the game anyway, but I do add a rider: it needs to be good

Test cricket. Since limited-overs cricket became part of the modern-day game, there has been a lot of good cricket at Test level and there have been many splendid one-day or day-night matches.

The argument is used to me that people will always remember a wonderful and close finish in a Test, whereas they will be pushed to talk at length about a pulsating finish in a limited-overs game. So what? When limited-overs matches came into vogue, no one claimed it was about to take the place of the Tied Test or the Old Trafford match when Australia beat England, nor, in modern times, the Edgbaston game in 1997 when England triumphed over Australia, or the 1981 Test at Headingley, Botham's match. I don't sit down in the evening with a glass of Chablis and start nattering about the day Viv Richards hit that wonderful century in Melbourne in the day-night game, nor the times there have been more than 50,000 spectators at the MCG for a limited-overs clash. But, and it is an important note, I haven't forgotten them.

We are living in a different era, a different world. It has been said to me that if God had meant us to be playing cricket at night he would originally have decreed cricket balls to be white. They *are* white, in fact, until those who run the game colour them red.

To some it was a crushing disappointment that Sir Donald Bradman should have given even the slightest hint of approval to limited-overs cricket when, twelve years ago, he wrote his thoughtful article in the 1986 edition of *Wisden*. Perhaps the disappointment is reflected in the fact that very few of the hardcore traditionalists quote from the article but often tell you the game isn't the same since Bradman stopped playing and Test matches began to be mixed up with what they call the one-day rubbish.

Sir Donald wrote that there was a stirring of emotions at the limited-overs game from those of a new and largely young audience, who yell and scream their support, and those dyed-in-the-wool lovers of Test cricket, who yearn for more peaceful, bygone days. He pointed out that, as with so many things, reconciliation between the factions is well-nigh impossible. And he added that, despite a deep feeling for the traditional form of cricket, his conviction was that we must accept we live in a new era.

He correctly noted the Achilles' heel of the limited-overs game, that premium is placed on defensive bowling and negative and defensive field-placings, so one can be bored by countless singles being taken with no slips and five men on the boundary. He pointed out that the limited-overs contest has done something else: it has got rid of the unutterable bore who thinks occupancy of the crease and his own personal aggrandisement are all that matter. He commented on the lift in the standard of fielding, and that running between the wickets has taken on a new dimension. Risks must be taken to maintain a run-rate.

As one might expect from Bradman, it was a perfectly balanced article and, more important, a constructive one. As a matter of interest, he suggested there would be no loss of face or pride if television were to be used to assist umpires in run-outs, stumpings or disputed catches, though it would not be possible to use the method in lbw appeals. All this he wrote twelve years ago. As has often been the case with Bradman, he was well in advance of others in their thinking on the game.

Four games to remember
Richie Benaud, *My Spin on Cricket*, 2005

It is possible to have a boring Test match but easier to have a boring one-day match because, if the team batting first suffers a collapse, then spectators and viewers on television will most times have a good idea of the result. Not always though. I have seen more Test cricket than most and I have, as well, seen more one-day cricket than most, though I didn't play it for NSW and Australia. More's the pity. I would have loved to be part of the tactical ploys, the big hitting, the brilliant fielding and trying to deceive the batsmen with legspin.

I've watched a lot of exciting games, with all their twists and turns, and four stand out of the pack. One of those was the first World Cup final [in 1975], with West Indies the victors over Australia at Lord's. Clive Lloyd hit a century, Viv Richards ran out three Australians and Alvin Kallicharran two, and Dennis Lillee and Jeff Thomson battled hard at the end but weren't quite good enough to hold out the Windies. This was the longest day's cricket in the history of the game, lasting from 11 a.m. to shortly before 9 p.m.

In 1984 at Old Trafford I watched one of the more remarkable games I had seen to that time and the key men were Vivian Richards and Michael Holding. It was a good batting pitch but there had been enough sweating under the covers overnight to add to the cloudy morning and to allow the England attack to rip through the West Indies. Bob Willis, Ian Botham, Neil Foster, Derek Pringle and offspinner Geoff Miller were too much for the visitors and, at 102–7, Viv Richards had played a lone hand. He had some assistance from that underrated allrounder Eldine Baptiste, who helped in adding 49, but it was still tough going when Holding came in at 166–9. At least, if the last wicket fell quickly, the bowlers would still have something at which they could aim, even though the sun breaking through the clouds was going to be in favour of England.

Richards and Holding shared a partnership of 106, with Michael making 12 and facing only 27 deliveries. He showed skilful defence and a keen appreciation of how to take the quick single if Viv generously allowed him to face a ball. Viv, at the other end, was simply magnificent and those at the ground or watching BBC Television had the treat of their lives. Not out 189 from only 170 balls is what it says on paper, but that doesn't go even part of the way to confirming the dominance of one batsman over the opposition, even though he was playing beautiful strokes, rather than bludgeoning the bowlers. It was an innings I'll never forget, nor will others at the ground or watching on television, including the man who was for the most part an interested onlooker from the non-striker's end.

One of the best limited-overs cricketers ever to walk on to a cricket ground is the Australian Michael Bevan who, over the years, has done some extraordinary things in the shortened version of the game. He used to play for NSW, now he has moved to Tasmania and is still very much in the business of winning matches for his new state, though not for Australia because the Australian selectors have given him the push. He showed he hadn't lost his touch in 2004–05 when he guided 'Tassie' to victory over Queensland in the ING final at the 'Gabba with a typical decisive innings of 47 not out.

Two of the most memorable innings he has played in this form of the game were in different competitions, one against the West Indies in a Sydney match when he was still in the Australian team. This first game [in 1995–96] was a low-scoring affair in slightly damp conditions, with West Indies making 172–9 after the game had been reduced to 43 overs a side, maximum. Carl Hooper made 93 of those runs in a very good attacking innings and Shane Warne took three wickets to contain the Windies to the reasonable target. West Indies bowlers just steamrollered Australia and had them 74–7 and looking for all the world a beaten side. Then Paul Reiffel made 34 out of an 83-run partnership and another two quick wickets had Glenn McGrath coming out to join Bevan in the final over. Roger Harper was to bowl it with the score 167–9 and McGrath somehow pushed a single to give Bevan the strike. Four were needed from the last ball and Bevan, as he always did, had his areas picked out depending on where the ball pitched. It went back past Harper at a rate of knots and finished under the sightscreen to provide a magnificent victory; a typical Bevan effort, timed to perfection.

In the World Cup in 2003 in South Africa, he conjured up a win from nowhere, one that left Michael Vaughan's England side flattened by the manner in which they had snatched defeat from those well-known jaws of victory. England made most of the running in this game played at Port Elizabeth on a very ordinary pitch. They did very well to make 204–8, although the Australian, Andy Bichel, turned in a sensational all-round performance of which he could be very proud. Nick Knight and Marcus Trescothick added 66 for the opening partnership, Andy Flintoff and Alec Stewart shared 90, with Flintoff making 45 and Stewart 46, but then Bichel, in an extraordinary last few overs of his permitted ten, finished up with 7–20. It didn't do the Australians much good because they quickly lost wickets until Darren Lehmann and Bevan pulled things around with a 63-run stand. Then three wickets fell for almost nothing and, when Bevan walked across to Bichel on his way out from the dressing-room, 69 were still needed.

Bichel hit 34 of those from 36 balls faced. Bevan controlled the bowlers with exquisite touches and their partnership was worth 73 and the game was won with three balls remaining. Bevan has the attribute of being able to bring mild panic to opposition teams because they know he is able to turn what seems a certain loss into an extraordinary victory. So it was this day in Port Elizabeth and it effectively put England out of the World Cup.

The limited-overs game that amused and thrilled me more than any other, though, was the 1999 semi-final at Edgbaston between Australia and South Africa. Steve Waugh had hit a century in the match between the two teams four days before the semi; that match was played at Headingley and was a high-scoring affair, with Waugh being dropped by Herschelle Gibbs, who was celebrating the catch before it was properly in his hands. Hence Waugh's alleged throwaway line of, '*You've just dropped the World Cup, Herschelle . . .*' The semi-final at Edgbaston was a much tighter affair than the match at Leeds, with Australia making only 213, Steve Waugh 56, Michael Bevan 65, and Shaun Pollock turned in a wonderful bowling performance of 5–36. Then South Africa several times looked as though they would make the runs in comfort. It was Shane Warne who turned it around for Australia after Gary Kirsten and Gibbs had added 48 and Jacques Kallis had made a very good 53. Warne bowled magnificently this day, but then it looked as though Lance Klusener would certainly win it for South Africa with some astonishing strokes off Damien Fleming's final over. The amusing side of things came in that final over with Klusener, having clubbed 31 from only 16 balls faced, being involved in the most extraordinary and completely unnecessary mix-up with South African number eleven, Allan Donald. This resulted in Donald being run out, still with two balls remaining in the over. Thus the semi-final was tied and the Australians, being ahead of South Africa in the Super Six table because of net run-rate, therefore went through to the final, where they beat Pakistan. The run-out was on a par with me running out Alan Davidson in the Tied Test in Brisbane, no sense in it at all. On reflection, my running-out of 'Davo' was not good cricket; South Africa's run-out at Edgbaston was unbelievably bad cricket. Fleming on the other hand performed with great skill and common sense. Taking the flick throw from Mark Waugh, he made certain there could be no way out for South Africa by rolling the ball along the pitch to wicketkeeper Gilchrist.

It is true that a thrilling Test match will stay in the memory for a long time because it is played over five days and the ebbs and flows of each day, rather than one day, will make a difference. The great thing about modern-day cricket for me, though, is that you can have excitement in both Test cricket and limited-overs cricket, and that will continue to be the case around the world. Never forget as well that only 50-overs-a-side limited-overs cricket can properly prepare teams for the World Cup. Anything less than that will be worth nothing by way of preparation.

The future of the one-day game

Richie Benaud, *Over But Not Out*, 2010

I may have seen more Twenty20 cricket than most people because I was around when the first proper game was played in England in 2003. It was a match at Chester-le-Street between Durham and Nottinghamshire and it finished in a win for the host team; the margin was 'five balls remaining'. I saw excerpts of it on television. Three days later I was at Trent Bridge for Nottinghamshire to host Lancashire. It was something different. Trent Bridge had laid on the entertainment, some dancing girls, who seemed to be having a hell of a time, as did the people who had paid their money at the gate. The ground holds, or held at that time, 15,000 spectators; there were 16,000 in attendance that evening.

They had come out of their offices at five o'clock, bought a packet of sandwiches, a few cans of beer for their mates, stepped on to the bus they had specially organised with a non-drinking driver and been driven to the

> ❝As long as the people who run the game have brains and keep three forms of the game I think it will be terrific.❞
>
> *RB on Twenty20*

parking area at the football ground next to the cricket ground. They watched the match, which was a very lively one, cheered their local heroes, returned to their bus and they were back in their villages or towns half an hour after the conclusion of the game. It was a daytime match put on for the people, on the basis that the hours of twilight in the United Kingdom offer the opportunity to have spectators come to the ground to watch 40 overs of quick-fire cricket after they have finished work.

It was regarded then as *not* being what you would call 'proper cricket', in the same way as when one-day cricket began in England in 1963. That was sneered at by some administrators who said rather wearily that they supposed they had better put it on but not many people would bother going to see it. That soon changed after an action-packed competition brought in big crowds, engendering great enthusiasm, and 25,000 spectators crammed into Lord's for the final between Sussex and Worcestershire. *Wisden* said of the first year:

> The new Knock-out competition aroused enormous interest. Very large crowds, especially in the later rounds, flocked to the matches and 25,000 spectators watched the final at Lord's where Sussex narrowly defeated Worcestershire by 14 runs in a thoroughly exciting match. It says much for this type of cricket that tremendous feeling was stirred up among the spectators as well as the cricketers with numerous ties being decided in the closest fashion. At Lord's, supporters wore favours and banners were also in evidence, the whole scene resembling an Association Football Cup Final more than the game of cricket and many thousands invaded the pitch at the finish to cheer Dexter, the Sussex captain, as he received a Gillette Trophy from the M.C.C. President, Lord Nugent.
>
> Sussex emphasised their superiority in the one-day game when they beat the West Indies by four wickets in a Challenge match at Hove on September 12.
>
> There were two points which invite criticism. Firstly, the majority of counties were loath to include even one slow bowler in their sides and relied mainly on pace and secondly the placing of the entire field

around the boundary to prevent rapid scoring – Dexter used this tactic in the Final – became fairly common. The success of the spinners at Lord's may have exploded the first theory.

There is no doubt that provided the Competition is conducted wisely it will attract great support in the future and benefit the game accordingly.

Since then, the one-day format has indeed attracted great support and benefited the game, yet recently there has sometimes been a campaign, mostly by the print media, to denigrate 50-overs-a-side Internationals and have them removed from the international cricket programme. This will best be countered by having, for the most part, good exciting matches for spectators at the ground or watching on television. Unfortunately, the problems associated with the 2007 World Cup in the Caribbean provided those critical of the 50-over game with plenty of ammunition. The tournament in the West Indies was an appalling piece of mismanagement by the ICC and their officials, and the Caribbean islands were done a complete disservice. I quailed when I saw the prices for admission tickets, and a listing of food and drink prices inside the grounds, which can simply be put down to monetary greed. It was done on the basis that it was a World Cup and that people would be desperate to get a seat and would pay anything for the 'privilege'. Only when the local organisers showed a little common sense and dropped the prices did reasonable crowds turn up. As it was, there was more than US$30 million in ticket revenue. The fact that many could not pay the prices of admission, and were not permitted to take their own food and drink into the ground, meant that a great deal of the wonderful Caribbean flavour of cricket was lost, not only at the grounds but also on television.

13
Technology

‘Richie never morphed into an old-school bore ... He admired the modern player; he loved Twenty20 and all the technological advances – especially his beloved Snicko.’

Mike Atherton, *The Times*

DRS and neutral umpires
Richie Benaud, *Over But Not Out*, 2010

The referral system is still very much a long work in progress at the time I am writing this paragraph. There has been a great deal said about it by a number of people, including players, captains, ex-players, ex-captains and a wide variety of media people, some of whom have played cricket, others who have not played but have watched a myriad of matches.

As might be expected, Ricky Ponting has a sensible approach, sharing my view that the trialling of the system should have taken place in one-day or T20 matches before being used in the Test arena. At the time, he was talking about the Australia v West Indies Second Test of the series in 2009 and he noted that the game just completed at the Adelaide Oval had been marred by inconsistency and then the departure of Mark Benson. There had been media speculation that Benson had returned to the UK because of the Decision Review System, which Benson categorically denied. In fact, he had been unwell at the start of the match and was to undergo a series of medical assessments. At the time he had not resigned as an elite panel umpire.

Ponting met with the umpires and stressed he was supportive of the system itself and felt that in the end it would have a good impact on the game. He talked with the umpires in Adelaide concerning additional technology which might be used, but stressed again that once the system was trialled comprehensively it would be for the good of the game. He said, 'We're all still coming to terms with it and the more we play with it the more we'll appreciate it.'

Ponting received backing from match referee Chris Broad in Adelaide, with the ICC representative saying the system itself needed reviewing. 'The use of technology is long overdue and this is the start of the process, but any new tool that comes into the game of cricket takes a while for everyone to understand the way forward,' Broad said.

One of the very best articles I read was from one of the finest umpires I have watched, Peter Willey, an Englishman. He was a good cricketer and when he became an umpire he had the respect of those who were playing. He eventually retired because of the time he had to be away from his own country, the system being that you are not permitted to officiate in matches in which your own country is participating.

It is one of the quaint things about cricket these days that an umpire like Simon Taufel, recognised as being the best in cricket, is unable to umpire in Test matches where the Australians are playing. When they brought in the concept of 'neutral' umpires I found the idea amusing, even though it was also insulting to umpires like Taufel, suggesting, as it did, that they would be biased towards their own country. When I played and captained, the two best umpires I knew were Syd Buller from England and Colin Egar from Australia. Buller started with Yorkshire as a youngster then moved to Worcestershire, where he played for eleven years and was county coach for four years before becoming an umpire. I first saw him in 1956 when he officiated at Trent Bridge in the First Test and at

Headingley in the third game of the series. Then, when I first worked for BBC Radio in 1960 when the South Africans toured England, Syd Buller stood in the Second Test at Lord's. Geoff Griffin, the South African pace bowler, was called eleven times for illegal bowling by Frank Lee, the umpire standing at square-leg. In a match arranged after the early finish to the Test, Buller called Griffin for the same offence. The bizarre follow-up to this was that Lee then umpired the following Test at Trent Bridge with Charlie Elliott; Buller was objected to by the South Africans and so didn't stand in the final Test at The Oval. Quaint, bizarre, stupid, take your pick.

Fortunately Buller umpired in 1961 when I captained the Australian side to England and we formed a very high opinion of him, Charlie Elliott, John Langridge, Eddie Phillipson and Frank Lee throughout the five-match series.

Two of those umpires, Buller and Phillipson, umpired in the first match of the tour against Worcestershire and they came to me with a very sensible and interesting piece of information before the start of play on the opening day. This was to the effect they had received advice that the English authorities intended to bring in a front-foot no-ball Law as an experiment. They told me the umpires had met and that in all the Test matches, and in other games where the Australians were taking part, they would be working off the back foot, trying to ensure the bowler's front foot landed somewhere on the batting crease. They would advise the bowlers when they were going a bit too far but would only no-ball a bowler for a blatant over-stepping.

A common-sense approach, which unfortunately in life these days, is not all that common.

There was only one no-ball bowled in the five Test matches; that was by Fred Trueman in the opening Test at Edgbaston. In all on that tour, with the common sense applied by the umpires, we played thirty-seven matches, one against the Club Cricket Conference, two

against Ireland, one against Scotland and one against Minor
Counties. There were thirty-two first-class matches including the
five Tests. In all those thirty-seven matches there were fifty-three
no-balls bowled during the whole six-month-long tour. And then
they brought in the worst Law of cricket ever produced, the front-
foot Law. A statistic of some consequence is that from 1876–77
until 1968–69 in Test cricket fewer than 5,000 no-balls were bowled.
Between 1969–70 and 2010 there were more than 30,000 no-balls
bowled.

Peter Willey suggested there may come a time when television
technicians responsible for providing the pictures for referrals will
need to be 'neutral', as is the case with the umpires. He also said that
increased use of technology has posed problems for umpires because
they have lost the art of being able to make run-out judgements. The
reason for that, he argues, is that the umpires never have to bother
because run-outs are now always referred. In his wide-ranging article
in *Wisden Cricket Monthly* he suggested it would be a good idea to
increase the number of Test match officials and have them standing
in only one Test in each series. There is certainly merit in that, as it
would make certain that if an umpire had an 'ordinary' match, he
didn't then have to back up again the next week. Willey added that
the more technology is brought into the umpiring part of the game,
the more umpires will relate simply to referrals rather than their own
split-second judgement.

There are many umpires who will definitely agree with Willey,
which brings me back to the ridiculous situation of the best umpires
not being able to stand in Test matches in their own country. Why
for heaven's sake can't that be overturned now that the ICC have
decided to use technology in this fashion and to this extent, where
referrals are the norm and the fielding and batting teams are allowed
to choose their moments to object to a decision? The ICC Committee
will have to make up their minds: is technology the only answer to

umpiring problems and, in fact, are those problems being magnified in order that technology can take over?

Somehow the two items should be intertwined so we have the best umpires standing plus the technology to back them up.

14
Board Games

Gilbert and Sullivan at their very best could hardly have done better.

Richie Benaud on an early experience with
the Australian Board of Control

The Barnes business
Richie Benaud, *My Spin on Cricket*, 2005

Although Australian administrators are occasionally put through the wringer in these modern times, they are light years better than in those far-off days of administrators versus cricketers. Then Australia's first-class cricketers were subservient to administration, and those in charge of it, and the administrators were not merely the gentlemen of the game but didn't mind letting you know that was the situation.

The one outstanding case in Australian administration in a file marked 'Appalling' remains vetoing the selection of opening batsman Sid Barnes in the aftermath of the invincibles tour of England in 1948. Barnes was chosen by the Australian selectors to play in the Third Test of the series against the West Indies in Adelaide in 1951–52, but his selection was refused by the Australian Board of Control, a move they hoped and believed would remain a secret.

When the Australian team had assembled without Barnes, the twelve consisted of Lindsay Hassett (captain), Arthur Morris (vice-captain), Jim Burke, Neil Harvey, Keith Miller, Graeme Hole, Ray Lindwall, Ian Johnson, Doug Ring, Gil Langley, Bill Johnston and

Geff Noblet – a good team with a balanced look about it. That idyllic state of balance lasted only until the practice the day before the game was due to start when Lindsay Hassett slightly strained a muscle in his hip and pulled out of the side on the morning of the match. The match itself involved an unusual arrangement as regards dates because it was played over the Christmas break and was scheduled to begin on Saturday, 22 December. There was no play on Sunday, 23 December, play resumed on 24 December and the match concluded on Christmas Day. The selectors chose Phil Ridings, a fine cricketer, as Hassett's replacement. However, not every single Board member around Australia was able to be contacted by telephone when doing his very important Saturday morning shopping, so what did they do? Well, they did something that was unbelievable. You may think they would have had in place a method whereby a small committee, say an executive committee, would have been empowered to ratify any selection changes needed; or the Chairman of the Board invested with some powers, or even the selectors given the responsibility. What, for example, if three players had been injured in a car accident?

As it was, so lacking in foresight were the Board that precisely the same twelve players as originally named *had* to represent Australia with what was now a very unbalanced line-up. Hassett had to be twelfth man even though he couldn't field and Lindwall was batting at number six. It was a crass piece of administration. The players knew it and the public knew it, but it made no difference. West Indies won the match by six wickets.

This was the same season I made my Test debut against West Indies in the Fifth Test at the SCG and in the following summer, 1952–53, when the South Africans toured Australia, there was the famous, or infamous, court case where, as a follow-up to being vetoed out of the team, Sid Barnes sued a member of the public, Mr Jacob Raith. Mr Raith, in a letter to a newspaper, had castigated Sid and supported the Board in their vetoing of him, suggesting that they had cause to do so.

Gilbert and Sullivan at their very best could hardly have done better than the Board with the ensuing events. They had started by refusing Barnes's selection but then wouldn't say anything about it and tried to pretend it hadn't happened. It later transpired that when the vote was taken it had been ten–three in favour of excluding Barnes, with Aub Oxlade, Sir Donald Bradman and Frank Cush voting against the motion put to the meeting. Bradman had been captain of the 1948 side which included Barnes as a player; Oxlade and Cush were two of the three NSW delegates. Oxlade later lost his place as Chairman of the Australian Board, and Chapple Dwyer, also of NSW, his position as Australian selector. It was very much, in Australian cricket administration, the night, week and disgraceful year of the long knives.

Furthermore the Board, incredibly, faked the minutes of a meeting in the most extraordinary fashion, producing a document which bore no relation to what had actually happened, and pretended there had been no discussion concerning Barnes and his exclusion.

In the court case, one of the odd happenings was that following the axing of Oxlade and Dwyer, Keith Johnson, the 1948 team manager and NSW Board representative, actually retained his Board place. He had voted against Barnes, had been party to the deception of the doctored minutes of the particular meeting and then, in court, agreed that in his end-of-tour review to the Board, after the 1948 tour, he had given every player, including Barnes, what was termed 'a glowing report'.

Chapple Dwyer, as honest a man as you would find in or out of cricket circles, said in the witness box of Sid, 'I have a high opinion of Barnes as a cricketer and no objection to him as a man.'

When the defence had disintegrated, Raith's Counsel made a statement to the judge and the defending Counsel's words should have reverberated around the walls of Cricket House, and every other administrative room in the land, but I doubt they did so. He said, speaking of the Board's actions and words, 'Seldom in the history of libel actions has such a plea failed so completely and utterly. The Board has presented an awful image of the chaos and bigotry under which Australian cricket is administered.'

No such reverberating happened. If anything the whole issue strengthened the power of the Board in that it could clearly be seen that anyone who had the hide to have a dissenting voice, or even a dissenting thought, may not be absolutely sure of a continuing career in the game.

Some years later, when writing about my own and other young players' thoughts at the time, I said of the Board: 'Those were the days when you spoke with a touch of reverence and a certain amount of humility to cricket officials in their navy blue suits, white shirts and strong leather shoes. Jack might have been as good as his mate in the outback of Australia in the 1800s but it took a while for the idea to permeate through to the various state associations and the Australian Board of Control.'

Prior to the start of that 1952–53 tour by South Africa, the Australian Board had also been in touch with their South African counterparts expressing their grave disquiet about the potential financial horrors of the tour. In South Africa there had been some conjecture about sending the team, and the South African players were hardly given an overwhelming vote of confidence by administrators around Australia. The South African Cricket Board, put under enormous pressure by the Australian Board, after the latter had repeated their disquiet in yet another letter to South Africa, secretly agreed to stand losses on the tour up to a figure of £10,000. No one on the Australian Board of Control bothered mentioning that information to the cricketing public; it was to remain a secretive agreement.

The Board's 'disquiet' is probably a low-key word because those Australian administrators actually feared, and said, the tour would be a complete failure. Among them was Sydney Smith, president of the NSWCA, and he had been charged with the task of proposing the *welcoming* toast to the South Africans at a function in Sydney prior to the match between South Africa and NSW. He spent most of his speech saying how bad South African cricket teams had been over the years. It was a delightfully ironic result that this South African team, led by Jack Cheetham, finished 2–2 with Australia, after a great win in the final Test at the MCG.

Certainly the Australian Board found it a difficult season. Their team had failed to win the series against a South African team rubbished by the Board itself. In the Barnes court case it had been shown that the Board had falsified minutes of a meeting in order to deceive people and, because of their own back-stabbing, they had lost two good men in Oxlade and Dwyer, the latter an outstanding Australian selector.

My international career was only one year old at that stage and I can assure you there was nothing at all comforting about Australian administration at that time.

The boots business

Richie Benaud, *Anything But . . . an Autobiography*, 1998

In 1970 we had the Boots Business in NSW, one of the more extraordinary matters of cricket administration in the time I have been in the game; hilarious, too, in many ways. As it happened, I was in on it right from the start. I was passing through the executive room of the NSW Cricket Association, in the old Members' Stand at the SCG, when a New South Wales player dropped a catch at first slip. Two of those present in the room were NSW delegates to the Australian Cricket Board. Their considered opinion on the matter was, as they conveyed it to me, that the reason the catch had been dropped was because the fieldsman was wearing the new-style boots with the ripple-rubber heels.

These boots were very popular with the players who wore them, and they were widely regarded by sports-medicine experts as being ideal for cricket, because they put far less stress on players' knees and some muscles than conventional boots. They were unpopular with the administrators because they were different, something new. I pointed out that I'd actually worn them and thought they were good, but there was no response: they were too busy talking about the benefits of sturdy boots, made of leather and with solid uppers and spikes in the sole and heel.

The administrators actually banned the NSW team from wearing the boots, and did so the day prior to a match. My brother tried a new pair of the sturdy jobs, and found they blistered his feet. Because he then switched back to the 'spikes in the sole, ripple-heels', he was dropped from the captaincy of the NSW team and from the team for the Southern Tour. One of the team on that tour, John Rogers, wearing the regulation boots which didn't violate any NSWCA by-laws, fell when fielding a ball in the WA second innings, tore ligaments in his ankle and therefore was unable to play in the following game against South Australia at the Adelaide Oval. This little mishap was then highlighted by the fact that South Australia beat the newly shod NSW cricketers by 195 runs, with ten of the 'Sacas' wearing the boots which NSW players were precluded from wearing.

All this was a total nonsense, brought on by an overwhelming and overbearing urge by administrators to stamp their authority on players – nothing new about that in 1970, but it did lead to some interesting aspects in the game and its sidelines.

Syd Webb, QC, was a keen racing man as well as a cricket administrator and, as noted earlier, he had been my team manager in 1961. He was surprised, shocked, and maybe even appalled, when he found that Australian cricket teams touring England had been traditionally known by English cricket followers as Darling's team, Noble's team, Gregory's team, Armstrong's team, Collins's team, Woodfull's team and Bradman's team. That had continued after Bradman with Hassett and Johnson and it was hardly likely to change with Benaud, no matter what the legal stature of the manager or his position as an administrator in Australia. When the Board, or rather those with a feel for these things, sent Ray Steele as assistant manager in 1961, it turned out they knew more than I did. The phrase, 'it's the Board's team not the captain's' has a memorable ring to it to this day.

Syd and I finished up OK, but we had our moments during that 1961 tour, with his claim prior to the Second Test that the Board had instructed him to take over all media announcements. The ensuing 'gagging of the captain' provided a lot of amusement for many people, but not quite as much for me because I was having awful problems with my shoulder and was trying to get fit for the Lord's Test.

Nine years later, in 1970, Syd was Chairman of the NSWCA Executive, and along with Alan Barnes, Secretary of the NSWCA, he was having a 'boots' disciplinary meeting with my brother John. The meeting began with Syd telling JB in firm and decisive tones where he had gone wrong with the boots business. Unfortunately, in the course of making his various points about immaturity and other demerits, he twice called John 'Richie' instead of John. It was that sort of meeting; things didn't improve.

Shortly after this, and following an Australian Cricket Board meeting, Syd met up with racing writer Pat Farrell at Randwick races. I knew Pat well because he was turf editor of the *Daily Mirror*, the afternoon newspaper in Sydney. Syd chatted to him and told him that, at the recent Board meeting, 'he and the other NSW delegates had received unanimous backing from the other Board members for sacking John Benaud because of the boots business, and the fact that he wasn't any good as a captain anyway.'

Pat, a cricket devotee as well as a racing journalist, listened and made his shorthand notes in the settling pages of his racebook, but was actually far more concerned about backing a winner in the next race than listening to Syd go on and on about the Board. At any rate, he detailed the conversation and a few other racing matters in a column the next day and it did catch my attention. So much so that I immediately telephoned two of the Board members and put Farrell's column to them and asked for their reaction to Syd's remarks.

'Absolute nonsense,' was the reply. 'The Board wasn't in the slightest interested in parochial NSW business, it was nothing at all to do with us and it simply wasn't mentioned at all.'

I phoned Farrell, had him read out to me his shorthand notes from the racebook and then I wrote a column of my own, setting out various matters.

The following Tuesday, at the NSWCA delegates' meeting, those present were told no one had spoken to Farrell about cricket. Many have said to me there seemed no need to resign my life membership of the NSWCA because JB had been banned. Quite right; it would have been needless and it would also have been stupid. I resigned the membership because it had been said that Pat Farrell was a liar and had published something he knew to be false. The NSWCA accepted that this was so.

15
My Greatest XI

As other selectors have recognised over the years, it is very difficult to have more than eleven players in a cricket team.

Richie Benaud on the challenge of picking his Greatest XI

Being a selector
Richie Benaud, *My Spin on Cricket*, 2005

In recent times it has become fashionable to choose best teams, greatest teams or most enjoyable teams, which is what I did with My Greatest XI. Also there have been countless players of the match, the series, the season and the year, not all the nominations free from controversy, as I have found.

The media, in all areas, are quite keen on choosing people to nominate important events and, in 2003, the Melbourne *Age* newspaper asked ten prominent cricket people in Australia to list their ten most important cricket moments relating to Australia from the time cricket was first played in that country.

1861 was chosen as the starting point as it was that year the catering firm of Spiers and Pond arranged for an English cricket team to go to Australia to play a series of matches. This was after they had failed to persuade Charles Dickens to make a tour and then George Parr also declined to take a cricket team because the financial terms were not what he and his Nottinghamshire players wanted.

H. H. Stephenson of Surrey eventually took a good team to play a series of matches and financially, for the players and for Spiers and

Pond, the tour was a great success. Those 1861 matches are regarded in Australia as being the beginning of international matches between England and Australia, though not Test matches.

The next international exchange occurred in 1868 when a team of Australian aborigines, under the leadership of Charles Lawrence – who had gone to Australia with Stephenson's side and remained out there as coach – toured England. The side was not capable of playing English first-class counties but opposed strong club sides and, in addition to cricket, gave exhibitions of boomerang throwing and other similar attractions.

James Lillywhite organised and captained the fourth English side to Australia in the autumn of 1876. The team were beaten by Fifteen of New South Wales in their second match and then by Fifteen of Victoria. This was followed by a crushing defeat in the return v Fifteen of New South Wales, who immediately challenged the tourists to an eleven-a-side game. The match was drawn, much in favour of Lillywhite's men, but it set the stage for the first proper eleven-a-side match between 'England' and Australia, which was played when the tourists returned from a visit, in mid-tour, to New Zealand. The match is regarded as the 'First Test' and was played at the Richmond Paddock, the fourth cricket ground owned by the Melbourne Cricket Club, which had come into existence in 1838. The first three grounds were where the Royal Mint now stands, Spencer Street Railway Station and an area close to Emerald Hill. The Richmond Paddock, now the Melbourne Cricket Ground, has changed to a marked degree over the years and will hold 100,000 spectators for whatever the activity in progress might be.

The ten cricket figures asked to nominate their most important ten events out of fifty listed for consideration by the Melbourne *Age* were:

Darren Berry (Victorian captain), Belinda Clark (Australian women's cricket captain), Dick French (Test match umpire), Dennis Lillee (great Australian fast bowler), Tim Lane (broadcaster and radio cricket commentator), Brett Lee (Australian fast bowler), Ashley Mallett (Australian offspinner), Steve Rixon (former Australian wicketkeeper, NSW, New Zealand and Surrey coach), Paul Sheahan (former Australian Test batsman) and Richie Benaud (former Australian Test captain and cricket commentator).

My list was:

1. Australia defeat England, The Oval 1882
2. Tied Test, Brisbane 1960
3. World Series Cricket 1977
4. First one-day International 1971
5. Bodyline 1932–33
6. The Inaugural Test 1876–77
7. The Centenary Test 1976–77
8. Australia makes 404–3, Headingley 1948
9. Old Trafford Test 1961
10. Australia regains Frank Worrell Trophy, Jamaica 1995

There were interesting choices in the other lists. Dennis Lillee had as number one the aboriginal pioneers of 1868; Belinda Clark went for Steve Waugh's 'Ton of Drama' 2003 as her top choice; Steve Rixon, Dick French and Brett Lee chose Bodyline. Tim Lane had at numbers one and two Bradman bats and bats and bats, 1930, and Bodyline 1932–33. To me a very thoughtful line of one naturally following the other.

It was one of the more interesting media promotions of the summer and produced a great deal of discussion, argument and provoking thought around the cricket community in Australia.

A summation of the choices of the ten judges was:

1. Bodyline 1932–33
2. World Series Cricket 1977
3. Tied Test 1960
4. Centenary Test 1976–77
5. Bradman duck, The Oval 1948
6. Underarm ball, MCG 1981
7. Steve Waugh's Year of 2003
8. Australia beat England 1882
9. Inaugural Test 1876–77
10. Warne bowls Gatting, Old Trafford 1993

Three years earlier *Wisden* embarked on what seemed at the time a task which was close to impossible, the nomination of the Five Cricketers of the Century. One problem they faced was that no one saw all the Test cricket played from 1900 to 2000 but, like most great ideas, it eventually worked.

Wisden asked 100 people to be selectors and, in a clever additional aspect, they weighted the numerical composition of the selection committee to reflect each country's playing role in International cricket over the century. There were three women selectors and 97 men, the committee covered all aspects of cricket, and the basis of asking people to contribute was either their having played Test cricket, watched a lot of it or being known for having contributed in the media and other areas.

In the end the 100 selectors cast votes for only forty-nine cricketers, a remarkably small number, but not one of the 100 selectors chose all the top five players, not even in a changed order. The five were:

Don Bradman	100 votes
Garry Sobers	90
Jack Hobbs	30

Every reason to celebrate – RB and Daphne after their wedding in 1967.

Left: 'That 1977 summer in England revolved as much around the High Court as the cricket field.' Kerry Packer, accompanied by RB, arrives at Lord's to discuss his proposed World Series Cricket tournament. The proposal was not well received.

Below: Australian jockey Arthur 'Scobie' Breasley after triumphing in the Derby at the age of 50. It was the first leg of a double that won RB and fellow journalist Bob Gray some useful spending money as they covered the 1964 Ashes.

'One of my best moments in sport.' RB and Daphne were thrilled to be covering the 1986 Masters for the Australian media when Jack Nicklaus pulled off a memorable victory at the age of 46.

Friends and respected colleagues: golf commentator Peter Alliss and sports journalist Ian Wooldridge.

To those like David Gower and Geoffrey Boycott who followed him from the playing field into the commentary box RB was happy to offer advice – if asked.

'My mantra is: put your brain into gear and if you can add to what's on the screen, then do it; otherwise, shut up.'

Glenn McGrath – 'one of the great pace bowlers' – in the 6th Ashes Test at The Oval in 1997, the days when officials such as Peter Willey – 'one of the finest umpires' – were still allowed to stand in home Tests.

Adam Gilchrist, wicketkeeper in RB's Greatest XI, after his final Test innings, against India at Adelaide in 2008. It was not one of the occasions when he bucked modern trends and chose to walk.

'He's done it. He's started off with the most beautiful delivery. Gatting has absolutely no idea what has happened to it. Still doesn't know.' RB delights in Shane Warne's Ball of the Century at Old Trafford in 1993.

RB and Daphne at the memorial service for Tony Greig at the SCG in 2013. Greig, like the Benauds, had an important role in the early days of WSC, and he went on to join RB in the Channel Nine commentary box.

RB addresses an appreciative audience after his induction into the Australian Cricket Hall of Fame at the Allan Border Medal ceremony in Melbourne in 2007.

The Channel Nine line-up for the 2014–15 season. From left, standing: Mike Hussey, Michael Slater, Mark Taylor, Mark Nicholas, James Brayshaw, Shane Warne, Ian Healy; sitting: Ian Chappell, RB, Bill Lawry, Brett Lee.

Left: As a tribute to RB and his ancestry, the French and the Australian flag fly at half mast on the Members' Pavilion at the SCG.

Below: The loss of RB was felt far beyond the world of cricket. Here, young and old pay their respects before a Super Rugby match between the Waratahs and the Stormers at the Allianz Stadium in Sydney.

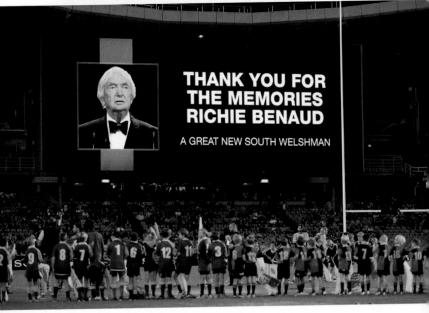

THANK YOU FOR THE MEMORIES RICHIE BENAUD

A GREAT NEW SOUTH WELSHMAN

Shane Warne   27
Vivian Richards   25

The most interesting aspect for me, in looking at the five, was that all of them had changed the game in some way during the time they played. A rare quality.

That the 100 selectors from all over the cricket world managed to encompass that attribute in the five choices was, to me, a remarkable achievement.

In 2004 I was one of a multitude asked to choose a personal best team of the century. There had already been teams of the century announced for England and other countries, some covering the thought of best team of the century.

I declined, on the basis that these similar combinations had already been produced, Australia's team of the century had been announced with a flourish four years earlier and had been along the lines of the Australian Hall of Fame Inductees.

The Australian team of the century was:

1. Bill Ponsford
2. Arthur Morris
3. Don Bradman
4. Greg Chappell
5. Neil Harvey
6. Keith Miller
7. Ian Healy
8. Ray Lindwall
9. Shane Warne
10. Dennis Lillee
11. Bill O'Reilly
12th man: Allan Border

Eventually I agreed to do it, but it had to be in my own fashion. I said it would be called My Greatest XI, and I decided that, as this was to be my team, it would be one I would like to watch and be with during whatever matches they might play. The players would be first of all brilliant cricketers; they would be characters as well and good mixers with the opposition. They would be representing me on the field.

I also decided to choose the final eleven in the same way I have always chosen teams, with, on the left-hand side, the team to take the field and then two back-up players, so that in effect I was looking at thirty-three players and I would finish up with three sides capable of taking the field and being reasonably well balanced. The criteria used were as follows: two opening batsmen, three, four, five batsmen, allrounder at six, fast-bowling allrounder at seven, wicketkeeper-batsman at eight, legspin bowler nine, pace bowlers ten and eleven.

I set down a rule that matches would be played on good pitches, allowing bounce for the bowlers and for the batsmen to play their strokes. Progressively through the match the pitch would allow spinners to come into the game. What you might term an ideal pitch in Australia.

I have met all of the final eleven I chose and, when I narrowed it down to thirty-three from sixty-six, I had met all but one in the three teams, each of which could give a good account of itself.

TEAM

1	2	3
J. B. HOBBS	L. HUTTON	V. T. TRUMPER
S. M. GAVASKAR	A. R. MORRIS	C. G. GREENIDGE
D. G. BRADMAN	W. R. HAMMOND	G. R. HEADLEY
I. V. A. RICHARDS	G. S. CHAPPELL	R. G. POLLOCK
S. R. TENDULKAR	F. M. M. WORRELL	B. C. LARA
G. St A. SOBERS	K. R. MILLER	I. T. BOTHAM

IMRAN KHAN	R. J. HADLEE	KAPIL DEV
A. C. GILCHRIST	R. W. MARSH	I. A. HEALY
S. K. WARNE	W. J. O'REILLY	ABDUL QADIR
D. K. LILLEE	R. R. LINDWALL	G. D. McGRATH
S. F. BARNES	F. S. TRUEMAN	H. LARWOOD

12th Man: K. R. MILLER

Manager: F. M. M. WORRELL

One of the aspects of my selection was that I would pay a great deal of attention to those players I believed had a beneficial effect on the game, those who stood out as champions and who are remembered as being outstanding in their own eras. Also, they had an influence on cricket itself.

For a start I looked for an opening combination and I could instantly see how difficult this was going to be as I narrowed it down to six players. One of those, Trumper, was the only one of the thirty-three I never met.

Victor Trumper: Trumper was a legend in Australia while he was still playing; the only other person I know to have achieved that was Bradman. It seems that Victor was not only a law unto himself with the bat, but was a batsman whose strokes knew no restriction. There have always been arguments in Australia about Trumper and Bradman but never other than that pair. There is no doubt who scored most runs but, in their different eras, each had the tag 'cricketing genius' attached to him.

Gordon Greenidge: There have been other batsmen who hit the ball harder or as hard as Greenidge, Everton Weekes is one who comes to mind, so too Adam Gilchrist. Greenidge though was like his fellow Barbadian Weekes, a butcher of bowlers and one whose ambition always was to entertain and remain on top of the opposing attack.

Arthur Morris: A wonderful attacking left-hander and I agonised for a long time over a left-hand right-hand combination, but in the end I had him on the second line with Len Hutton. Arthur was my first captain and a very good one too, but after NSW had one of their best seasons, Morris with both bat and captaincy, surprisingly he was removed and Keith Miller was made skipper of the state side.

Len Hutton: Len had a wonderful technique, orthodox but not restricted in the sense that when he wanted he could be a dashing stroke-player. He was also the first professional captain of England in the proper sense, captain by appointment, and this before the difference between amateur and professional players was lifted. He not only regained the Ashes in 1953, but retained them in 1954–55 in Australia, and that after he had predicted in 1950–51 in Australia that England would bring a fast bowling attack to Australia four years later and pose problems for the Australians. At that stage he had no idea he would be captaining them. One of the most famous of England's performances was when they achieved a draw under Hutton at Lord's in 1953, with Watson and Bailey batting most of the final day. Never forget that without Hutton's chanceless 145 in the first innings, there would have been *no* final day. It was the best innings I saw him play.

The two openers I finally chose were Jack Hobbs and Sunil Gavaskar.

Jack Hobbs: Hobbs was far more than the best batsman of his generation, and possibly other generations as well, but he was a player who bridged several eras. Before the First World War he was regarded as an outstanding player. He played in fourteen Test series for England and no one to whom I spoke when I first came to England in 1953 was in the slightest doubt that he was the best. He played his first match for Surrey against a team captained by W. G. Grace. This was against the Gentlemen of England in 1905, when he made a sensational start to his first-class cricket career. His first Test was against Australia in 1908 at the MCG, when England won by one wicket and Sydney Barnes and Arthur Fielder added an unbroken 39 for the last wicket to win the exciting game. His last Test was against Australia at The Oval in 1930, Bradman's first tour, where he watched Bradman make 232. He seems to me to have been not only a genuinely great player, when the word 'great' is often used so loosely, but a wonderful team man who would be of value in my team dressing-room. He made nine hundreds against Australia and Bradman was of the opinion that two of them, on treacherous pitches, provided some of the finest batting he ever saw. One was at the MCG in 1929, where some balls, with the wicketkeeper standing up and the batsman playing forward, went over the 'keeper's head. England had to make 332 to win, Hobbs opened with Sutcliffe and they put on 105 on the Melbourne 'sticky'. Bradman never forgot it. One of the reasons I have chosen Hobbs is that I don't believe cricket to be a game necessarily meant to be played only on covered pitches.

Sunil Gavaskar: I have always been a fan of Gavaskar, who came into the Indian team seven years after I retired. I saw more of him in England than Australia, when I was covering cricket for the BBC, but his most memorable effort for me was in Melbourne in 1980–81, where, as captain, he lifted his team to victory. He had been given out lbw to Dennis Lillee when he nicked the ball on to his pad and he was so livid he tried to take Chetan Chauhan, his fellow opening batsman, off the field with him. The team manager, not knowing whether to laugh or cry, stopped Chetan at the gate and sent Sunil off, not quite with a red card but, at least, fuming to the dressing-room. Sunil, still seething the next day, closed the Indian innings and, with Kapil taking 5–28 and Dilip Doshi, who opened the bowling, 2–33, India bowled out the Australians for 83 and a famous victory.

*   *   *

Don Bradman: There is hardly likely to be an easier choice than the number three batsman, yet the two I narrowed it down to with Bradman were **Walter Hammond** and **George Headley**, wonderful players in their own right. Headley was known as the black Bradman and, in their time as contemporaries, no one pressed Bradman harder as a run-scorer. There is some significance in the fact that the Australians of the time tried to keep both Headley and Hammond tied down by bowling at their leg stump, but had no marked success in doing so. Headley played only twenty-two Tests, Hammond eighty-five, each of them with great batting averages and ratios of centuries and fifties to the number of games played.

There will be many people who would have selected Wally Hammond in their team of all-time greats, most of them as a batsman; some would have put him up against the allrounders. Bradman was one who had a very high opinion of Hammond as an all-round cricketer. The Don remarked that he was one of those bowlers for whom the ball seemed to make pace after it hit the pitch, even though he concurred with the scientists who tell us that is impossible. Bradman said of him that generally he was too busy making runs to be bothered about bowling, but when he did he was very difficult to play: 'He was a far better bowler than he was given credit for.' Alec Bedser thought Hammond was the best allrounder he had ever seen and Bill O'Reilly listed him as the finest England batsman he bowled against, yet it was O'Reilly who occasionally caused Hammond most frustrations. Bradman was of the opinion that Hammond was the strongest offside player he had seen and I imagine Bradman therefore would have had a hand in O'Reilly bowling at Hammond's leg stump. It certainly appeared that the tactic frustrated Hammond, even though he still made a lot of runs. His 231 not out at the SCG in the 1936–37 series, and the 240 in 1938 at Lord's, add weight to those who claim him as a magnificent player, one of the real greats.

Bradman was something else. I first heard of him when I listened to my initial cricket broadcast in Jugiong (south-west New South Wales), in 1936–37, when 'Gubby' Allen's side toured to play for the Ashes. Mel Morris, a deep-voiced Victorian, was the first commentator I heard on our five-foot-high Kreisler radio which sat in the corner of the living-room. I was six at the time and was only seven when we moved to Parramatta. I was nine when I watched my first Sheffield Shield match and Bradman was captaining South Australia at the SCG. Stan McCabe was captain of NSW. Grimmett took 6–118 and 5–111, then O'Reilly ten wickets, Pepper six and Ward four, which meant legspinners cleaned up thirty-one of the forty wickets to fall. Rather a good way to influence a young cricketer to become an over-the-wrist spinner.

I saw Bradman in a Test at the SCG in 1946–47 when he and Sid Barnes each made 234 and, in the final match of the series when Australia won by five wickets, Bradman top-scored in Australia's second innings. I was standing below the old Sheridan Stand at the Randwick End and Doug Wright, bowling from the Paddington End and turning the ball viciously, had Bradman dropped by Edrich at slip. It was costly at a time when England had a real chance of victory and Bradman top-scored with 63. I first met Bradman in December 1949 as a member of the NSW side in Adelaide. Everyone who bowled against him, or played against him when he made runs, which was most of the time, said that he was the best and, although statistics don't always tell the tale, they did with Bradman. Statistics roughly twice as good as any other batsman.

He was Chairman of the Australian selection committee when I was surprisingly made captain after Ian Craig contracted hepatitis in 1958; he was Chairman of Selectors and of the Australian Board when the Tied Test series was played between Australia and the West Indies. He delivered the short speech at the team dinner the night before that Tied Test, where he told the Australian players the selectors that summer would be looking in kindly fashion upon players who set out to entertain the spectators, and in less kindly fashion on those who didn't. A great cricketer and, as he showed in that short speech in 1960, he had a very good grasp of what was needed in cricket.

The six batsmen vying for the numbers four and five spots are just as high quality as the ones we have been talking about earlier. **Greg Chappell, Graeme Pollock, Frank Worrell** and **Brian Lara** all fit into the category of being match-winners, a prime ingredient in this team choice, and they all batted with grace and wonderful skill.

When Lara made his 375 against England in St John's, Antigua, in April 1994, it was only fifteen months after he had made 277 at the Sydney Cricket Ground before he was run out. I won't say it was the only way the Australian bowlers looked like dismissing him, but it was close. It was one of the best innings I've ever seen and I was unlucky not to be there to see him break Garry Sobers's record in the later Test against England. Both innings were played as part of drawn matches and I know, through having been there, that the one in Sydney was on a beautiful batting pitch. I assume the one at St John's was of similar quality. Certainly that was the case when I watched him in St John's in 2004 when, in scoring 400 not out, he broke Matthew Hayden's 380-run record and again established himself as the highest innings-scorer in Test matches. There is no doubt his dominance with the bat kept West Indies going at a time when the national team had an extraordinary amount of trouble in winning *any* matches. Lara was an outstanding player of spin bowling, and brilliant footwork and great judgment of length made him a very difficult proposition even for the best spin bowlers in the opposition teams.

I first heard about Graeme Pollock when Frank Worrell's team played in Australia in the Tied Test series in 1960–61. He was nothing to do with those matches but three years earlier his older brother, Peter, had been the young room attendant for the Australian team in Port Elizabeth when we played the final Test of the series at St George's Park. Ian Craig's 1957–58 touring team only knew the older Pollock as Peter, a lad from the Grey College in Port Elizabeth, and some of the uncomplimentary conversation about Adcock and Heine, and the spate of bouncers they bowled in that match, had Peter vowing that one day he would be a fast bowler for South Africa and he'd give the Australians a bit of hurry-up. When we were playing the Tied Test series in Australia, South African friends who were watching the matches told us about the Pollock brothers, that Peter was a fast bowler but his younger brother Graeme, then sixteen, was going to be a champion left-hand batsman.

I stored it away and heard that he played a few matches for Sussex 2nd XI when I was captaining Australia in England in 1961. Then, when New Zealand toured South Africa in 1961–62, I saw Peter had made a very successful debut to Test cricket and that Graeme made 78 for Eastern Province against the touring side and also an unbeaten half-century for the South African Colts XI. The first time I saw him play was when I went to South Africa at the end of the 1962–63 Australian season as captain of Ron Roberts's Cavaliers' XI. We dismissed him cheaply in the Eastern Province first innings and then he hit the most majestic double-century against us, 209 not out of 355–5. I knew I was watching a champion. When he toured Australia in 1963–64, my last summer in first-class cricket, he showed how good he was. The selectors asked me to fly to Perth at the start of this South African tour so I could play in the Combined XI and Graeme and I each made centuries. I thought I did well to make 132 in what seemed quite brisk time, 205 minutes. Graeme's 127 not out was blasted in less than two hours and I knew we were in for some tough times over the next thirteen weeks.

In the third match of that Test series he hit a glorious 122 out of 186 added while he was at the crease, then made 175 in Adelaide playing one of the finest innings I've ever seen in Test cricket. The pity was that he was only able to play twenty-three Tests, but there's no doubt he was one of the best ever to walk on to a cricket field.

I finally chose **Viv Richards** and **Sachin Tendulkar** to occupy those four and five places.

I have seen a considerable amount of both of them and Australians, in fact, were responsible for Viv Richards becoming one of the greatest batsmen and entertainers the cricket world has seen. My first sighting of him was in 1975–76 in Australia when Greg Chappell was captain of the home side and Viv was only a year into Test cricket. The West Indian selectors had given him a tough initiation in November 1974 with a debut against Chandrasekhar in Bangalore, where the brilliant spinner dismissed him twice for 4 and 3. He made 192 not out in his next innings, so suddenly a great deal of notice was taken of him in Australia because West Indies were touring there a year later. When I first saw him he was all attack and disdained any form of shackling by the bowlers but, in 1975–76, Dennis Lillee, Jeff Thomson and Gary Gilmour sorted him out and he made only 137 runs at an average of 19 in the first four Tests.

Then Clive Lloyd, in desperation, or with a touch of genius, opened the batting with him in a couple of minor matches. He was successful and, opening in the final two Tests, he made 30, 101, 50 and 98, even though Australia still won both matches and the series 5–1. This was the summer which started Lloyd thinking that pace bowling would win Test series and that winning was far preferable to losing! The Australians, having got Viv into the right frame of mind, watched with interest as West Indies toured England in 1976 and he hit 829 runs in four Tests at better than 100 an innings. He never looked back and remains one of the greatest batsmen I have ever seen.

So too Sachin Tendulkar, though they are completely different types. Tendulkar made his debut against Pakistan as the third youngest player in history and that too made interesting newspaper copy in Australia. I was covering Test matches for the BBC in England and Channel Nine in Australia at the time, and this happened just after Australia's wonderful tour of England in 1989 when they regained the Ashes. I knew Sachin was to come to Australia in 1991–92 but, before that, he played against England in England in a high-scoring series and I watched one of the best innings imaginable in the Old Trafford Test, where he made 119 not out and was partly responsible for the saving of the match.

When he came to Australia he made two centuries, one at the WACA in Perth and the other in Sydney. This was the better innings, although Perth too was good. The one in Sydney though was flawless. It had everyone in raptures, an innings of 148 not out which, to my mind, could not have been bettered, with an incidental note that, at eighteen years and 256 days, he was the youngest player to hit a Test century in Australia. It was Shane Warne's first Test, so being privileged to see the innings and note the legspinner's debut was a highlight.

Keith Miller was the greatest allrounder I ever played with or against, but bear in mind that the period covered there embraces Miller retiring in 1956, which was only two years after Garry Sobers made his Test debut. Sobers was more my time, and then a considerable distance past, but Miller was an extraordinary cricketer. He, Arthur Morris and Ray Lindwall were my mentors, three great cricketers and outstanding people. Miller succeeded Morris as captain of NSW and was the best captain I have known and certainly the finest captain never to have captained Australia.

It was a freakish and much appreciated happening that in later years I was able to watch four extraordinary allrounders in action in the one period: **Imran Khan, Richard Hadlee, Ian Botham** and **Kapil Dev**. Fancy having them all playing in the same era. It is normally regarded a great bonus to have just one in action over a similar time.

Three of the Hadlee family played for New Zealand. Walter, the father, made his debut in England in 1937 and then captained his country for the first time in the Test against Australia straight after the end of the Second World War. His eldest son Barry didn't play for New Zealand but Dayle and Richard did and Richard brought left-handedness into the world of all-round cricketers and was a splendid player.

It was unusual that the four allrounders of that era each reached the milestone of the 2,000 runs and 200 wickets 'double' in consecutive years in the early 1980s. Ian Botham was the first in 1981–82, then Kapil Dev in 1982–83, Imran Khan in 1983–84 and Richard Hadlee in 1984–85. No wonder it was such a good time to be around the commentary box.

Botham's most extraordinary Test series was the one in 1981 against Australia where all the points one makes about cricket being 'a funny game' were underlined at the one time. The game at Headingley has always been known as Botham's Match and the circumstances were extraordinary. It was a six-Test match series and Australia won the First at Trent Bridge by four wickets, with Terry Alderman taking nine wickets on his Test debut. Botham was captain of England and had just returned from the England tour of the West Indies, where he had also been captain and West Indies had won 2–0, with one Test abandoned without a ball being bowled. This happened when the Guyanese government withdrew Robin Jackman's visitor's permit and deported him. When England and Australia met at Lord's in the Second Test in 1981 the match was drawn but Botham collected a 'pair'. It is a moot point whether Botham then resigned as captain or received the push from Alec

Bedser but, for the following Test at Headingley, Mike Brearley was reinstated as skipper. Brearley's opposite number, Kim Hughes, had won the loss and fielded in the opening two Tests with Botham leading the opposition but, in this one at Headingley, Hughes won it and batted. Australia made 401 and then bowled out England for 174 and made them follow on.

To create some form of history, England needed to win, since only one other team had ever been victorious after following on: England at the Sydney Cricket Ground in 1894–95. When Botham came in to bat in the

> ❛Don't bother looking for that, let alone chasing it . . . It's gone straight into the confectionery stall and out again . . . A beautiful hit.❜
>
> *RB describes a six during Botham's 149 in 1981*

second innings, England were 105–5 and they quickly lost two more wickets for 30. Then Botham hit a century from 87 balls and shared a partnership of 67 with Graham Dilley. Botham remained 149 not out and this all happened after the England team had booked out of their hotel on the fourth morning of the match. Bob Willis then bowled out Australia for 111, returning his best-ever figures of 8–43, and suddenly the Test series was 1–1. England won by 29 runs at Edgbaston in the Fourth Test, with Botham bowling out Australia in their second innings with 5–11 from 14 overs. Australia, needing 151, lost their last six wickets for 16, with Botham's haul 5–1 from 28 balls. Quite extraordinary. Botham then hit 118 and took five wickets in England's triumph at Old Trafford and, when he went to The Oval for the final Test, he had the chance of reaching the 2,000 runs and 200 wickets 'double' in that game. It was a pity he didn't quite manage it on the last day. He made it as regards the wickets, but was 23 short with the runs; something he redressed in the following Test against India at Wankhede Stadium in Bombay.

Kapil Dev was playing in that latter game and it was only two months later he also reached the landmark against the touring West

Indian team led by Clive Lloyd. I always thought Kapil better suited with both bat and ball to pitches in England and India, though he certainly turned in some fine efforts in Australia at different times. He was a magnificent striker of the ball and could there be any more spectacular way to save a follow-on than what he did at Lord's in 1990? With 24 needed, and last man Hirwani at the other end, he hit Eddie Hemmings for four successive sixes. Great allrounders, all of them!

Garry Sobers, in my view, is the greatest all-round cricketer the world has seen. He was certain to be in my team as one allrounder; a brilliant batsman, splendid fielder, particularly close to the wicket, and a bowler of extraordinary skill, whether bowling with the new ball, providing orthodox left-arm spin or over-the-wrist spin. It is in the latter category I would use him in this team, though he might also be given the new ball on occasions if Bradman could extract it from the hands of Lillee, Barnes and Imran.

It was a matter of choosing one other out of Hadlee, Imran, Botham and Kapil and I selected Imran Khan. Imran was the only one I saw reach the 2,000-run and 200-wicket milestone; that was in the match between Australia and Pakistan at the MCG and he was playing as a batsman, having been injured prior to the tour with a stress fracture to his left shin. It was, even by Pakistan administrative standards, an extraordinary set of circumstances. Originally Zaheer Abbas had been named as captain by the selectors, then the president of the Pakistan Board sacked the selectors and made Imran captain. Sarfraz Nawaz had also been banned from the tour because of criticism he had made of the Pakistan selectors who had not chosen him for the tour of India which preceded the Australian tour. When it was seen that Imran's X-rays would not allow him to bowl, possibly for the duration of the tour, Sarfraz was instantly un-banned but he appeared in Australia at such a time that he had missed playing on the pitches which would have best suited his bowling. As it happened,

Imran's batting in Melbourne saved the team from defeat. In the Pakistan second innings Lillee took two quick wickets and Lawson one, and Pakistan were 81–5 when Imran came to the crease. He added 79 with Zaheer Abbas and then 53 with Salim Malik and, in the course of making his 72 not out, became only the fifth player, and the first from Pakistan, to achieve the double.

I didn't see him make his debut for Pakistan at Edgbaston in 1971 when Zaheer Abbas hit his magnificent 274. He was run out for five by Zaheer and didn't take a wicket, nor did things immediately progress a great deal because it was six years before he was able to force his way back into the team and share the new ball. It was against Australia in Australia in 1976–77 that he really caught my eye and continued to do so for another seven years. In the Third and final Test of the short series, Pakistan achieved their first-ever Test victory over Australia in Australia and Imran took 6–102 and 6–63, bowling his team to victory in 46 overs of sustained hostility. He fits in nicely for me in this side as the pace-bowling allrounder to go with Garry Sobers.

There have been many fine wicketkeepers from all countries over the years but Australia have been particularly well served in this regard in the past thirty years. In other countries Godfrey Evans and Alan Knott were very good over long periods, Jeffrey Dujon, Wasim Bari and others have impressed but, in Australia, **Rodney Marsh**, then **Ian Healy** and now **Adam Gilchrist** have been outstanding. My vote goes firmly and quickly to Gilchrist, a fine wicketkeeper who had to move from NSW to Western Australia to have his chance of representing Australia, and then proceeded to keep wicket and bat magnificently. In fifty years of playing and watching, I have never seen anyone strike the ball *more* cleanly than Gilchrist and no one has reached 'keeping dismissals and batting targets faster in the history of the game as far as 'keepers are concerned. He has kept brilliantly to Shane Warne and Glenn McGrath, and even stumped Craig McMillan off McGrath in a limited-overs match in Wellington, New Zealand, in February, 2005. Some of his batting in the last few years has been as good as I have seen from anyone, particularly in turning his team's problems into a winning position by the most attacking batting imaginable.

Shane Warne is the best legspin bowler I have ever seen. He has also had a great influence on boosting the art and in persuading young cricketers that it is a good thing to be a slow bowler rather than one who runs from 30 yards and bowls at something like 85 mph. There is no doubt legspin bowling is an art, and a very difficult one at that. Over-the-wrist spin puts tremendous pressure on shoulders, elbows and fingers; fingers imparting fierce spin are torn and bleeding before a day is completed and there have been many bowlers over the years who have had short careers because of this.

Bill O'Reilly was all flailing arms and legs and aggression, and no lover of batsmen. He played against Don Bradman in 1925. Bradman, playing for Bowral, took an unbeaten double-century off him on the first day of the match and the following week O'Reilly, playing for Wingello, bowled him first ball. Both were country boys living no more than 20 miles from one another in the south-west of NSW. I have talked about 'Tiger' O'Reilly elsewhere but one thing remains clear: that when he and Clarrie Grimmett were playing for Australia, Australia's spin-bowling fortunes were at their peak. The fact that he and my father both went to Teachers' College around the same time gave me some feeling of family connection and made me enthusiastic as a youngster when I was able to see St George play in the Sydney club competition. 'Tiger' made his Test match debut against South Africa in 1932 and it was there his partnership with Grimmett was forged, Grimmett having already been seven years in the Australian team. I was only a year old when 'Tiger' made his debut and my father was teaching at Warrandale, outside Koorawatha, very much in the far south-west of NSW. O'Reilly took his 144 Test wickets in just twenty-seven Tests and knee problems forced him into retirement after the one post-war Test match in Wellington, New Zealand. He was rated by Bradman as the finest of all bowlers.

The other legspinner for whom I have great regard is **Abdul Qadir** of Pakistan, who never for an instant stopped attacking the batsmen. He first came on to the Test scene in 1977–78 in the series against England and he bowled with attacking verve for thirteen years, right up to the time Warne made his first Test appearance.

There have been others but in my view none to match Warne, who is my number nine.

There has been no shortage of fast bowlers and fast-bowling combinations over the years. Australia started it off with Gregory and McDonald in the 1920–21 period, then Lindwall and Miller 1946–56, Lillee and Thomson 1974–1982. Larwood and Voce, Trueman and Statham were pre-eminent in England and, for a short time, Frank Tyson blasted all-comers. Alec Bedser, on the other hand, was for much of the time from 1946 just about on his own and was a magnificent bowler at medium-fast pace. **Harold Larwood** and Bill Voce were too much for Australia in the Bodyline tour, leading an attack quickly to be banned. Bradman's batting average in that series was merely half what was considered normal for him.

> ❛Glenn McGrath dismissed for two, just 98 runs short of his century.❜
>
> *RB on bowler Glenn McGrath*

Ray Lindwall was a great fast bowler with a slightly round-arm action that allowed him to bowl wonderful outswingers to the right-hand opening batsmen.

Glenn McGrath is, in my opinion, one of the great pace bowlers the cricket world has seen. Not blisteringly fast, he is beautifully accurate and with a host of variations that make him a real danger to batsmen, even on the best of batting pitches.

It is always worth keeping one's own statistics, particularly on bowlers. McGrath, in the list I keep of bowlers with at least 100 Test wickets, is quite outstanding and is a model for all young bowlers. One of the aspects of his bowling which can't be quantified by a figure is his superb control of change of pace. This part of any bowler's armoury must always be subtle in the longer version of the game, though it is obvious that many varieties of slower balls can, and will, be produced in one-day matches. Many times I have seen McGrath use subtle changes of pace, particularly a slightly faster ball, to have the batsman hurry his stroke. Glenn has been playing Test cricket now for ten years and the manner in which he has come back from injury setbacks simply underlines that he is not only a great pace bowler, but a courageous one as well. I've been very fortunate to have been there on his debut against New Zealand in Perth in 1994 and to see him in action with Shane Warne. It is one of the greatest bowling periods in Australian cricket history, with Warne the world's highest wicket-taker and, at the start of the 2005 Ashes battle, McGrath needed only one wicket to reach the 500 milestone.*

Fred Trueman remains for me one of the finest fast bowlers of the post-war period, a classic action, plenty of pace and no one has had a better outswinger, except perhaps **Dennis Keith Lillee**. Lillee is the first of my pace-bowling attack. I saw him make his Test debut in Adelaide in 1971 and the only time he faltered was when he suffered severe stress fractures to his back and the medicos said it was unlikely he would play again. He fought his way through that injury, came back in triumph against England in 1974–75, and then played

---

* Glenn McGrath's final Test was against England at Sydney in 2006–07, in which he took his total of Test wickets to 563.

another nine years before retiring as the world's leading wicket-taker at that time.

To join him in leading the attack is **Sydney Francis Barnes**, a bowler I met but never played against but one who, from the time I have talked about cricket to older and more experienced people in Australia and England, is said by them to be the finest bowler of all time. I met him in 1953 at Stoke-on-Trent, where the Australians were playing Minor Counties and Barnes bowled the first ball of the match. He had turned eighty years of age a couple of months earlier and the ball he bowled landed on a good length and the batsman played it defensively. Even then he was a tall, straight-backed man with big hands, very long, strong fingers and a firm handshake. Ability to swing the ball with great control and cut it off the pitch made him a formidable proposition. Barnes's record in Test cricket, at a time when the Australians had a splendid team, very strong in batting, and South Africa, the other nation of the time, were very good, was quite astonishing.

He played only twenty-seven matches, a mere ten of which were in England, over a period of thirteen years up to the start of the First World War. He took 189 wickets. When he went to Australia in 1911–12 he was up against the cream of Australian batting, including Trumper, Bardsley, Hill, Armstrong, Kelleway, Ransford and the young Macartney. Thirty-four wickets at 22 on shirt-front pitches. He must have been some bowler!

When Barnes made his debut in a three-day Test at the SCG during the 1901–02 tour, he took 5–65 and 1–74. He took 13 wickets in his next Test, which was played at the Melbourne Cricket Ground, but damaged his knee two weeks later in Adelaide and played no more cricket on the tour. The MCG was a favourite ground for Barnes and ten years after his Test debut he routed the Australians pre-lunch on the first day, taking 5–6 from 11 overs. Those present said he was as close to unplayable as could be imagined. England won by eight wickets, with Jack Hobbs, included in My

Greatest XI, making the first of his twelve Test centuries against Australia, an unbeaten 126.

It would be superfluous to have a coach with a team of this quality and character, but I do have two men I would appoint to other positions: Keith Miller as twelfth man and Frank Worrell as manager. My experience with Miller as player and captain showed me that he could, if necessary, fill any position in the team and Worrell was the best I ever saw in man-management. He was the first black West Indian cricketer to be allowed to captain a team away from the Caribbean and he was one of the reasons the face of cricket in Australia and perhaps in other parts of the world was changed for ever because of that Tied Test series. No one but Worrell could have done it for the West Indies.

TEAM

J. B. HOBBS

S. M. GAVASKAR

D. G. BRADMAN

I. V. A. RICHARDS

S. R. TENDULKAR

G. St A. SOBERS

IMRAN KHAN

A. C. GILCHRIST

S. K. WARNE

D. K. LILLEE

S. F. BARNES

12th Man: K. R. MILLER

Manager: F. M. M. WORRELL

Choosing eleven players out of sixty-six, eventually narrowed down to thirty-three, simply showed me three things. First, I wouldn't want to be an official selector, though sometimes I have had the task of choosing teams for various media.

Second, no matter how you twist and turn and burn the midnight oil, you can only fit eleven players into a team. And third, that exactly one hundred per cent of the people who read the final list of names will instantly be able to come up with their better eleven and that, in those selections, all thirty-three of the names will appear!

III
THE MAN

‘Away from the microphone, he was always fine company . . . he was kind, generous and simply loved talking about the game. Brian Johnston, the late *Test Match Special* commentator, held a birthday party at his house in London during the Lord's Test every year and I will always remember simply sitting in the garden chatting about cricket with Richie. It was invariably a pleasure.’

Jonathan Agnew, BBC

16
Away From Cricket

'He was also knowledgeable in areas other than cricket. He loved his wine and keenly followed the horses. He would set up his desk at the back of the commentary box when he was not in front of the microphone and check on his laptop to see how the horses were going, without ever failing to keep an eye on the game that was being played out in front of us.'

David Gower, *Sunday Times*

Tales of the turf
Richie Benaud, *Anything But . . . an Autobiography*, 1998

Nineteen sixty-four was an interesting year. The Australians toured England and Glamorgan beat them at Swansea. Any Australian would excuse the defeat because of the wonderful sound made by the massed Welsh choirs at every bar in the country. It was very impressive on and off the field.

Then, at Old Trafford, Bob Simpson made 311. If you are going to make your first Test century, and have waited a while to do it, you might as well go on with the job.

This tour was my first full-time stint as a journalist with an Australian team and I found it extremely interesting being on the road for a full six months. In those days the filing of copy was done either by telephone or by telex through Cable and Wireless, with no computers to facilitate sending of stories. As before, I was with the Sydney *Sun*, and Bob Gray was working for the Sydney *Daily Mirror*.

We had some good battles, because although we were close friends we never once shared a story on any tour.

Gray and I often travelled together during that tour, though the Benaud–Gray caravan was no model for rally drivers. Bob, sensibly, has never driven any vehicle in his life, other than a golf cart backwards at the Paradise Island Golf Club in the Bahamas. The main problem with this was that he actually wished to go forward, but his snap decision, as to which was the correct way to point the direction lever while his foot was on the accelerator, turned out to be slightly astray. This was emphasised by the cart rocketing across the practice putting green, fortunately skirting the bunker.

He had a similar driving problem seventeen years later when Daphne and I, and Bob's wife Grace, were in Port Hacking in a small boat with an outboard motor, trying to make it to his cruiser *Pistasnute*, which was moored fifty yards away to the left. He turned right instead of left, the boat rose high above the jetty and we were all unceremoniously deposited in the water.

In 1964 in England it was a case of Gray navigating, Benaud driving, and this gave us a little scope for studying the fields for race meetings and keeping abreast of various 'good things' through that splendid publication *Timeform*.

Gray and I had a stroke of luck during that tour, in that we backed the Derby–Oaks double, Santa Claus and Homeward Bound. Keith Miller had already slung Gray and me the tip of Santa Claus for the Derby, to be run on 3 June, and a couple of days later, 'Flipper' Lewis told Miller that Homeward Bound must have a good chance in the Oaks, but the proviso was that it must be soft going. At the time there had been very little rain in England in the lead-up to the major races, and the tracks, and training tracks as well, were bone hard. Gray and I decided to take the odds on offer about the double, which at that stage amounted to 7–1 and 25–1, with a point added to each because of the generosity in those days of the bookmakers with antepost doubles. It meant, in rough terms, Gray and I were to collect about £1,300 each if both steeds obliged.

We watched with interest when Santa Claus at evens thrashed a good field in the Irish Two Thousand Guineas on 16 May, beating Young Christopher by three long-looking lengths. He instantly shortened to 2–1 for the English Derby and finally started at 6–4. That was no surprise because of his effortless victory at the Curragh.

Ridden by Scobie Breasley, aged fifty, Santa Claus won the Epsom Derby after a few heart-stopping moments. Now all we needed was for Homeward Bound to swoop down the outside in the Oaks.

Gray and I were at the Trent Bridge Test during Derby and Oaks week, and as the race broadcaster Peter Bromley was calling the last two furlongs, we were on opposite sides of the Trent Bridge ground. We had already selfishly cheered the news that a cloudburst had hit Epsom an hour before the Oaks was due to be run.

With no play possible at Trent Bridge because of showers, I was climbing a ladder to do an in-vision piece for BBC and had to go up one-handed because I had a radio to my ear. On the other side Gray, half leaning out of the press-box window, was oblivious to everything but the race and finding some decent reception from his own radio. When Bromley's voice rose several decibels, with the filly swooping on the leaders and winning with plenty in hand, Peter, with a slight touch of patriotism, cried, 'And it's Homeward Bound for England.'

'Pigsarse it is,' came the unbridled yell of joy from Bob at the press-box window. 'It's Homeward Bound for Gray and Benaud.'

It wasn't that, in fact, but it was some useful spending money for the tour, and a little punting money as well, and the spectators standing on the ground in front of the press box were left shaking their heads about the strange behaviour and language of that chap wearing the bright check cashmere sports jacket and shouting at them.

*   *   *

On 10 July Gray and I set out from Leicester for Southampton for the game between Hampshire and Australia, having made some modest investments on a four-horse Yankee bet which finished with two horses, Nanda Devi and New Sovereign, trained by Johnson-Houghton and Elsey and running at Beverley and Chester. Racing by this stage was affecting our navigation, and we found ourselves on the A604 heading east instead of on the A1 going south. We knew the first two horses in our Yankee, one of them Althrey Don, had won at short prices and, just south of Cambridge, by now on the A10, we stopped at Trumpington, where a phone call to the bookmaker established that Nanda Devi had bolted in.

New Sovereign, a two-year-old bay filly and our final bet, was running in a maiden a few minutes later, and it must have been a sight for the good folk of Trumpington village to see these two Australians in the old red phone box outside the pub, holding one telephone receiver to two ears whilst cheering on the gallant steed to its splendid length-and-a-half win over Star Money.

I was part-lessee with Ray Steele, Barry Jarman and Norman O'Neill of a horse called Pall-Mallann, which was coming along well, and we had high hopes of it winning a race at some stage in the summer. We had Ron Hutchinson ride it, Sid Dale was the trainer and eventually it saluted in a handicap, run whilst the Australians were playing Yorkshire at Bradford, on Saturday, 8 August.

On the morning of the match I was entrusted with the task of putting £200 on this conveyance with Messrs Ladbrokes, the genial offerers of odds of 5–1. It was difficult getting through to them on the telephone, and the time for the race was drawing very close when Denis Compton opened the door of the telephone booth and said, 'Put fifty on for me, will you?' At that moment Ladbrokes answered and I said I wanted to take the 5–1 and I'd have £200 on it thanks.

As it went past the post, and we were cheering it on, a slight chill ran up my spine as I suddenly realised I hadn't put Denis's money on. Pall-Mallann won, not with its head on its chest, but it beat Dinner Gong by three-quarters of a length, putting in a strong run to lead close to home. All that happened was that it cost me 250 big ones once I had paid the four winning bets to Steele, Jarman, O'Neill and 'Compo'. It was a little lesson in concentration – costly, but a good lesson.

My best friend in life
Jack Bannister, *Guardian*, 2015

WHEN THE YOUNG Australian batsman Phillip Hughes tragically died last November, my dear friend Richie Benaud was asked to provide the voiceover for a short tribute video. As always, it was pitch perfect.

Afterwards, his fellow commentator Bill Lawry asked about Richie's own condition – he had been receiving treatment for skin cancer – and queried whether a refusal to wear a sun hat during his playing career, which Richie blamed for the illness, was due to a commercial deal with Brylcreem.

In true Richie fashion he paused and considered the response. 'I'm not going to tell you whether I had a contract or not, Bill . . .' he replied with a glint in his eye. 'Nor am I going to tell you how much the fee was.' That was the humour of the man – always slightly off-key and understated.

> 'A boy just beginning. Twenty-five years of age. Baggy Green number four zero eight. His father's best mate. Son, brother, fighter, friend . . . inspiration. Phillip Hughes. Forever rest in peace, son.'
>
> *RB's tribute to Phillip Hughes*

As a commentator you arrive early before the start of play and often finish past seven in the evening. That was a long time for seven or eight people to share a small space and often tempers would fray, fallouts would occur. But never involving Richie. He was always the coolest of the lot.

After every stint on air he would simply retire to a small table in the corner of the room to watch the play, quietly reading the newspaper or studying the *Racing Post*. He always brought sandwiches to the ground and was so meticulous when it came to organising his day.

Richie became my best friend in life. We first met when I was playing club cricket in Johannesburg during the 1957–58 season and the Australians were touring. He took more than 100 first-class wickets on that trip – a feat I do not believe has been achieved since. I then played against him for Warwickshire in the early 1960s before I joined him on the BBC television team in 1987 following a spell with the radio team. That was where I really got to know him.

We discovered early on in our time working together that we shared two passions away from cricket: golf and horseracing. We would play a round of golf before every Test at Trent Bridge, Headingley and Edgbaston and Richie, who had a single-figure handicap, won more often than not.

His love for horseracing was infectious. And from 1987 to only three weeks ago we had a personal nap competition. Every Saturday for twenty-eight years we would talk on the telephone and swap the names of our horses, totalling up the wins from April to September in England and October to April in Australia, with the winner buying a slap-up meal for the other. I would study the form day and night and still the bugger would win.

His other big passion was his car, a 1963 Sunbeam Alpine, and when he crashed it eighteen months ago he was more concerned about it than his own health. He had a great sense of humour but would never set out to take the mickey. That did not stop him making gentle, witty points about people or situations, though.

In short, Richie Benaud was a true gentleman.

17
Family

❝Benaud, who was born in Penrith, just west of Sydney, into a family of Huguenot origin, had a keen cricketer for a father. Lou Benaud, who had once taken all twenty wickets in a bush match, keenly and wisely guided his two sons.❞

David Frith, *Guardian*

The Benauds and the Savilles: pioneers
Richie Benaud, *Over But Not Out*, 2010

Penrith in the 21st century is a thriving centre, thirty-four miles to the west of Sydney in New South Wales. At high noon on Monday, 6 October 1930, it was a small and serene town close to the Nepean River, with High Street as its main thoroughfare and several other streets running off what was a friendly hive of activity. There were the usual businesses, an hotel, a newsagent, some general food and produce stores, eating places including Mrs Tipping's popular 'Star' Refreshment Room, and some shops listed as 'Baker and Pastrycook', a saddler's noted as a 'Practical Saddle, Harness and Collar Maker', two cinemas, four shops selling meat and ham, and the business premises of a watchmaker and jeweller, Richard Benaud, full name Richard Grainger Napoleon Benaud, who lived in the flat above with his wife, Nellie. Their daughter-in-law, Irene (*née* Saville), was staying with them because she and her husband, Lou, were about to become parents.

Rene had travelled by train a week earlier from Koorawatha, where there was no resident doctor, and within hours was to have a baby. However, her husband Lou was still in Koorawatha, two hundred miles south-west of Sydney, in the tiny local town of Warrandale where he was the only schoolteacher for a small number of children. School holidays would not start for another six weeks, so there was no chance of modern-day paternity leave for him. Lou received the news the following day that his son Richard had been born, but that it might be some time before we set eyes on one another. During October and November 1930 I stayed in Penrith with my mother, who had been strictly forbidden to take me back to Koorawatha because I was looking, as they say nowadays, 'not too crash-hot', having gone down with a severe bout of gastroenteritis. When eventually, six weeks later, my mother and Lou's sister, Gladys, were allowed to take me back to Koorawatha on the steam train and in a severe heatwave, the medico wished my mother well, but was said to have voiced the private opinion to friends of my grandparents that, sad as it may be, and though he had done his best, he wasn't holding his breath about seeing me again.

It was both an exciting and an unhappy time in Australia; unhappy because of the Great Depression which saw businessmen ruined, families split, and the picture for the future was very gloomy and problematical. Country areas were particularly hard hit, but with many of the residents descended from pioneer stock, they were very resourceful. Living off the land was never better exemplified than in those years in Australia when the Great Depression didn't merely hover over everyone, it wrapped itself around the country, and for a time the continent was all but smothered. Money was scarce, and employment of any kind, along with reasonable health, was the greatest thing that could happen. A two-year drought had turned country areas to a mixture of burnt grass and dust.

It was an exciting time because Australian sporting heroes and aviation pioneers took people's minds off their problems, and the year I was born a youngster named Donald Bradman captivated the country with his batting exploits on the 1930 cricket tour of England.

Around the time that Bradman and others enjoyed the nervous excitement of their first air flights, Major Charles Kingsford Smith was making headlines by flying from England to Australia in an Avro Avian sports plane, and three other British pilots, C. W. Hill, C. J. Chabot and C. E. Pickthorne, were attempting the same journey: Hill, in a Moth, hoping to beat the fifteen days set as a record by Bert Hinkler; the other pair in a two-seater trying to do it in seven days.

The endeavour to conquer the skies reached a climax on the evening of Monday, 6 October 1930, with the numbing news of the crash and explosion of the R101, the world's largest airship, which came to grief near the French village of Beauvais. Buffeted by high winds and heavy rain it was flying at 55 mph at an altitude of only 300 feet when it hit a hill, forty miles north of Paris. Of the fifty-four on board, forty-six perished in the flames and huge explosions.

On the day I was born this was front-page news around the world in newspapers large and small, one of the latter variety a pink newspaper, pink in colour that is, not politics, the conservative *Richmond River Herald*. It was published in Coraki and had been established by my great-uncle, Louis Ferdinand Branxton Benaud, in 1886. The first issue was a test of nerve and willpower, because the office and the newspaper plant went up in smoke and flames a few hours before the presses were due to run. He set his jaw and pinned on the wall the phrase 'do your best and never give up'.

Louis Ferdinand was the brother of my grandfather, Richard Grainger Napoleon Benaud, and the son of Captain Jean Benaud, who had named his children so his original French heritage would be maintained.

*   *   *

My ancestors the Benauds and the Savilles had come to Australia at roughly the same time. James and Martha Saville had seventeen children in the sixty-nine years they were married before James passed away aged ninety-four. Martha died three years later aged ninety-two. Ten children survived James and there were seventy-eight grandchildren and seventy-six great-grandchildren. The eleventh of the seventeen children was George Saville, born on 28 January 1872, and he married Lillian White; they were my mother's parents.

The Savilles journeyed on the SS *Euphrates* in 1855, after emigrating from England, where the family farmed in Langley in Essex and Ely in Cambridgeshire. At Langley, in the mid-1800s, living conditions were said to be mediocre and wages poor, and in the case of the Saville family, there were now too many children to farm the same amount of land. Their new life in Australia must have been something of a shock to them, and despite their determination and acceptance of the obvious challenges, they knew what they were undertaking would be far from easy.

The Savilles were pioneers, in the sense that almost immediately following their arrival in Sydney they joined a bullock wagon-train and made their way 500 miles to the north. James Saville worked for five years for a farmer, Mr Ogilvie, as stockman, blacksmith and general factotum at 'The Ten Mile' station. James's wages were 25 shillings a week and a double ration of flour, tea, meat and jam. They then moved to Gordonbrook station, which was owned by Mr Frank Bundock, for another ten years, where James continued his work.

There was nothing fancy about the food in those early days in Australia. It was said the outback was under the yoke of a 'muttonous' diet, and the Savilles and other newcomers quickly became used to its chewy qualities. I particularly like the name given to one such dish: they called it 'The Old Thing', and it consisted only of mutton and damper, a light, flat bread about two inches thick and eighteen inches wide, which if poorly cooked in the campfire was heavy enough to be known as 'buggers on the coals'. As a schoolboy, I had a liking for damper, but it has gone out of fashion now with the arrival of some very good hot bread shops, such as Baker's Delight, the one we use in Coogee Bay Road.

In September 1861, six years after the Savilles arrived in the area, Casino's first representative cricket match was played, a return game for one played in Grafton in July that year; the matches were between two teams from the districts of the Clarence River and the Richmond River. To travel to Casino from Grafton, the Clarence team had to ford rapid-flowing creeks, boggy roads and rest jaded horses. On arrival all the problems were forgotten in the euphoria of the contest and the festivities which were held in their honour at the Durham Ox hostelry opposite the ground.

The cricket ground with the pub alongside was a reminder of their English village life, something jealously guarded by writers of the time. Four years before the Savilles' arrival in Australia, the Rev. James Pycroft, BA, wrote in *The Cricket Field* in high praise of the English heritage, but with scant regard for the enthusiastic and ambitious Associate and Affiliate European Members of the modern-day ICC, 'No single cricket club have we ever heard dieted either with frogs, sour crout or macaroni.'

Eighteen sixty-one was an important year in Australia: the first Melbourne Cup had already been won in November by Archer, but sadly, 1861 also marked the deaths of the two explorers, Burke and Wills, who perished trying to cross the continent so others would eventually know the extent of the vast land.

In cricket, that first representative match in the Northern Rivers area preceded by only 116 days the first game of cricket ever played between an English team and one from an Australian colony. It was in late 1861 that Spiers & Pond, the British catering firm with a branch office in Melbourne, decided to sponsor a team to visit Australia. The players departed England on the steamship *Great Britain* on 18 October 1861, arrived in Melbourne to a tumultuous welcome on Christmas Eve, were magnificently fêted during most of the hours between then and the start of their match, and still managed to win! They were 116 years in advance of World Series Cricket, for they played in coloured clothing with different coloured hatbands and sashes so they could be identified by spectators.

After their ten-year stint was up at Gordonbrook, the Savilles applied, with a mixture of trepidation and excitement, to select, or to be allowed to purchase a lease on, a block of farming land at One Tree in the Richmond River area. It was as it sounded, land with one proper tree, a solitary and large gum on an open flat, and much frequented by the cattle for the shade it afforded. In 1870 they moved on to the bare land at One Tree Farm seven miles from Casino, and it was thirty-two years before they actually owned the selection.

The Savilles eventually moved into dairy farming, which was all done by hand, and James Saville's six horses and flat dray were a familiar sight as he took his cases of butter and cheese into the co-op or to private sale. All travel was by spring-cart, horse and dray, horseback, or by Shanks's pony. The production of the cheese was a good example of pioneering and innovation: it was made in the stump of a hollow tree, with a block of wood at the cool base on which the cheese vat was placed. A bag of stones was then lowered on to the vat by use of a long pole and pressure was exerted. They were able to make only one cheese a day using that innovative method, although no one in the family now seems certain if that was because there was only one suitable hollow tree stump or that the volume of available curds was insufficient for something more grandiose.

Life was interesting for my mother's antecedents the Savilles: James, a tall, sinewy character with a built-in refusal to be beaten at anything, and Martha, hard-working and supportive, and, judging from a glance at the family tree, keen to start some kind of minor dynasty in the new country. Life was also tough.

Captain Jean Arthur Albert Benaud, born in Bordeaux, became a naturalised citizen of Australia in 1849, nine years after he arrived on the vessel *Ville de Bordeaux*. For many years Captain Benaud traded between Sydney and the Richmond and Manning Rivers in his ketch *Lightning* and was one of the characters of the Northern Rivers. His son Louis Ferdinand was only three when Jean died, but Louis made sure twenty years later that the shipping section of the *Richmond River Herald* was outstanding and interesting reading, although that always sounded a complete contradiction in terms to me, until I read E. Annie Proulx's *The Shipping News*.

Jean Benaud loved horses and was a keen horseracing man. As soon as any ship of which he was captain reached Taree on his trips up and down the coast, he would rent a horse and go for long rides in the bush. He was killed in an accident when thrown from a horse in Pulteney Street, Taree, after returning from a race meeting in nearby Wingham on 3 July 1866. He was in a coma for three days before the effects of the fractured skull proved too much. Two of his children were Louis Ferdinand the newspaper founder and Richard Grainger Napoleon the jeweller and watchmaker, my grandfather.

On 18 July 1925, in Sydney, there was some laughter and chiacking when the assembled Teachers' College graduates heard the first announcement of their initial postings and that their co-graduate Lou Benaud would be going to what sounded a remote spot, One Tree. In fact, they had forgotten he was born down the road from what was to be his first teaching school. Coraki might have been a very small place, but it made up in warmth and care what it might have lacked in numbers and my father often told me of what a wonderful childhood he was given there by his parents and his friends. Perhaps that was one of the reasons he and my mother tried to make the same thing happen for me and for John in later years. Lou was one of a number of kids in the town who played cricket on the grassy area between the main street and the river. The south arm of the Richmond River was joined at Coraki by the north arm and then it was used by ships and river boats as a way to reach Lismore. 'Coraki' itself is an aboriginal name which means 'meeting of the water'.

Richard and Nellie Benaud, and their children Jack, Gladys and Lou, lived on the western bank of the river in a weatherboard home with a surrounding verandah, with the front facing in such a way that the sun burst on them early in the morning. In the account left by my father, *The Kid From Coraki*, the children never seemed to have a moment to spare in any day. They were always *doing* something, making their own fun. Cricket was played using bats home-made from carefully cut packing case material, knotty riverbank willow or lantana roots. Stumps were kerosene tins, and tennis balls were used.

Richard Grainger Napoleon Benaud, my grandfather the watchmaker, made Lou and his brother Jack a clockwork boat each, which they started sailing in a large bathtub before graduating to the river, where they always made certain they had strong, light thread attached to the tiny vessels so they could be retrieved in case of sinking in some rough water. Sugarcane was shipped downstream on the south arm of the river and pieces were thrown on to the bank for the congregating children to sample, and every weekend picnics were organised by the Benauds and their friends the McCallums to go up the South Arm. The two large rowing boats went up the river past the goannas lying along the tree limbs, past the masses of redbills, water hens and shags, and the clever thing was to spot the mopokes high in the trees, the birds' feathers blending perfectly with the foliage.

Richmond Terrace was the hub of Coraki and Lou's favourite shop was the one owned and run by his mother Nellie. Many of the items in the shop were still brought by ship from Sydney, in the same way as, many years earlier, Captain Jean Benaud had brought goods up the coast. In 1910 there was Turkish Delight, Bulgarian rock, marshmallows, Tobler's Swiss chocolates, diamond jubes and liquorice belts and pipes. The most popular items, and the best sellers, were Nellie Benaud's home-made meat pies, plus her special vanilla ices, which were churned by whichever member of the family might be available – these were regarded by customers on the river as outstanding.

Aged sixteen, older brother Jack left school wanting to be a postmaster and accepted a job in the post office at Bangalow, a town near Byron Bay north of Casino.

Richard Grainger Napoleon Benaud accepted the position of manager of a jewellery and watchmaking business at Grafton, a hundred miles to the south on the Clarence River. Nellie, Glad and Lou went to Penrith on holiday to have a look, for the future, at a town my grandmother knew well, as she had been born not far away on the other side of the Blue Mountains, at Lithgow. Lou thought he could never feel sadder than when Jack went to Bangalow, but the day the family left Coraki for ever, he felt, aged thirteen, his heart would break. He had to say goodbye to his schoolboy friends, farewell to the place he loved and to the newsagent's little fox terrier called Toby who, for most of both their lives, had followed Lou all around Coraki every day.

Just as twilight was settling, the three Benauds went to Government Wharf and the drogher took them to Oakland, where the steamer was already loading cargo. Nellie, Glad and Lou boarded the ship and went to their cabins.

'That night, as the ship steamed down the Richmond, I lay on my bunk and wept quietly in the realisation that it was farewell to Coraki and all it meant to me – a beautiful place where two streams met, inhabited by wonderful, happy and friendly folk who had made my boyhood a time to cherish.'

Eight years later, in 1925, he was to return, not as a boy, but a man, and was to start a new, exciting and, at the same time, frustrating period of his life.

Reasons to celebrate
Richie Benaud, *Over But Not Out*, 2010

In 1967, Daphne and I were married, and not long ago we celebrated forty years of being together at home and in business. Daph started with the BBC in the mid-1950s, then worked for E. W. Swanton, which is a good grounding for anyone. She has been personal assistant to several international cricket team managers over the years. Somehow she manages to unravel the chaos I produce, though I imagine it is no easy task.

Nineteen sixty-eight proved to be a momentous year, and not just because it was the year Bob and Grace Gray were married in London and Daphne and I were appointed official caterers to the event. Gray had been best man for me when Daph and I were married the previous summer. The Grays' wedding ceremony was held at St James's, Spanish Place, on Sunday afternoon, the rest day of the Lord's Test, and the reception was at Bob's flat near St John's Wood.

The Benauds decided not to try to outdo Fortnum & Mason, and instead provided smoked salmon sandwiches and a bathtub full of crushed ice, champagne, Foster's and soft drink. The assembled guests included all the members of the Australian team playing at Lord's at the time, bar the skipper, Bill Lawry, who was spending the day with fellow pigeon fanciers.

The early-afternoon reception was timed so the players were all able to have an early night prior to play resuming at Lord's on the Monday. This was very important because Australia were one-nil in the series at that stage, having turned in an outstanding performance at Old Trafford to win the opening Test by 159 runs. In the rain-marred first three days at Lord's, England had moved to 351–7, and that was when they declared on the Monday morning, at which point the Australians were bowled out for 78. I am able to say, hand on heart, that the festivities the previous day, particularly the catering, had nothing to do with it, and Bill Lawry, who hadn't attended the nuptials, was the only batsman to make a duck.

A splendid piece of advice

Richie Benaud, *My Spin on Cricket*, 2005

One of the most pleasant times we've had in recent years was when Daphne and I went with an ITC-organised trip to watch England play West Indies in Barbados and Antigua. This was as a preface to the 2004 English summer, when I was due to cover for Channel 4 and *News of the World* the two series, seven Tests in all, between England, New Zealand and West Indies. As New Zealand were due to tour Australia in October, and then West Indies were going to be there for the triangular series, there was plenty of information to be gained from watching at Kensington Oval, Bridgetown, Barbados and then at the Recreation Ground, St John's, Antigua.

In addition there was the good fortune of having Tony and Joan Lewis and David and Thorunn Gower on the ship and also Laurence and Val Parry from Sarasota, Florida, where I am the Patron of the cricket club which they started many years ago.

The organisation was brilliant, as is always the case with Drew Foster, who was responsible for a splendid piece of advice at the pool-deck bar when we were having a rum punch or two made to the bartender's special recipe. The subject was cricket and Drew asked me a question which I couldn't answer without checking some records. I said to him that he should ask Daphne, who was further along the bar chatting to Val Parry. He did that, received the answer, came back and asked me another question and I said Daph would have the answer. He came back happy with the second answer and asked me a third question. Again I said Daph would definitely know because she had checked the particular Test match only a couple of days ago.

Drew said, 'I'll catch up with everyone at lunch,' and turned to go down the stairs. Then he stopped, walked slowly back to the group at the bar, looked hard at me and said, 'Rich, do you mind if I offer just a small piece of advice? *Don't leave home without Daphne . . .*'

A sad farewell
Richie Benaud, *Anything But . . . an Autobiography*, 1998

By 1992, my parents had been living at Parramatta for fifty-four years, fifty-two of them at Sutherland Road, and they had witnessed all the changes in the city and its surrounds. The vast areas of paddocks had become built-up streets and the place was now a modern bustling metropolis.

Mum and Dad had been healthy for most of the time other than for the occasional problem, but my father began to struggle a little during this year, and much as he disliked medical examinations, he had to have one and the news was bad. It was cancer of the oesophagus and further tests led the doctors to tell him he needed a major operation, one which would take many hours, and there was no subsequent guarantee that it would be successful. Recuperation would be long and painful, if there were to be recuperation.

My parents told John and me the bad news, and my father added that he had decided not to have the op, and that he would be trying to beat the problem in his own way, mind over matter. He had always been very good at that.

At the team meeting he had told us that we were to continue doing the things we would normally do, and that he would be staying at Parramatta, not in hospital, and he and Mum would spend every possible moment in their garden, which is something they had always loved doing. He was brave, as many others have been in the same situation, but it was all to no avail.

In early 1994, I saw him before flying to Brisbane, and I knew he had only a short time. He told me to keep working and make certain I continued to work well, and to do it enthusiastically. He, too, knew time was short.

JB phoned me a few days later in the 'Gabba commentary box during the one-day double-header matches between New Zealand, South Africa and Australia and told me he thought it might be a good idea if I came back to Parramatta. Channel Nine's organisational whiz of that time, Gary Shaw, organised a taxi and a seat on a plane. Ian Chappell and the other commentators handled all the things I would have been doing, and I was off on what was a very sad pilgrimage.

At the time bushfires were sweeping through metropolitan Sydney and the tinder-dry areas of the Blue Mountains, and were threatening John's home at Valley Heights. As we approached Sydney airport from the north, there was a haze covering the city and a red glow away to the right in the Penrith area where I had been born.

Mum and John were there when I arrived at Parramatta, and Dad stayed with us only for another hour, time to say goodbye to a man who had guided us protectively and educationally through our lives and had done his very best for all three of us.

I stayed with Mum until four in the morning, when John returned from Valley Heights where he had been hosing his home, keeping at bay the flames sweeping down the valley, and then I went back to Brisbane.

Lou had told me, 'Remember, do not miss a match under any circumstances,' something he had often said when I was playing, though he needed to backtrack once or twice when injury produced a few chaotic moments in the family. He was one of the best, and it says so where he rests these days.

Another sad farewell
Richie Benaud, *Over But Not Out*, 2010

We were lucky to have them. Mum and Dad were as good as you could have as parents and they looked after JB and me and made certain we understood that there was no more important aspect of life than people. Mum passed away in October 2008 and we gave her a good send-off: seventy people at the crematorium where Dad had been farewelled in 1994, aged eighty-nine. Although Mum didn't drink alcohol, there were many glasses raised to her at the Mean Fiddler, all by people who hadn't reached her age.

She was 104 when she left us. The last five years of her life were spent at an aged care facility at Greystanes, not far from North Parramatta, where she and Dad had spent fifty-eight very happy years. She went there when she realised she had forgotten how to use the microwave and she felt it was time to be looked after.

She had her 100th birthday at the care facility surrounded by relatives and friends and looking at a signed photograph from Her Majesty the Queen wishing her a happy birthday. She was in excellent shape until a bad fall incapacitated her and a few months later it was a merciful release. She was a splendid lady.

IV
TRIBUTES

‘There would be very few Australians who have not passed a summer in the company of Richie Benaud. His voice was even more present than the chirping of the cicadas in our suburbs and towns, and that voice, tragically, is now still. But we remember him with tremendous affection. This is the greatest loss for cricket since Don Bradman.’

Tony Abbott, MP

Richie Benaud, cricket's philosopher king

Gideon Haigh, *The Australian*, 2015

RICHIE BENAUD WAS a stranger to winters, experiencing few as a cricketer in a 63-Test career, and none after 1963 when his life as a commentator and critic began. Instead he became a constant of summers in Australia and England as his era's most celebrated sports broadcaster.

John Arlott has been garlanded as the 'voice of cricket'; Benaud was indisputably the 'face of cricket', being involved in the telecasts of Test matches and one-day internationals by Australia's Channel Nine, the BBC and Channel 4 for half a century.

Behind the microphone, Benaud was a mix of the pithy and the oracular, relying on no particular motifs and no special catchphrases. He drew simply on a lifetime's knowledge, applied pertinently and phrased economically.

In a way, because his opinions so often became gospel, he was as influential as any cricket administrator of the post-war period. In *Wisden Australia*, Dr Greg Manning once denoted him 'cricket's philosopher king'.

The citation for his 2003 lifetime achievement award from the Royal Television Society summed Benaud's style up succinctly: 'No man is better prepared. Never mind the statistician alongside him, providing information – he's already worked out all the information for himself.

'He also manages to make the modern game as compelling as the old game – every day for this remarkable person is as exciting as the day before.'

Benaud the commentator seldom referred to his on-field experiences and accomplishments – a shrewd expedient which had the effect of making him seem almost ageless – and was amused when young admirers inquired innocently whether he had been a player.

In fact, Benaud would rank among Test cricket's elite leg-spinners and captains had he never uttered or written a word about the game.

Benaud's great-grandfather Jean was born in Bordeaux and left France for the Antipodes in 1840. Benaud, born in Penrith, grew up in a classically Australian setting: the country towns of Koorawatha and Jugiong, where his father Lou spent twelve years as a schoolteacher.

He received his first bat at the age of four, cut from the timber of a packing case; he played his first competitive game as a six-year-old on a coir mat pitch with a compressed cork ball.

Youthful memories influenced him strongly, both the recollection of listening to radio broadcasts of cricket from far away, and the dawning awareness that Lou had sacrificed his own cricketing aspirations for the sake of stable employment. Benaud remembered his father's vow to ensure that any sons of his would have the chance to make a cricket career.

As a teenager out of Parramatta High School, Benaud then worked in an accounting firm where he met his first wife Marcia Lavender, but where he was sacked when his absences playing cricket intensified after selection for New South Wales in January 1949.

This, too, left a mark. Benaud was critical of the sacrifices his semi-amateur cricket contemporaries had to make in order to play, asserting as far back as 1960 that 'some players . . . made nothing out of tours' and that 'cricket is now a business' – statements prefiguring his progressive attitudes to cricket's commercialisation when he was a commentator.

For the initial five years of his Test career, which began in February 1952, Benaud was something of an enigma.

He spun and hit the ball hard, and caught superbly in the gully. He exhibited the same positive charge as his idol Keith Miller.

But the dean of English cricket writers, Neville Cardus, found him 'inexplicable', capable of deeds 'which nobody merely talented is able to do', but then guilty of 'gross and elementary errors'. His returns were modest: twenty-seven matches, seventy-three wickets at 28.9, 868 runs at 20.7.

The trajectory of Benaud's career altered utterly with seniority. Upon Australian captain Ian Johnson's retirement in October 1956, Benaud became his country's chief slow bowler.

Under the leadership of Ian Craig in South Africa a year later, he practised tirelessly and ripened rapidly, taking 106 wickets at 19 and scoring 817 runs at 50 in eighteen first-class matches on tour.

When Craig contracted hepatitis on the eve of the 1958–59 Ashes series, Benaud took his job with alacrity, impressing with his tactical legerdemain and irrepressible self-confidence.

Before the Tests, it was rumoured that England's captain Peter May had advised his players: 'Play Benaud down the line. He won't worry you.' He had been thinking of the old Benaud not the new; Australia's captain claimed 31 wickets at 18 in the 4–0 series victory.

Benaud's strengths as a captain extended beyond all-round skill and tactical acumen. He led by both example and empathy, inaugurating the custom of pre-Test dinners, contending that 'cricketers are intelligent people and must be treated as such', and recommending 'an elastic but realistic sense of self-discipline'.

Players reciprocated his trust. He had greats in his corner, such as Neil Harvey, Alan Davidson and Wally Grout. But he was adept at getting the best of modest talents too: on the 1961 Ashes tour, eight players made two hundreds or more, and nine took 40 wickets or more.

Benaud was equally popular with crowds and critics. Usually bareheaded, shirt open as wide as propriety permitted, he was a colourful, outgoing antidote to an austere, tight-lipped era.

Jack Fingleton likened Benaud to Jean Borotra, 'the Bounding Basque of Biarritz' over whom tennis audiences had swooned in the 1920s; he has been credited with originating the demonstrative celebration of wickets and catches that is today de rigueur.

As a journalist himself – for some years an ambulance-chasing police roundsman on Sydney's *Sun* – Benaud was also masterful in the presence of the media, even hosting them in the Australian dressing room.

'I never knew him to squib an awkward question,' remembered the Australian cricket writer Ray Robinson. 'He often came up with answers that defused harmful slants . . . In public relations to benefit the game, Benaud was so far ahead of predecessors that race-glasses would have been needed to see who was at the head of the others.'

Benaud's cricket and public relations zenith was Australia's 1960–61 series against Frank Worrell's West Indians, which encompassed Test cricket's first tie and perhaps its tensest draw.

In the captains' public commitment to entertain with fast scoring and over rates, Fingleton wrote, they 'set an example which other cricket countries will ignore at their peril'. London's *Evening News* acclaimed Benaud as 'the cricketer who has done most to restore life to the game'.

The vibrancy of the cricket actually proved something of a false dawn, though Benaud's leadership in the Ashes series in England in 1961 again occasioned admiration, particularly the fightback he engineered at Old Trafford when the hosts were 2–150 on the last day, requiring only 106 to win at not quite a run a minute.

Benaud, having taken 0–40 from 17 overs, told his vice-captain Harvey: 'We've had it as far as saving this, Ninna. The only way we're going to get out of it is to win.'

Indulging a hunch by coming round the wicket to exploit loose turf outside the right-hander's leg stump, he retained the Ashes for Australia with a match-winning 5–13 from twenty-five deliveries. After the tour he was made an Officer of the British Empire.

Benaud's reputation as a gambling captain has probably been overstated. On the contrary, he planned fastidiously and executed clinically. English writer Alan Ross thought that there had 'never been such a calculating cricketer'.

Off the field, likewise, he impressed as planning his life to the finest degree. 'As a person,' commented his successor Bob Simpson, 'I think he planned every move from the time he got up to the time he went to bed.'

This forethought was evident in Benaud's transition from player to pundit when he retired from cricket in March 1964 with a then-Australian record of 248 Test wickets at 27, 2201 runs at 24.4 and unbeaten in a series as captain. He had already explored his options meticulously.

After the 1956 Ashes tour, Benaud had undertaken a BBC television training course, studying the commentary styles of the likes of Henry Longhurst, Peter O'Sullevan and Dan Maskell in order to understand sport 'from the commentator's point of view'.

He then accepted BBC invitations to England in 1960 as a radio commentator and in 1963 as a television commentator, between times writing the books *Way of Cricket* (1960), *Tale of Two Tests* (1962), *Spin Me A Spinner* (1963) and columns in Sydney's *Sun* and London's *News of the World*.

Ultimately, astute as he was in print and on radio, television was Benaud's calling, suiting his captain's spontaneity and intuition. He was authoritative but not pedantic, dignified but not pompous, and never spoke unless he had something to say. He was so popular that many humorists strove to imitate him, so distinctive that none ever quite got him right.

Again, too, Benaud was broader than the average broadcaster. In 1969, he published the wide-ranging *Willow Patterns*, and left the *Sun* to form a sports marketing consultancy with second wife Daphne (cricket writer E. W. Swanton's secretary, whom Benaud married in July 1967).

Long-held Benaud views about professionalism obtained an outlet when D. E. Benaud & Associates was recruited by Kerry Packer's World Series Cricket in April 1977.

This controversial breakaway circuit, wrote Benaud, 'ran alongside my ideas about Australian cricketers currently being paid far too little and having virtually no input into the game in Australia'. And as consultant and commentator, he contributed inestimably.

To the organisation, he brought cricket know-how; to the product, he applied a patina of respectability. He was the front man to changes wrought in cricket over two years – night play, coloured clothing, the white ball, field-restriction circles, even television coverage from both ends of grounds – that would have taken decades under the game's existing institutions.

The crowd in excess of 50,000 at the SCG's first night match in November 1978, he wrote in *Benaud on Reflection* (1984), was something he'd not forget 'until the moment comes to make my way to that great vineyard cum cricket ground in the sky'.

Benaud's work estranged him from some in cricket's establishment. He described the period as one of 'making new friends and losing old acquaintances'.

But in a way, he joined a new establishment, a sporting-industrial complex that came to hold almost as much sway over cricket as its nominal governors.

And while great players came and went, Benaud remained, always spruce, never at a loss, pervading cricket in both hemispheres, and spanning generations.

Though he published three other compilations of his views on the game, *The Appeal of Cricket* (1995), *My Spin on Cricket* (2005) and *Over But Not Out* (2010), and a somewhat reticent memoir, *Anything But . . . an Autobiography* (1998), he was finally identified almost exclusively with television and its tropes.

Channel 4 changed many aspects of cricket coverage in England when it replaced the BBC in 2000, but made sure to recruit Benaud as a signifier of continuity.

He was its senior commentator for another five years, finally signing off to English audiences at The Oval, whereupon the crowd and the players of both sides stood as one to salute him.

In Australia, Benaud seemed to be continuing into perpetuity when his half-century of broadcasting was curtailed by an accident. In October 2013, aged eighty-three, he crashed his 1963 Sunbeam Alpine into a wall near his Coogee home, sustaining painful breaks.

This entailed a lengthy convalescence, punctuated by talk of comebacks that never eventuated. His voice was last heard in an Australian cricket ground at Adelaide Oval in December: a moving recorded recitation of a tribute to the late Phillip Hughes.

By passing away himself after one of Australian cricket's longest summers, Benaud ensured, as ever, that the game took precedence.

A fond farewell to the quiet voice of an English summer

Mike Atherton, *The Times*, 2015

'WATCH RICHIE.' Like most sportsmen starting out on a second career in broadcasting, I did so without any formal training. So, like any sensible novice, I sought advice. Gary Franses was the producer of Channel 4's cricket coverage in 2002 and that was the advice he gave me: 'Watch Richie.'

So I did. One of my early broadcasts was from Lord's and, before the game began, the cameras were to alight on each of the commentators in various parts of the ground, from where they were to analyse a particular aspect of the day's play.

We were to come to Richie last of all, up in the commentary box, and he was to be the scene-setter for the day – the last voice to be heard before live play began.

I had finished my segment down below and hurried up to the commentary box to listen to the great man do his bit – to watch and learn, as I had been instructed. I stood behind the camera at the back of the box and waited. Richie's turn came; on the director's cue, he turned to the camera, with that one-eye-half-closed look, and began to speak.

Maybe Richie thought he had a lapel microphone attached to his jacket. He did not. Richie spoke, but the viewers heard nothing.

Franses stood behind the camera, waving frantically and pointing to the hand-held microphone on the desk, instructing Richie to pick it up.

Without moving his stare from the camera [. . .] Richie felt around blindly on the desk, picked up what he thought was the microphone, lifted it to his mouth, and began talking into his glasses.

He didn't miss a beat, later laughing the mistake off and happy to be the butt of everyone's jokes for a while. Therein, I suppose, lies Richie's first law of broadcasting: 'It's live telly, mistakes happen'. It's also sport on telly and not the most important thing in the world, so don't get too hung up about it and don't imagine yourself to be more important than you really are. You are only a television commentator.

This humility is closely linked to Richie's second law: 'Remember, above all, that you are a guest in someone's living room, often for six hours a day. Try not to irritate them.'

Not irritating the viewer may sound like a limited ambition for a commentator but – as countless fans of live sport would attest, no doubt – it is not as straightforward as it sounds, especially in cricket when a game can go on for six hours a day for five days.

Ideally, you don't want the viewer switching off – or over – or turning the sound down. So remember, above all, that the viewer is there to watch the action and the cricketers and not to listen to you. Don't impose yourself too heavy-handedly between the viewer and the action. You are a conduit – no more, no less.

If you have been successful so far, Richie may allow you to progress to his third law: 'If you can add to the picture, do so.'

Aside from not irritating the viewer into switching off, you are there to add some insight and to inform, based on your knowledge and experience. That insight may be in the form of an anecdote, or a technical, tactical or human observation, and may be suited to a slow moment or a dramatic one, according to your discretion. But anyone can read the score and tell the viewer what has just happened. It's not radio.

Richie's third law links to his fourth: 'Michael, always engage brain before speaking.' I can't remember what particularly in my commentary prompted that remark, but it is sound advice. Radio demands immediacy as, obviously, people cannot see what is happening. Television occasionally allows for a brief distancing from the action, just enough time for the brain to function. Use it.

Richie's fifth law – 'nobody ever complained about silence'

– is an old-fashioned notion these days, as increasingly television companies move to three commentators in action rather than two and there is a battle for air time. It also might not apply to an Indian audience who, I am told, enjoy a full-on visual and audio experience – one reason perhaps why Bill Lawry, say, was always more popular on the subcontinent than Richie was.

Richie has always been immensely popular in England where, I think, audiences enjoyed his understated style, pauses and silences.

And Richie's final law of broadcasting: 'Never use the term "We" when talking about a team.'

Neutrality and fairness were non-negotiable for two very good reasons: first, you are an observer not a cheerleader; second, although there will be a home audience, within that there may be many people cheering for the other team. You need to be fair to both sides. Most broadcasts these days go around the world in any case, and so you are speaking to cricket-lovers of all nationalities.

Richie understood television. He played in an era before television gripped cricket, became a key mover in the Packer revolution and he knew how television could help to sell and grow the game.

He was not averse to a little understated showmanship: the beige jackets that came to define him, the sayings – 'morning everyone' – that did the same. He worked the camera beautifully. The best commentators provoke imitation and Richie had thousands of imitators. Who among us has not said some phrase or other in Benaud-speak?

He saw television commentary as a craft, and one to be excelled at. In meetings before the start of a test series he was meticulous about the pronunciation of names, especially if, for example, Sri Lanka were touring. And I have lost count of the number of times he said to me: 'It's a pitch, Michael, not a wicket. The three bits of wood are wickets.' Or: 'Please don't start interview questions with "must".' ('You must be pleased with . . .' being a statement and not a question.) Small things, but important.

Richie never morphed into an old-school bore. He rarely talked about his playing days, or his considerable achievements as a player. He never began a commentary stint or a sentence with 'in my day. . .'. He admired the modern player; he loved Twenty20 and all the technological advances – especially his beloved Snicko. He wore his playing achievements lightly.

He recognised that times change and that comparisons are pointless. Because of that, the modern players loved him.

He was loved. For longer than people care to remember he was the voice of the English summer, just as he was in Australia. Thinking back now, I can hear him in 2005, at the culmination of the greatest test match I have seen at Edgbaston, exactly the right man for the moment as he followed the pictures with succinct but dramatic precision: 'Jones! Bowden! Kasprowicz the man to go and Harmison has done it! Despair on the faces of the batsmen and joy for every England player on the field!'

Richie's laws distilled.

For the pleasure he gave as a great player and as a wonderful commentator, and for the kindness and consideration he showed to this young commentator trying to make his way in the game, a belated 'thank you' to Richie Benaud.

Richie Benaud
David Frith, *Guardian*, 2015

Richie Benaud was perhaps best known latterly for his work as a global cricket commentator, with his distinctive voice, familiar fixed gaze, prominent bottom lip and carefully tended coiffure. But he had been a distinguished performer for Australia on the cricket field himself, playing for his country for twelve years until 1964.

The best of his career hung principally on the exhilarating Test series of 1960–61, when he captained Australia against the visiting West Indies side led by Frank Worrell. Some tedious contests had been inflicted on the watching public, with more to follow in the 1960s. But that extraordinary five-match encounter produced electrifying batsmanship, and bowling that was less concerned with shutting the game down than keeping it moving.

The opener at Brisbane delivered the thrill of cricket's first tied Test match. At Adelaide, a nation was brought to a standstill during a long, pulsating last-wicket stand between Ken Mackay and the near-hopeless No 11 Lindsay Kline as they secured an unlikely draw for Australia. When, a few months later in England, Benaud took veteran Ray Lindwall's advice and bowled his legspin around the wicket into the rough, when all seemed lost in the Old Trafford Test, his wicket-taking that afternoon ensured that Australia retained the Ashes and raised the captain close to sainthood in the estimation of his team and his country.

Benaud, who was born in Penrith, just west of Sydney, into a family of Huguenot origin, had a keen cricketer for a father. Lou Benaud, who had once taken all twenty wickets in a bush match, keenly and wisely guided his two sons. John, who played in three Tests, was thirteen years younger. After attending Parramatta High School, Richie made his New South Wales debut on the final day of 1948. Three years later, against the West Indies at Sydney, he first played for Australia. His selection was frequently questioned in those early years, when much other flowering talent was evident in domestic cricket. In 1952–53 Benaud played against

South Africa, recording a duck and having his front teeth smashed while fielding at gully in the Sydney Test, which coincided with his honeymoon. It was not the first time he had been hospitalised by a blow to the head. Four years previously he had been hit in the face while batting for New South Wales 2nd XI in Melbourne.

Then came the 1953 tour, the first of three he was to make to England as a player. In his three Tests he averaged just three runs with the bat – scoring 15 runs over five innings – and took two wickets for 174 before ending the long tour in glory with 135 in a festival match at a crowded Scarborough ground, hitting eleven sixes to equal the world record at that time. Against Len Hutton's dominant England tourists in 1954–55 he again did little with bat or ball, just as he struggled in 1956 on his second tour of England, the Lord's Test apart: having taken a memorably sharp reflex catch in the gully to dismiss Colin Cowdrey, Benaud was at his cavalier best in an innings of 97, ended by a top edge as he tried to reach his hundred in the grand manner by hooking Fred Trueman.

On the way home Benaud finally fulfilled his potential by taking 7–72 (this remained his best Test return) at Madras to set up an Australian innings victory over India, the short series being sealed at Calcutta in the third Test when Benaud took 11 wickets for 105. Having helped Australia win the 1955 series in the West Indies (Benaud's century in Jamaica, one of five in an innings of 758–8 – still Australia's highest total in Tests – came in a mere 78 minutes), after four years and twenty-seven Test matches it was felt at last that he truly belonged in the side.

His performances in South Africa in 1957–58 reinforced that belief. Often bare-headed, and a somewhat stooping, rangy figure at the crease, he cracked a century in both the Johannesburg Tests, averaged 54 in the series, and took 30 wickets at a rate of just under 22 runs each in the five Tests. Time and again he and fellow bowler Alan Davidson took the opposition by storm, and the Australians, led by 22-year-old Ian Craig, finished the tour unbeaten. Then, within the year, Richie Benaud became captain of his country. Craig had fallen ill, and just when the senior player, Neil Harvey, was expected to succeed to the leadership, Benaud's name was announced. The selectors' long-term planning had reached fulfilment.

His first series as skipper was remarkable for a number of reasons. A strong England party, led by Peter May, were widely expected to retain the Ashes. But some of them played below expectation, and Australia's attack contained several bowlers whose actions were perceived as highly suspicious. Benaud's crew cruised to a 4–0 victory, the skipper taking 31 wickets for an average of 18.83 runs each. Within the year he had spun his way to a further 47 wickets in eight Tests in Pakistan and India, and all was set for what was perceived as a world championship contest against the visiting West Indies team. The chairman of selectors, Sir Donald Bradman, made it clear that he was keen to see Test cricket rescued from a period of dull introversion, and the two captains approached the series in a positive frame of mind.

By that summer's end, with the beaten but popular West Indies having had a tickertape motorcade send-off in Melbourne, Richie Benaud's own popularity was sealed. He had brought novel flashes of exhibitionism into play on the cricket field, racing over to embrace a fieldsman after a catch, his own shirt unbuttoned almost to the navel. Soon after television came to Australia he appeared in a commercial, tending his garden with a Victa lawnmower. In 1961 he was made an OBE for services to cricket.

The Ashes were retained in England in 1961, though a shoulder injury kept Benaud from the Lord's Test, which was won by Australia under Harvey. The decisive victory came in the fourth Test, at Old Trafford, when Benaud's 6–70 and an unlikely Australian 54-run victory shamed England, who fell from 150 for one to 201 all out.

In his final Ashes series, in 1962–63, the tempo reverted to that of the bad old days. Three of the Tests were drawn, Australia's Bill Lawry, Bob Simpson and Ken Mackay scoring at a snail's pace (matched by Geoff Pullar, Ken Barrington and Cowdrey for England). Although the shoulder injury had affected him, Benaud did produce a memorable piece of bowling in the New South Wales match against England, taking 7–18, his best figures in first-class cricket.

The next season saw the last of Benaud on the field of play, apart from some later charity matches and light-hearted private tours. He played three Tests against South Africa in 1963–64 under his successor as captain, Simpson, whacking a memorable 90 on his home ground, Sydney, having calmly endured the trauma at the start of the season of captaining for the last time while his key fast bowler, Ian Meckiff, was repeatedly called by umpire Colin Egar for throwing. Benaud removed Meckiff from the attack and did not recall him.

His career in television then took off, while his contract with the *News of the World* was to proceed for half a century until the paper closed in 2011. That TV commentary style lent itself to much mimicry, and his pronouncements, carefully rationed, were widely regarded as gospel. He was shrewd not only from the weight of experience but in the cautious way he rationed opinions. Such guarded humour as he evinced bore the touch of a man who was keen to be seen above all else as discerning.

Although Benaud preferred to avoid controversy, he waded in when covering Australia's tour of the West Indies in 1965, taking eye-opening photographs of the fast bowler Charlie Griffith and writing of his concerns over the legality of the Barbadian's action.

His major advisory work for Kerry Packer during cricket's revolutionary upheaval in the late 1970s alienated him in some traditional quarters, one consequence being an outcry for Benaud to be removed from BBC's television commentary panel. But he was a survivor, even if his friendship with Bradman never quite recovered from that cricket civil war.

He wrote a number of books ... and there were two books about him, one by A. G. Moyes and a later study by Mark Browning. While a move to preserve Benaud's childhood home failed, he was honoured with a life-size statue at the Sydney Cricket Ground, his spiritual home.

A true one-off

Jonathan Agnew, *BBC Sport*, 2015

RICHIE BENAUD was the doyen of cricket commentators.

He was quite simply peerless. Nobody else had his authority, popularity and skill. If you speak to any broadcaster from any sport, they will point to Richie as the standard-bearer. He had this unique style – the choice of words, how he delivered them, the way he looked – and it all came together to make him one of the most recognisable people on television.

His incredible knack was knowing what to say and when to say it – usually as briefly as possible. Richie's basic premise was not to speak unless he could add something to the television pictures. He was brilliant at saying just what was required and you knew that with Richie at the microphone the broadcast was complete.

The cream jacket, the steely grey hair and his clipped voice made him a mimic's dream. Rory Bremner and company had an easy job. But his gravitas meant he became an icon among fans, myself included. He was the face of my childhood and for millions of others. He *was* cricket on the

TV in England. He was our Richie – and that is the ultimate compliment for an Australian.

For my generation of commentators coming through, he was the man. I had the privilege of working with him for BBC TV at the 1999 World Cup, when he was my rock. As a radio commentator, I was a novice on TV and anxious about presenting with him. My first programme was a shambles. I missed the countdown to zero in my ear from the producer and was still talking as the show ended. The next time, Richie simply asked me how long I needed for my final comments. I added them up to seven seconds. Every time we were on air from then onwards, he stopped talking at eight seconds and let me sign off on the button. He was so good that he could edit his own comments down in his head to the precise second.

I never saw him as anything but unflappable. He was the face of calm. No matter what chaos was going on in the background – and there is plenty during a live broadcast – as long as Richie was at the helm, you knew that everything would be fine. He was a natural in front of the camera, but you also could learn so much from his discipline, preparation and application.

As a trainee journalist with the BBC while he was still an international player, he was knocking on doors asking for quotes, conducting interviews or writing obituaries. How many commentators have done that? When he was writing for the *News of the World*, he may have had only 300 words to file. Yet he was still the first person in the press box every day, poring over his notes. He took his work incredibly seriously.

Interestingly, Richie the broadcaster – so disciplined, so self-restrained – was quite a contrast to Richie the player – a daring, dashing captain who loved taking chances. He was a typical legspinner, tossing up a bit of bait to the batsmen.

Away from the microphone, he was always fine company. Although not a back-slapping and laugh-a-minute kind of guy, he was kind, generous and simply loved talking about the game. Brian Johnston, the late *Test Match Special* commentator, held a birthday party at his house in London during the Lord's Test every year and I will always remember simply sitting in the garden chatting about

cricket with Richie. It was invariably a pleasure.

You never heard him say the game was better in his day. He was a great moderniser and a key figure in the start of World Series Cricket, which revolutionised the sport in the 1970s and 1980s.

He could give strident opinions when he had to. He hated bad behaviour on the field and described the infamous underarm ball which gave Australia victory over New Zealand in a one-day international in 1981 as 'one of the worst things I have ever seen done on a cricket field'.

Whenever Richie spoke, whether it was on TV or not, you listened.

The fact he was still broadcasting until the age of 83 was extraordinary. It is only a shame he did not get the send-off he deserved – the game of cricket has not had a chance to say goodbye. Knowing Richie, he would have taken it in an embarrassed, humble sort of way with as little fanfare as possible. That was the type of man he was.

Captain of his country, one of the finest allrounders of his era and a broadcaster beyond compare for five decades ... there will never be another Richie Benaud. He was a one-off.

Australia's master commentator

Mike Selvey, *Guardian*, 2015

THE TRUE VOICES of sport, the really memorable ones, are those who transcend a catch-phrase or a personality trait, to become recognisable not only for that voice but for the way in which they are imitated. We have all tried the impressions, and they are few: John Arlott's Hampshire burr ('shirt flapping, elbows working, he runs in . . .'); Murray Walker's nasal delivery as a complement to the engine noise around him ('and *there* goes Ayrton Senna . . .'); Geoffrey Boycott's 'techneeeeque' perhaps or Henry Blofeld's 'dear old thing'.

But then there was Richie. Always Richie, not Benaud. Perhaps the most imitated of them all, from the comedian Billy Birmingham to just about anyone who has ever followed cricket. Richie was not just a voice or a memorable turn of phrase, but a visual personality too, arguably the most cele-brated television commentator of them all.

So when we imitate Richie we do it wearing an imaginary pastel jacket, body turned side-ways at 45 degrees but head to the camera, with bottom lip protruding. That in itself would be sufficient to identify him. Then, though, came the words and the manner in which he enunciated, totally distinctive, quite unlike any other: the way in which he alone could say 'siveny chew for chew' or 'morn-ing everywunnn' or 'maaarvellush'.

I can still remember with clarity one of the first pieces of commentary I heard from him, as he did a voiceover for high-lights of the 1970–71 Ashes tour: 'We pick up play in the seventh over of the day, and it's Snow bowling to Stackpole'. Shnow. Shtackpole.

Richie's stock-in-trade was always economy of words, an old-fashioned virtue in an age when one aspiring cricket commentator of my acquaint-ance was told by prospective employers, following a meas-ured, understated debut, that he wasn't 'loud enough. Every ball has to be an event'.

Richie saw himself as a complementary figure to the television pictures rather than the main event with the cricket as a sideshow. He let the pictures do the talking, as it were, and offered nothing that he did not consider would add value to what the viewer could already see. It wasn't about him.

Which do you think would sit in the memory thirty-odd years on? 'Great shot by Botham, huge, a maximum' or simply a silence and then 'that's gone into the confectionery stall ... and out again'. Who, indeed, would call it a confectionery stall in the first place? Economy of words and a picture painted for ever.

I was struck by the manner in which Richie would always tend towards overstating the skills of players while fighting shy of criticising, as if he felt he was an ambassador for them. There was always mild amusement when he talked about a bowler sending down a 'leg-cudder' and 'rolling his fingers across the seam' to do so, when we knew the ball had just gone off the seam in the first place. He was investing in them a skill they did not possess, but in so doing was adding mystique.

There were times, too, when he could enter the world of hyperbole and invention, but even then it merely seemed to add gravitas and deep knowledge. So, for example, with not the slightest piece of empirical evidence, a sliding piece of fielding would have 'saved, oh, point two of a second' but because Richie said so, that is what it did. And there was never a new non-existent delivery that Shane Warne had apparently developed with which to taunt England before the Ashes that nonetheless Richie was not subsequently able to pick with authority during the series.

It is for others to expand on how wonderful a cricketer he was, and a captain to rank with the finest. The series in which he led Australia against Frank Worrell's West Indians remains iconic and his post-series broadcasting with Worrell already a masterful piece of what we would now call media relations.

By then Richie was already carving out an alternative career as a journalist, something that he pursued almost to the end. In England he was the figurehead for the *News of the World*'s cricket coverage, and if this might seem to have been incongruous in a world where ghosted columns tend to rule (and he was incredibly loyal to that particular employer), then those who frequented the press box on a Saturday would always see him set up at a desk, dutifully filing his 800 or 900 words of considered copy, knowing that only a couple of hundred would be extrapolated. He was that diligent.

I have a small personal story of his totally meticulous nature. My family had come to Australia for Christmas during the 2006–07 series, and one of my sons had a book, *100 Greatest Australian Cricketers*, into which he was hoping to get as many relevant signatures as he could.

The morning after the Melbourne Test we arranged to see Richie in the lobby of the Langham hotel prior to him returning to Sydney. He arrived promptly to the second, chatted in a fatherly way to what was then an overawed nine-year-old, insisted on using his own pen (fountain, of course) and asked whether Josh was short for Joshua. He wanted to get things right. And so there it is, in a proper, cultured, legible hand: 'To Joshua, Always enjoy the game no matter what. Best wishes. Richie Benaud.'

'Enjoy the game' could almost be his epitaph.

My friend the colossus

Henry Blofeld, *Daily Telegraph*, 2015

IT IS NOT EASY to do justice to Richie Benaud. His record as a captain and an all-round cricketer was more than remarkable, and he went on to reach heights as a television commentator that had not previously been scaled.

His second career made him even more famous than his first, and gave him just as much pleasure. Benaud had as light a touch in the commentary box as he appeared to have when purveying cricket's most romantic and generally unreliable product: wrist spin. This lightness of touch, on the field or in the box, was the product of great thought combined with hard work and an extraordinary dedication to both subjects. He was also intensely human – persuading you rather than trying to ram something down your throat.

When Benaud, the legspinner, brought up another close fielder it was the product of as much perception and preparation as when Benaud, the commentator, paused for a purposeful ten seconds. Less gifted colleagues would have rambled on without adding anything very much.

No one can have understood the game as well or have appreciated better what was required at any given moment of a player or a commentator. Indeed, the two roles required many common qualities to carry off, of which humour, patience, unflappability, persistence and, of course, ability were the most important.

I am sure there is no successful and long-standing cricket commentator who has not profited from Benaud's example. Television and radio are different, but he influenced both. Television requires the commentator to analyse the picture the viewer can see. He must try and point out things the viewer may not appreciate on his own; direct his eyes to something significant he might miss. Above all, he must not describe the action, for that the viewer can see for himself.

Benaud was a master of this. He never wasted words, and understood better than anyone before or since the value of the pause. Sometimes silence underlines and emphasises a point just made. At other times there are deeds which simply speak

for themselves and do not need to be cluttered up with words. On radio, of course, the commentator has to describe everything. 'And he comes into bowl . . .' is essential on radio just as it is superfluous on television. Nonetheless, Benaud's economy and choice of words, together with the occasional brief pause, are legacies which he passed from the television to the radio box.

He understood both of these worlds.

I was lucky to get to know Richie quite well on my first tour of Australia. As an impecunious freelance, I watched the West Indies play there in 1968–69. I had met Benaud playing for former *Telegraph* cricket correspondent E. W. Swanton's Arabs, and when he heard I was going out to Australia, he and his wife, Daphne, once a long-serving secretary of Swanton's, asked me if I would like to save on hotel bills and stay with them in their apartment in the Sydney suburb of Coogee.

To be asked to stay with Richie Benaud on your first tour of Australia was a bit like being offered board by W. G. Grace in the 1880s on your first visit to Bristol. There were two Tests and a New South Wales match in Sydney on that tour. I must have stayed for nearly a month in all and I learned so much from my charming, considerate, immensely generous and always interested host.

Conversationally, at home, he seemed to choose his words almost as carefully as he did on air, although the pauses were fewer. What he said was inevitably to the point. He loved having people to dinner just as he enjoyed his food and wine – Daphne's cooking was high up the Richter scale of these things. He knew lots about wine too, and shrewdly put Australia's produce into a new perspective for me. There was never any side to Richie when he was telling you something: just a charming certainty.

Talking about each day's cricket over dinner was an object lesson. He pointed out so many things I had not even noticed. He talked in that inimitable and highly imitable voice of the intricacies of placing a field. His analytical brain taught me to interpret what would be going on in a captain's mind when he brought up, say, an extra short

leg or put a man in at short straight mid on. It was fascinating object lesson, so gently taught, and suddenly thanks to Richie, my own personal cricketing map expanded.

You never knew who was coming to dinner. One evening it was Don Bradman, who was then chairman of the Australian Test selectors. The Don, in his surprisingly squeaky voice, and Richie pulled each other's legs a fair bit. There was much laughter and also interesting technical matters were discussed. It was obvious that the Don hugely respected Richie.

A few years later I was commentating for a commercial radio network in Australia and Richie joined us for the games in Sydney. It goes without saying that he moved brilliantly and seamlessly from one box to the other.

The world of commentating and the world of cricket have both lost a colossus. Richie Benaud was a world champion both on the field and in the commentary box. The game's most famous voice has been stilled.

What an innings

David Gower, *Sunday Times*, 2015

THE FIRST THING to say about Richie Benaud as a broadcaster – and perhaps as an all-round cricketer of the late 1950s and early 1960s, although that was a little too long ago for me to judge first-hand – is that he was, quite simply, the best. He was the best at finding the right word at the right moment, at catching the mood, and at knowing when to speak and when not to speak.

The key bit of advice he gave me when I sat alongside him for the first time in a commentary box while working for Channel Nine at the 1992 World Cup in Australia was to always engage brain before speaking. Never were truer words spoken.

A lot of what we hear on television today, not just in cricket and not just in sport, is very instinctive and reactive. Richie was the master of taking a moment, without letting it pass, to find the right phrase and to say precisely the right thing. He also had the rare ability to say nothing when there was nothing to say.

He had the self-confidence to know that if he was caught out or made a mistake (and that was rare), he would cover it seamlessly or carry on as though nothing had happened.

One of his expressions was: 'We'll just let the viewer worry about that one.' It is why he was held in such affection because getting it right counts for a lot. The ability to take everything in your stride, coolly and calmly, is an absolute bonus on live television.

Some of his phrases seemed to linger for ever, such as his comment during Ian Botham's famous innings at Headingley in 1981 when the ball went 'into the confectionery stall and out again'. Then there were his unique pronunciations such as '222 for two', and his very particular way of looking at the camera with his gimlet eye – a trick he picked up even during his time as Australia captain. He knew the power of the camera and how to make it work to his advantage. He connected with the nation and the viewer. He was an innovative captain, a strong competitor and highly successful, which meant he had a good background as a player, but he also trained properly as a broadcaster and journalist.

In his early days on the Sydney *Sun* he worked as a crime reporter and suchlike. To make things look as effortless as he did takes hard work.

Working in Australia during our winters and in England during our summers, and with jobs as a writer and broadcaster, he was so thoroughly involved in the game that he was a master of his subject. He probably watched or played in more Tests than anybody else. He also possessed a very good memory for events and conversations that had taken place many years earlier – an invaluable asset for a broadcaster. He had a wealth of stories.

His vast experience served him well when a big story broke. He was far too shrewd to rush into a judgement that he might swiftly have regretted as events continued to unfold.

He was also knowledgeable in areas other than cricket. He loved his wine and keenly followed the horses. He would set up his desk at the back of the commentary box when he was not in front of the microphone and check on his laptop to see how the horses were going, without ever failing to keep an eye on the game that was being played out in front of us.

When I joined the BBC commentary team after retiring as a player in 1993, Tony Lewis was the presenter, and Richie was the senior figure. I had already spent a couple of winters with him in Australia, where he was the main presenter. So as far as I was concerned, it was simply about looking and learning from the master. Every movement was unhurried yet precise. The microphone was picked up, and put down again. The words came out clearly and properly, and succinctly.

How does this man do it?

He epitomised the saying that practice makes perfect. In his case it really did. He was always happy to impart words of wisdom to those trying to follow in his significant footsteps, and he was very easy to get on with.

Richie was always adaptable to changes in broadcasting styles, too. In the 1990s he would be working for the BBC, where there were no advert breaks between overs, as well as Channel Nine in Australia, where there were. And he sailed through it, without any issues at all. More recently he worked as one of three Channel Nine commentators who were on air at one time, which was not easy given how sparingly he used words. He was able to accept developments on and off the field, and appreciate them. It was a great gift.

This was never more evident than when Kerry Packer arrived on the scene. While others saw him only as a threat, Richie became a key adviser and ultimately shaped the way the game was played in Australia. One of Packer's rewards was to make him the number one figure on his Channel Nine commentary team. Another, perhaps less welcome, was being sent up in Billy Birmingham's Twelfth Man spoofs.

Given his astonishing output, his mistakes were incredibly rare. I saw him once in Sydney make an error reading out the bowling figures and he asked the producer if he could do it again, only to be told: 'No, Richie, we're live.' He continued as though nothing had happened.

Also, in the build-up to the start of his final day of commentary in England, during the Oval Test of the 2005 series against Australia, he began by picking up his pen and speaking into that rather than his microphone. Given the circumstances, it was an entirely understandable mistake.

A true leader

Geoffrey Boycott, *Daily Telegraph*, 2015

I WOULD LOVE TO HAVE played under Richie Benaud. He would have been firm and very clear-thinking. I have talked to Bill Lawry and Bobby Simpson, Ron Harvey and Ray Lindwall, and they say he gave his players clear instructions – and that's all you ever want from a captain.

Richie would get a table when his team were batting and do his mail but always made sure his players could watch him. He was a leader, not just a captain in name only. If you can carry your men with you, in business or the armed forces or sport, it is a gift and he had it. You might not always agree with him but he gets you to play for him – that's the key to leadership.

One time, when he was leading Australia in Pakistan, he told his twelfth man that he was the most important player in the team. When we are batting, Richie said, I want you to go down to the ground ahead of the team in the morning and make sure the matting is pulled tight – there was no grass in Karachi in those days. If the ground staff were allowed to leave the matting loose the Pakistan bowlers would be able to make the ball move all over the place. The twelfth man hadn't to leave until the umpires came out, then he could have the rest of the day off.

The first couple of times I met him was when I was playing for Yorkshire and England, but injured. When John Snow broke my arm in 1967 and I missed the Gillette Cup final, and when Bob Willis broke my finger in 1972. Both times I got invited as a special guest commentator with Richie and Jim Laker at BBC TV, which was then black and white.

The thing about Richie was that he very rarely offered advice until he was asked to. When you asked him, he was very generous and helpful. I was interested in commentating long before I finished playing because I loved cricket and it seemed to me a job in summer and winter that was not exactly work.

He gave me advice that has stayed with me for ever. He said: 'Don't talk too much, let people enjoy the pictures, and when you speak, try and give the viewers something to add to their experience of watching. Always remember to speak about the picture that the viewer sees, never talk about things the viewer can't see, and the viewer is paramount. Pause just before the bowler gets to his delivery stride – this allows the editors to cut for highlights and replays, and be aware in commentating that microphones may be live even when they shouldn't be. If you swear off mike in the commentary box, never assume that it's switched off and it might go out to the public.'

Richie was a man of careful delivery, very succinct, with a dry sense of humour, and very astute about everything going on. When he was not on air he often gave the impression that he was working on his computer and might have missed something, but it was a big mistake to assume that. He never missed a trick.

I remember once, when England had been beaten very badly by Australia at Lord's. The next day there was a NatWest match televised at Edgbaston, and at teatime someone thought about Tony Lewis interviewing Richie to get an Australian view, to fill fifteen minutes of the interval, which is a long time on TV. Tony Lewis said to Richie, 'What do England have to do to improve?' Richie replied, 'They have to practise their batting, their bowling and their fielding.' Tony said, 'Anything else?' Richie said, 'No, that's enough to be going on with.' Then there were thirteen minutes left to fill!

He was respected, adored and loved by an older generation who had known him almost since the start of cricket on television. Cricket-watchers felt comfortable with him on air. He fronted the BBC highlights show for years and became an institution, an icon.

Although a former Australian cricketer – and deep down he admitted he always wanted Australia to do well – he made a point of staying neutral in his commentary, and I think this endeared him to everybody.

TV has changed: in this modern era we have got music between overs, DRS and spider-cams, players miked up during matches, and Richie just embraced it all. He accepted that these new-fangled gimmicks affect how some people view the game, especially young people,

but he knew they didn't change the game itself. So he took it in his stride and he didn't change his style.

I only batted against him once because 1961 was his last tour of England and he finished Test cricket in 1963. It was on the MCC tour of Australia in 1965–66 and he played for the Prime Minister's XI in Canberra. Wally Grout was the wicketkeeper, and I remember Richie set me up with a couple of legspinners just short of a length, which I jumped on and pulled for boundaries. Then a third one, very similar, I went to pull and it was a fast topspinner and hit me on top of the back leg right in front. Luckily it was too high and going over the top and I got away with it. He just looked at me, and I knew he was a crafty bugger, even though he had been retired for two years.

He was like Peter Alliss, part of the fabric of his sport. You cannot think of cricket without Richie. Peter, still going strong, and Richie have made such a fantastic impression that they will be remembered and loved for ever.

Listening to Richie was like having your neck gently massaged

Angus Fraser, *Independent*, 2015

AS A RATHER LIMITED lower-order batsman I did not have many bat-makers asking me to use their equipment. Because of this I spent the last few years of my career having a bit of fun with my bats. Each season Salix would supply me with a plain, stickerless piece of willow and I would then have a caricature carved into the back of it.

The caricature varied from season to season but above the carving was an empty box where I could place a message on a piece of tape. The aim was to catch the attention of the stump cameras that were present at international matches and to have a bit of fun with the commentary team. The first message I placed in the box was for the attention of Richie Benaud. It simply read 'G'day Richie'. I believe my slightly childish behaviour got a response from the great man, probably nothing more than 'G'day Angus'.

That Richie was the commentator I tried to engage with highlighted the impact he had obviously had on me. It is only now as I sit back and think of my summer holidays as a teenager and the hours I spent lying on the sofa watching England play that I realise how his description and summary of the game helped grow my love for it. It was also the way in which he presented the Channel Nine highlights packages wearing his cream blazer.

Richie's style was unique. Unlike in the modern era, where three commentators are at times competing to be heard and attempting to out-quote each other, Richie only spoke when he had something to add to the pictures.

His was a style wonderfully suited to cricket. Unlike many sports, cricket is not always a 100 mph, in-your-face, confrontational game. The sport ebbs and flows. It has quiet periods, sessions where stock is being taken and the next move thought through. Many people attend or watch cricket matches to relax, which seems the polar opposite to football, where fans turn up to get things off their chests by screaming and shouting at their team or the opposition for ninety minutes. Listening to Richie, however, was soothing. It was a joy. There were occasions when listening to a thirty-minute commentary stint of his was like having the back of your neck gently massaged.

Only the other day I came across a clip of myself bowling on YouTube. The clip was in the summer of 1990 when Sachin Tendulkar drove me through mid-off for three to complete his first international hundred. Richie was commentating at the time and he summed up the situation magnificently. 'Tendulkar on 98,' as I ran in to bowl. 'And there it is ... a Test match hundred for Tendulkar ... aged 17 years and 112 days ... one of the youngest ever to hit a Test match hundred ... an innings of temperament, skill and delightful strokeplay.' As ever he summed up the moment beautifully. The commentary was calm. There was no screaming or hyperbole. It was factually and technically accurate. It was simple.

That I want to refer to him as Richie in this article says something, too. The reason for this was that I, and I would imagine millions of others, almost feel that I had a personal relationship with him. It was his voice that guided me through my early years of watching cricket on television. It is his catchphrases that I can still remember. Each morning during the summer school holidays Alastair, my brother, and I would roll downstairs at about 10.30 a.m. and spend the next few hours lazing around on the sofa. He was always the commentator you wanted to listen to and the person we tried to imitate.

I would not describe myself as a good friend of his but I remember the first time I met him at the Sydney Cricket Ground in the winter of 1988–89. I was playing Grade cricket for Western Suburbs but had gone to the SCG to watch Australia play West Indies in a one-day international. I was chatting to a mutual friend in the Don Bradman Stand when Richie walked past. Recognising my friend, he stopped and chatted for five minutes. During the conversation I said I would one day love to play out there, under those lights in such a wonderful arena. As he left he just said: 'Work hard and you will.'

While playing for England and during my time working for the *Independent* I was fortunate enough to spend a couple of lunches and dinners in his company. Away from commentary he was exactly the same as when he was on air. He was polite, immaculately dressed and did not dominate conversations or want to be the centre of attention. Even though he was an outstanding cricketer and captain he was very modest and said little.

But when he did speak or tell a story you listened. And it was in his storytelling that his genuine love for cricket came through. The tales came from his heart, as did the fond way he talked about those he played against.

'Legend' is a word that is too often used to describe the achievements of an individual but cricket has lost a legendary figure.

The wonderful thing is that his contribution to this great sport has been only positive and the game has profited hugely for his involvement.

A cry for our lost youth
Oliver Holt, *Mail on Sunday*, 2015

WHEN WE GRIEVE for Richie Benaud, some of us grieve for ourselves, too. For what we have lost. For what is past and can never be recaptured. Mourning is often that way.

Benaud's voice is my time machine. It carries me back to the Seventies and Eighties and the front room of our house 100 yards from the village cricket club, the school holidays and the golden summers of youth.

It takes me back to Doug Walters and Chris Old, to Lillee and Thomson, to Geoff Arnold and John Snow and my favourite batsman, Dennis Amiss, and his shuffle at the crease.

It carries me back to the sofa and the fresh A4 notepad on my knee and the simple thrill of the theme music to the BBC's Test match cricket coverage beginning to play.

Peter West, whose pate is always impossibly bronzed in my recollection, making the introductions and then Benaud taking over. 'Morning everyone,' he would say. 'Beautiful day here at Edgbaston.'

And that was it. Benaud had you straight away. It was the lilt in his voice, the cadence, the stress he put on certain syllables. There was magic in that voice and what I recognise now as understated wisdom.

He seemed to relish the language. He loved the pronunciation of his words. And he had that gift that the great commentators have of being able to say an awful lot by not saying very much at all.

He had my undivided attention, too. I didn't have a computer on my lap back then. I didn't feel the need to punch stuff into Twitter while I was watching the Test and listening to Benaud. It was just me and him and the game.

And he had my youth, too. 'I don't love golf as much as when it was just pure joy to get on to the course to play,' said Rory McIlroy last week. Sport is still beautiful and compelling as an adult but other stuff crowds in. Back in the Seventies, it was just me and Richie.

We have great commentators now, too, particularly in cricket. Men like Michael Atherton, David Lloyd and Nasser Hussain are bred in the tradition of Benaud. It is not their fault that our attention spans are shorter and that we flit from screen to screen, diluting their effect.

As I grew up, I loved Benaud more and more. I didn't even know he had been a fine, fine cricketer in his own right until I was older. That made me admire him even more. The fact that he was Australian never occurred to me, either. He was always scrupulously impartial. What an achievement to be cherished by both sides of the Ashes divide.

Benaud was not afraid to offer an opinion and to be trenchant but he was never sanctimonious. He never allowed self-aggrandisement to creep into his commentary. Never. He never suggested the game was not as good as it had been in his playing days.

He never gave the impression of saying anything for effect or for a gimmick. He did not have phrases stored up ready to trot out when an event occurred. He prepared meticulously and his knowledge was the fount of his spontaneity.

Benaud's delivery was so distinctive, so clever, so evocative that he was ripe for mimicry. It was always affectionate. I remember simple things when I think back. 'Bowled 'im' or 'Got 'im'. Some of my friends had' more complex, more reverential party pieces. 'I once had the great pleasure of watching Clarrie Grimmett take 7–40 on a sticky dog,' one used to say regularly, apropos of nothing.

He also remembered how Benaud's voice used to rise a

little when one of England's great fielders exploded into action. 'Randall,' he would say. Nothing more. He didn't need to say any more.

He had that in common with the great Dan Maskell, the best tennis commentator there has ever been. Neither was afraid of silence. They were happy to let the game speak when there was nothing to add.

Because of the mellifluousness of Benaud's voice, because of the cadence, he could make ordinary phrases dance and sing. 'Late in the day, he's got a beauty through Kevin Pietersen,' he observed of a Glenn McGrath ball in the 2005 Ashes series and his voice evoked the timelessness of a summer evening, a dying sun and a great bowler getting the better of a great batsman.

Benaud brought great joy to a lot of people. His voice is one of the reasons why many of us love the game.

It is in my head every time I go to a cricket ground, every time I see a wicket fall or a six hit. Amid the grieving, that is a happy consolation.

Photographic
Acknowledgements

The author and publisher would like to thank the following for permission to reproduce photographs:

Associated Newspapers/REX Shutterstock, Chris Barham/Daily Mail/REX Shutterstock, BBC, Joe Castro/EPA/Corbis, Central Press/Getty Images, Patrick Eagar/Getty Images, Fairfax Media/Getty Images, Fox Photos/Getty Images, Dan Himbrechts/AAP/PA Images, Phillip Jackson/Associated Newspapers/REX Shutterstock, KeystoneUSA-ZUMA/REX Shutterstock, Ron Lovitt/Fairfax Media/Getty Images, Mark Metcalfe/Getty Images, Mirrorpix, David Munden/Popperfoto/Getty Images, Greg Newington/Newspix/REX Shutterstock, Newspix/REX Shutterstock, Sydney O'Meara/Evening Standard/Getty Images, Dennis Oulds/Getty Images, PA Archive/PA Images, Ray Saunders/Newspix/REX Shutterstock, Tom Shaw/Getty Images, Peter Sheppard/Mirrorpix, Prakash Singh/AFP/Getty Images, Sport & General/PA Images, Brandon Voight/Splash News/Corbis.

Other photographs are from private collections.

Index

Abbas, Zaheer 256, 257
Abbot, Tony 289
ABC TV 186–7
Adcock, Neil 155, 156, 201, 202, 251
Adelaide Oval 38, 44, 67, 87, 88, 89, 184, 185, 195, 226, 227, 231, 236, 249, 252, 260, 261, 296, 300
Agnew, Jonathan 265, 304–5
Alderson, Bert 21, 28, 38
Alexander, Gerry 109, 112, 151
Allen, David 12
Allen, 'Gubby' 149, 249
Allis, Peter 174, 315
allrounders, achieving the 'double' 254, 255, 256
Amiss, Dennis 202, 318
Appleyard, Bob 60, 61
Archer, Ken 37, 64
Arlott, John 64, 291, 306
Armstrong, Warwick 62
Ashes matches/tours xi, 3–5, 7, 8, 11, 12, 13, 24, 39, 67, 90, 123, 124, 140, 149, 150, 153, 156–7, 177, 199–200, 206, 217, 228, 245, 247, 248, 249, 254–5, 260, 261, 293, 294, 301, 302
  1953 series 46–56
  1956 series 60–5
  1958–59 series 74–89

1961 series 112–16
in ten most important cricket moments 241, 242
Atherton, Mike 176, 226, 296–9, 319
Atkinson, Denis 170
Australia, see also Ashes matches
players' records 38, 58, 62, 88
players' remuneration 76–7
v England, World Cup 221
v India 253, see also India
v New Zealand 74, 204, see also New Zealand
v Pakistan 256–7, see also Pakistan
v South Africa 23, 82, 232, 234, 235, 303, see also South Africa in World Cup 221–2
v West Indies 5, 8, 13, 23, 43, 44, 123, 140, 168, 170, 185, 222, 231, 232, 250, 252, 294, 300, 302, see also West Indies one day 220–1
  tied test 103–6, 107–9, 111 164, 184, 185, 217, 222, 241, 242, 249, 300
in World Cup final 219
Australia, team of the century 243
Australia, ten most important cricket moments 239–42

Australian Board of Control and
        Sid Barnes veto 231–5
Australian Cricket Board 76–7, 82,
        90, 92, 93, 94, 103, 106,
        149, 151–2, 154, 187,
        189, 192
    and player-journalists 82
    and the Boots Business 235–8

Bailey, Trevor 54, 55–6, 85, 86,
        87, 149, 246
Bangalore 252
Bannister, Jack 271–2
Baptiste, Eldine 219
Barbados 110, 170, 283
Bari, Wasim 257
Barnes, Alan 77
Barnes, Harold 17–18
Barnes, Laurence 17
Barnes, Sydney (Sid) 7, 38, 44, 60,
        82, 245, 247 249, 256,
        261–2
    selection vetoed 231–5
Barnes, Tieffie 215
Barrington, Ken 114, 115, 302
BBC 3, 49, 148, 150, 158, 159,
        160, 166, 175, 179, 180,
        181, 182, 192, 196, 228,
        247, 253, 269, 272, 282,
        291, 294, 295, 296, 303,
        304, 305, 312, 314, 315,
        318
Bedser, Alec 54, 248, 254–5, 259
Bell, Ronnie 207
Benaud, Daphne (wife) 19, 110,
        111, 125, 128, 154, 162,
        65, 164, 166, 178, 191,
        192, 194, 268, 282–3,
        295, 309, 310

cricket knowledge 283–4
Benaud, John (brother) 19, 209,
        236, 237, 285, 286
Benaud, Louis Richard (father) 6
        14, 17, 18, 19, 21, 22, 23,
        25, 26, 27, 28, 34, 39, 40,
        58, 179, 205, 209, 258,
        259, 273, 273–4, 280,
        284–6, 292, 300
Benaud, Rene (mother) 273–4,
        284–6, 286–7, 379
Benaud, Richie
    accountant, trains as 28, 143–6
    and Charlie Griffith 303
    and golf xii, 122, 162–6, 174,
        176, 197, 268, 272
    and Kerry Packer, see Kerry
        Packer
    and World Series Cricket, see
        World Series Cricket
    appointed Australia captain
        79–80, 301
    initiates changes 83–4
    arts, taste in 162
    as captain 313
    best figures in first-class cricket
        302
    biography to 1962 6–10
    from Cumberland Club to
        NSW 23–31, 31–6, 41,
        42, 44
    bowling advice from Bill
        O'Reilly 56–8, 119
    boyhood 14–18, 18–22, 300
    captains NSW 77
    career turning point 183
    changes run up 66–8, 82
    cricket statistics 10, 129–40
    cricket awards 291

cricket performances
v England 7, 8–9, 301, 302
v India 8, 301, 302
v Pakistan 8, 302
v S. Africa 7, 301, 303
v W. Indies 8, 301, 302, 307
horse racing in England 267–71
ill with fever 66–7, 68–9
injuries 9, 10, 23, 33–6, 43, 98,
    102, 111, 112, 301
legspinner 9, 300, 315, *see also*
    on legspin
media career
broadcaster 166–80, 182–3,
    283, 291, 295, 296–9,
    303, 304–5, 306–7, 308–
    9, 311–13, 314, 316–17,
    318–20
broadcasting anecdotes 167–9,
    170–1, 173–4, 174–5,
    180, 297
innovations 175
RB's final words 177
RB's guidelines to 171–3,
    175–6, 311, 314
training as 159–61, 179, 181
writer 82–3, 146–9, 154–5,
    157, 161–2, 183, 267–8,
    283, 293, 295, 296, 303,
    307, 312, *see also News
    of the World, Sun* at the
    Masters 164–6
on Australia's ten most impor-
    tant cricket moments 241
on Sid Barnes selection veto
    231–5
on Bodyline tour 27, 241, 242,
    259
on Boots Business 235–8

on captaincy 74
on Trevor Chappell's underarm
    ball 197, 305
on death of father 284–6
on death of mother 286–7
on DRS 226–30
on family history 273–82
on first airflights 275
on focussing 117
on front-foot no-ball 228–9
on future of one-day game
    223–5
on International Cricket Coun-
    cil (ICC) 116, 151–4, 189,
    225, 227, 229, 277
on legspin 81–2, 117–20
on limited-overs cricket 216–
    25
one-day cricket 51, 93, 156,
    170, 185, 186, 213, 216,
    217, 218, 219, 223–225,
    226, 241, 260, 285
Twenty20 216, 223, 226, 229
on My Greatest XI 239–63
on neutral umpires 229–30
on no violence in cricket
    211–12
on players' salaries 192, 194
on playing in South Africa
    212–15
on sledging 198–203
on Spirit of Cricket in Australia
    208–11
on televised cricket, in Australia
    183–9
on throwing 151–3
on topspin 118
on umpiring technology 229–30
on walking 203–6

on wedding 282–3
on World Series Cricket 187–
    94, 241, 242, *see also* Kerry
    Packer
background 181–7
High Court hearing 193, 194
inaugural match 190
records 58, 62,
spinning-finger remedy 69–70
Test debut 44
Wisden on 60
TRIBUTES TO RB by:
  Tony Abbott 289
  Jonathan Agnew 265, 304–5
  Michael Atherton 296–9
  Jack Bannister 271–2
  Scyld Berry 3–5
  Henry Blofeld 308–10
  Geoffrey Boycott xi, 313–15
  Neville Cardus 65, 292
  Ian Chappell 195–8
  Tony Cozier 110–12
  Wally Edwards 181
  Jack Fingleton 293
  Angus Fraser 316–18
  David Frith 23, 273, 300–3
  David Gower 143, 267,
    311–13
  David Gyngell on 188
  Gideon Haigh 3, 291–6
  Oliver Holt 318–20
  Justin Langer 158
  Bill Lawry 1
  Darren Lehmann 159
  Vic Marks 154
  Jim Maxwell 141
  Johnnie Moyes 145
  Michael Parkinson xi–xiii
  Mike Selvey 306–8

  Shane Warne 128
  Ian Wooldridge 178–81
    Wisden 6–10, 60
Benson, Mark 226
Berry, Darren 241
Berry, Scyld 3–5
Bevan, Michael 220–1
Bichel, Andy 221
Blofeld, Henry 308–10
Bombay 39, 66, 91, 100, 101,
    102, 155, 255
Border, Allan 122, 125, 174, 243
Botham, Ian 217, 219, 244,
    254–5, 256, 307, 311
Boycott, Geoffrey xi, 167, 209,
    306, 313–15
Bradman, Donald 16, 27, 28, 29,
    30, 37, 38, 51, 76, 88, 90,
    103, 104, 105, 106, 115,
    128, 151, 152, 153, 192,
    233, 237, 241, 242, 243,
    244, 245, 247, 248–50,
    256, 258, 259, 262, 275,
    289, 302, 303, 310
  on limited-overs cricket 217–18
Brearley, Mike 255
Brisbane 30, 43, 79, 83, 94, 107,
    110, 164, 202, 222, 241,
    285, 286, 300, *see also*
    Gabba'
Broad, Chris 227
Brown, Bill 27, 41
Brown, Freddie 87–8
Buller, J.S. 152, 153, 207, 227–8
Burge, Peter 60, 81, 113
Burke, Jim 29, 30, 31, 43, 50, 60,
    64, 67, 78, 81, 84–5, 86,
    104, 200, 231

Calcutta 91, 102, 301
Cardus, Neville 64–5, 292
Chanderpaul, Shivnarine 123
Chandrasekhar B.S. 252
Channel 4 TV 3, 166, 283, 291, 296
Channel 5 TV 3
Channel 9 TV 3, 61, 110, 160, 162, 166, 168, 170, 174, 175, 181, 186–8, 215, 253, 285, 291, 311, 312, 313, 316
Chappell, Greg 127, 197, 243, 244, 250, 252
  underarm incident 197, 242
Chappell, Ian 127, 195–8, 285
Chauhan, Chetan 247
Clark, Belinda 241
Clarke, Michael 4
Close, Brian 5, 114
Clues, Arthur 25
Cohen, Mort 16
Cook, Alastair 3, 5
Courcy, Jim de 32
Cowdrey, Colin 62, 63, 78, 84, 86, 87, 149, 202–3, 208, 211
Cozier, Tony 110–12
Craig, Ian 7, 50, 69, 74, 77, 78, 80, 249, 251, 293, 301, 302
Cumberland Club 6, 7, 16, 18, 19, 20, 21, 23, 25–8, 29, 32, 34, 38, 40, 41, 48, 209
Cush, Frank 233–5

Dacca 91, 93, 94, 95, 155
Daniel, Jack 32, 33
Davidson, Alan 4, 5, 8, 12, 41, 42, 43, 48, 60, 61, 71–3,

80–1, 86, 87, 89, 99, 104, 108, 109, 114, 115–6, 222, 293, 301
  RB on, *Wisden* Cricketer of the Year 10–13
Delhi 99
Denness, Mike 203
Depeiza, Clairmonte 170
Derbyshire 152
Dev, Kapil 245, 247, 255–6
Dexter, Ted 5, 114, 157, 208, 211, 224–5
Dickens, Charles 239
Dilley, Graham 255
D'Oliveira, Basil 213
Donald, Allan 222
Doshi, Dilip 247
Dujon, Jeffrey 257
Durham 223
Dwyer, Chapple 233, 235

Ebrahim, Baboo 215
Edgbaston 124, 125, 149, 217, 257, 221, 222, 228, 255, 257, 272, 299, 314, 318
Edrich, John 202, 249
Edwards, Wally 181
Egar, Colin 227, 303
Elliott, Charlie 228
England 74, *see also* Ashes matches
  C19th sides to Australia 239–40
  v Australia, World Cup 221
  v India 149, 253
  v Pakistan 149, 257
  v South Africa 149, 202, 228
  v West Indies 149, 150, 252, *see also* West Indies
  one-day 219–20
Essex 150

Evans, Godfrey 5, 87, 88, 149, 200, 257

Farrell, Pat 237–8
Feherty, David 163
Fielder, Arthur 247
Fingleton, Jack 27, 82, 293, 294
Flavell, Les 102
Fleming, Damien 222
Fleming, Stephen 204
Flintoff, Andy 221
'flipper', the 9
Flockton, Ray 43–4
Ford, Doug 156
Foster, Neil 219
Fraser, Angus 316–18
French, Dick 241
Frith, David 23, 273, 300–3
Fry, C.B. 28

'Gabba' 36, 37, 38, 41, 42, 77, 85, 93, 123, 164, 174, 184, 185, 197, 198, 204, 220, 285, *ssee also* Brisbane
Gatting, Mike xi, 123, 242
Gavaskar, Sunil 209, 244, 246, 247, 262
Georgetown 170
Gibbs, Herschelle 221–2
Gilchrist, Adam 203–5, 222, 245, 257–8, 262
Gillespie, Jason 38
Gilmour, Gary 252
Glamorgan 56, 166, 267
Gooch, Graham 124, 127
Gower, David 143, 267, 311–13
Grace, W.G. 27, 246, 309
Graveney, Tom 12, 78, 86, 87, 149–50, 155

Gray, Bob 267–70, 282
Great Depression 274
Greig, Tony 177, 193, 203
Greenidge, Gordon 244, 245
Gregory, Jack 39, 259
Griffin, Geoff 152, 153, 228
Griffith, Charlie 303
Griffiths, Alan 166, 7
Grimmett, Clarrie 16, 39, 82, 88, 119, 120, 249, 258, 319
Grout, Wally 12, 81, 87, 108, 109, 293, 315
Gyngell, Bruce 181
Gyngell, David 188

Hadlee, Richard 245, 254, 256
Haigh, Gideon 3, 291–6
Hall, Wes 108, 109
Hammond, Wally 49, 244, 248
Harper, Roger 220
Harvey, Neil 4, 5, 8, 47, 50, 51, 64, 69, 76, 77, 78–80, 81, 86, 89, 90, 95, 98, 99, 101, 113, 114, 115, 126, 127, 162, 206, 231, 243, 293, 294, 301, 302
Harvey, Ron 313
Hassett, Lindsay 7, 16–17, 42, 43, 50, 51, 52, 54, 55, 56, 57, 231, 232, 237
Hawke, Neil 115
Hayden, Matthew 250
Hazlitt, Gerry 26
Headingley 5, 52, 55, 112, 113, 149, 158, 167, 217, 221, 228, 241, 254, 255, 272, 311
Headley, George 244, 248
Healy, Ian 243, 245, 257

Heine, Peter 201–2, 251
Hemmings, Eddie 256
Hill, Jack 32
Hobbs, Jack 242, 244, 246–7,
       261, 262
Holding, Michael 219
Hole, Graeme 32, 46
Holt, Oliver 318–20
Hooper, Carl 220
Howell, W.P. (Bill) 26
Hughes, Kim 255
Hughes, Merv 38
Hughes, Philip 271
Hunte, Conrad 108, 109, 112
Hutton, Len 4, 7, 39, 52, 244,
       246, 301

Illingworth, Ray 75, 185
India 53, 67
       v Australia 8, 13, 39, 66, 91,
              98–103, 301, 302, see also
              Australia
       v West Indies 252, 255, 301
Insole, Doug 149, 150, 193
International Wanderers Team
       213–15
Iredale, Frank 26

Jackman, Robin 254
James, C.L.R. 106
James, Ivan 69, 71, 98
Johannesburg 140, 202, 214, 272,
       301
Johnson, Ian 44, 170, 231, 237,
       293
Johnson, Keith 233
Johnson, Mitchell 4, 38
Johnston, Bill 42, 44, 51, 54, 56,
       231

Johnston, Brian 265, 305

Kallicharran, Alvin 219
Kallis, Jacques 189, 222
Kanpur 99–100
Karachi 93, 94, 96, 98, 155, 314
Kensington Oval 170, 283
Khan, Imran 245, 254, 256, 257,
       262
Kirsten, Gary 222
Kline, Lindsay 81, 94, 95, 99, 102,
       109, 185, 300
Klusener, Lance 222
Knight, Nick 221
Knott, Alan 257

Lahore 95
Laker, Jim 4, 5, 60, 67, 74, 75, 79,
       80, 82, 83, 85, 87–9, 149,
       199, 314
Lancashire xi, 121, 195, 223
Lancashire League 39
Lane, Tim 241
Langer, Justin 158
Langley, Gil 231
Langridge, John 228
Lara, Brian 127, 168, 244, 250
Larwood, Harold 245, 259
Lashley, Peter 110
Lawrence, Charles 240
Lawry, Bill 1, 113, 122, 162, 271,
       283, 298, 302, 313
Lee, Brett 38, 241
Lee, Frank 228
Lehmann, Darren 4, 159, 221
Leicestershire 150
Lewis, Tony 167, 312, 314, 315
Lillee, Dennis 125, 126, 203,
       214–15, 241, 243, 245,

247, 256, 257, 259–60, 262, 318

Lillywhite, James 240

Lindwall, Ray 10, 13, 21, 31, 36–9, 40, 42, 47, 50, 53, 60, 61, 62, 77, 80, 88, 113, 125, 155, 198, 219, 231, 232, 243, 245, 252, 253, 259, 300, 313
  bowls Len Hutton 52

Lloyd, Clive 209, 219, 252, 256

Lloyd, David 203, 319

Loader, Peter 85, 86, 88

Lock, Tony 60, 61, 78, 79, 84, 87, 113, 149, 152, 200

Longhurst, Henry 161, 179, 182, 294

Lord's 5, 7, 48, 50, 53, 55, 60–5, 86, 112, 113, 125, 152, 153, 157, 173, 122, 175, 182, 183, 186, 193, 201, 209, 219, 224, 228, 225, 237, 246, 248, 254, 256, 265, 282, 283, 297, 301, 302, 305, 314
  the slope 49

Loxton, Sam 90, 92, 96, 98, 100, 101

Luckhurst, Brian 202–3

Lush, 'Ginty' 145

Mackay, Ken 'Slasher' 12, 62–4, 81, 89, 93, 94, 98, 102, 114, 115–6, 185, 300, 302

Mackenzie, Keith 166, 173

Madras 66, 67, 91, 101, 102, 301

Malik, Salim 257

Mallett, Ashley 203, 241

Marks, Vic 154

Marsh, Rodney 77, 245, 257

Marshall, Roy 155

Maskell, Dan 161, 179, 182, 294, 320

Matthews, Greg 62

Maxwell, Jim 141

May, Peter xi, xiii, 5, 53, 55, 63, 67, 78, 81, 84, 86, 87, 150, 293, 302

MCC 24, 27, 49, 53, 75, 78, 79, 82, 84, 151, 152–3, 157, 315

McCabe, Stan 16, 249

McCool, Colin 69, 70

McCormack, Mark 162–3

McDonald, Colin 32, 44, 45, 52, 81, 84, 86, 87, 96, 97, 200, 206, 207

McDonald, Gregory 259

McDonald, (Dr) Ian 32, 33, 34, 90, 91, 95, 96, 98, 108

McDonald, Ted 39, 259

McGrath, Glenn 177, 220, 245, 258, 259–60, 320

McKenzie, Graham 114, 157

McLean, Bob 11, 41

McLean, Roy 12, 155

McMillan, Craig 204

Meckiff, Ian 4, 81, 87, 105, 108, 109, 151, 184, 303

Melbourne Cricket Ground (MCG) 12, 30, 38, 43, 44, 88, 91, 121, 123, 140, 183, 184, 185, 186, 217, 235, 240, 242, 247, 256, 257, 261, 301, 308

Middlesex 55

Miller, Geoff 219

Miller, Keith 10, 13, 17, 30, 31,

36, 37, 39, 40–1, 41–42,
44, 47, 50, 52, 61–2, 63,
64, 144, 145, 231, 243,
244, 245, 246, 253–4,
259, 262, 268, 292
Wisden on 17
Milton, Arthur 88, 149
Morris, Arthur 31, 36, 37, 39–40,
41–2, 44, 52, 59, 126,
127, 170, 231, 243, 244,
246, 253
Moyes, Johnnie 144–5
Murray, John 114

Nawaz, Sarfraz 256
New South Wales (NSW) 4, 7,
10, 11, 15, 16, 19, 23, 24,
25, 27, 29, 30, 31, 32, 33,
36, 37, 38, 40, 41, 42, 43,
44, 72, 73, 77, 78, 80, 90,
102, 103, 121, 183, 184,
195, 198, 199, 200, 209,
219, 220, 233, 235–6,
238, 240, 246, 249, 253,
257, 258, 259, 292, 300,
301, 302, 309
New Zealand v Australia 69, 74,
see also Australia
News of the World 150, 154, 155,
283, 295, 303, 305, 307
Noble, M.A. 10, 62
Noblet, Geff 232
Norman, Greg 164
Northern District 27, 41
Nottinghamshire 9, 11, 53, 153,
223, 239
Nurse, Seymour 110

Oakman, Alan 207

Old Trafford xi, xiii, 4, 5, 8, 12,
55, 80, 89, 112, 113, 114,
116, 123, 167, 199–200,
202, 217, 219, 241, 242,
253, 255, 267, 283, 294,
302
one-day cricket 291, 305, 317, see
also RB
O'Neill, Norman 81, 95, 108,
114, 207, 270, 271,
O'Reilly, Bill 16, 40, 82, 243, 245,
248, 249, 258–9
advices RB 56–8, 119
O'Sullevan, Peter 160, 161, 179,
182, 294
Oxlade, Aub 233, 235

Packer, Kerry xiii, 181, 187–8,
189–94, 295, 298, 303,
313, see also RB - World
Series Cricket
Padgett, Doug 75
Pakistan 67
v Australia 8, 13, 39, 91, 93–8,
140, 302, see also Australia
delaying tactics 95–6
Parkinson, Michael xi–xiii
Parr, George 239
Patel, Jasu 102
Pepper, Cec 16, 249
Phillipson, Eddie 228
Philpott, Peter 127
Pietermaritzburg 12
Pietersen, Kevin 177, 320
Pollock, Graeme 244, 250,
251–2
Pollock, Peter 251
Pollock, Shaun 222
Ponsford, Bill 243

Ponting, Ricky 204
    on DRS 226–7
Port Elizabeth 213, 221, 251
Preamble to the Laws of Cricket
        211–12
Pringle, Derek 219
Procter, Mike
Pullar, Geoff 302

Qadir, Abdul 245, 259
Queensland 11, 29, 30, 31, 36, 37,
        41, 42, 77, 85, 106, 116,
        175, 184, 220,

Raith, Jacob 231, 233–4
Ramadhin, Sonny 44, 90
Reiffel, Paul 220
Rhodes, Harold 155, 156
Richards, Barry 209
Richards, Vivian 217, 219, 243,
        252, 262
Richardson, Arthur 29
Richardson, Peter 12, 86, 129, 149
Richardson, Richie 123
Ridings, Phil 232
Ring, Doug 16, 44, 56, 231
Rixon, Steve 241
Roberts, Ron, touring teams
        155–6
Rogers, John 236
Rorke, Gordon 102

Scarborough 4, 9, 56–8, 119, 301
Selvey, Mike 306–8
Shastri, Ravi 122
Sheahan, Paul 241
Sheppard, Rev. David 200
Simpson, Bob 62, 81, 103, 108,
        267, 294, 302, 303, 313

Sincock, David 127
Skelding, Alec 150
sledging 4, 210, see also RB
Smith, Cammie 110, 112
Smith, Sydney 235
Snow, John 193, 306, 314, 318
Sobers, Garry 61, 104, 108, 109,
        110, 127, 196, 242, 244,
        250, 253, 256–7, 262
Solomon, Joe 104–5
Somerset 167
South Africa 53, 213–15
    v Australia 7, 13, 29, 42, 67, 72,
        74, 83, 140, 202, 251–2,
        301, see also Australia
    v New Zealand 251
    in World Cup 221–2
South Australia 15, 27, 28, 44
Sporting Life 144–5
Sri Lanka v Australia 122
Statham, Brian 12, 61, 84–5, 86,
        87, 88, 116, 259
Steele, David 203
Stephenson, H.H. 239–40
Stephenson, Harold 156
Stevens, Gavin 102
Stewart, Alec 221
Sun (Sydney) 5, 10, 30, 32, 79,
        107, 143, 144, 146, 147,
        150, 154, 267, 293, 295,
        312
Surrey 26, 53 61, 239, 246
Sussex 75, 207, 224, 251
Sutcliffe, Herbert 149, 247
Swanton, E.W. 49, 110, 282, 295,
        309
Sydney Cricket Ground (SCG) 15,
        16, 21, 23, 27, 30, 38, 41,
        42, 43, 44, 72, 78, 79, 84,

87, 113, 115, 117, 123,
140, 168, 184, 188, 189,
190, 198, 232, 235, 248,
249, 261, 295

Taber, Brian 121
Tasmania 24, 32, 220
Taufel, Simon 227
Taylor, Mark 122, 176
Te Kanawa, Kiri 163
Tendulkar, Sachin 122, 126,
127, 244, 252, 253, 262,
317
Test, The Inaugural 241
Test and County Cricket Board
193
The Oval 26, 53, 56, 61, 121,
177, 186, 228, 241, 242,
247, 255, 296, 313
Thomson, Ian 207
Thomson, Jeff 203, 219, 252, 259,
318
tied matches 184, *see also* Australia
v West Indies
Trent Bridge 11, 54, 61, 223, 227,
228, 254, 269, 272
Trescothick, Marcus 221
Trueman, Fred 5, 75, 79, 85, 87,
145, 200, 202, 228, 245,
259, 260, 301
Trumper, Victor 244, 245, 261
Twenty20 299, *see also* RB
Tyson, Frank 87, 145, 198, 259

Valentine, Alf 44, 109, 112
Vaughan, Michael 221
Victoria 11, 16, 31–2, 76, 80, 90,
91, 121, 122, 183, 184,
199, 200

Voce, Bill 259
Vorster, John 215

WACA 202, 253
Walker, Alan 29, 30, 42
Walker, Max 203
Wardle, Johnny 61, 75–6, 82
Warne, Shane 38, 121–8, 128,
222, 243, 258, 259, 262,
307
300th Test wicket 189
bowls Mike Gatting xi, 123,
242
Watson, Trevor 85, 86
Watson, Willie 12, 55, 85, 86, 88,
149, 246
Waugh, Mark 127, 176, 222
Waugh, Steve 62, 221–2, 241, 242
Webb, Syd 113, 237–8
Weekes, Everton 110, 155, 245
West Indies 74
v Australia 64, 83, 140, 301,
see also Australia in World
Cup final 219
v England 250, 254, *see also*
England
Western Australia 24, 41, 46, 78,
115, 121, 257
Willey, Peter 227, 229
Willis, Bob 219, 255, 314
Wisden 5, 6, 10, 17, 60, 206, 217,
224, 242
five cricketers of the century 242
on RB 60
Wisden Australia 291
Wisden Cricketer (magazine) 178
Wisden Cricket Monthly 229
Wisden Cricketer of the Year 6–10,
10–13

Wood, Barry 203
Woolridge, Ian 192–3
Worcestershire 51–2, 152, 254,
          227, 228, 304, 311,
World Cup 186, 203, 212, 219,
          221–3, 225
World Series Cricket 295, 305, *see
          also* RB
Worrell, Frank 5, 8, 44, 105, 106,

          108, 110, 112, 151, 185,
          241, 244, 245, 250, 262,
          294, 300, 307
     Frank Worrell Trophy 106, 241
Wright, Doug 249

Yardley, Norman 52
Yorkshire xi, 32, 39, 52, 65, 75,
          167, 227, 270, 314

An invitation from the publisher

Join us at www.hodder.co.uk, or follow us
on Twitter @hodderbooks to be a part of
our community of people who love the very
best in books and reading.

Whether you want to discover more about a book
or an author, watch trailers and interviews, have the
chance to win early limited editions, or simply browse
our expert readers' selection of the very best books,
we think you'll find what you're looking for.

And if you don't, that's the place to tell us what's missing.

We love what we do, and we'd love you to be a part of it.

www.hodder.co.uk

@hodderbooks

HodderBooks

HodderBooks